The
High Heeled
Guide to
Enlightenment

First published by O-Books, 2009
O-Books is an imprint of John Hunt Publishing Ltd., Laurel House, Station Approach,
Alresford, Hants, SO24 9JH, UK
office1@o-books.net
www.o-books.com

For distributor details and how to order please visit the 'Ordering' section on our website.

Text copyright: Alice Grist 2008

ISBN: 978 1 84694 221 1

A CIP catalogue record for this book is available from the British Library.

Design: Stuart Davies

Printed and bound by CPI Group (UK) Ltd, Croydon, CR0 4YY
Printed in the USA by Offset Paperback Mfrs, Inc

We operate a distinctive and ethical publishing philosophy in all
areas of our business, from our global network of authors to
production and worldwide distribution.

CONTENTS

Endorsements

"Intimate, wise and sassy! The High Heeled Guide to Enlightenment leads us gently by the hand through an otherwise overwhelming array of spiritual and healing approaches. Alice Grist is humorous, frank and insightful. Through the lens of her own experience, Grist cuts to the heart of what it means to be a spiritual seeker in a modern world – unabashedly inviting every contemporary woman, whose soul sings for more, to do the same. A great contribution, delightful to read!"
Llyn Roberts, author of *The Good Remembering*, *Shamanic Reiki* and *Shapeshifting into Higher Consciousness*

"The High Heeled Guide to Enlightenment is a powerful and wonderfully entertaining journey into spirituality. I suspect that many readers will see it as the true path to 'women's liberation'!"
John Perkins, NY Times Best Selling Author of *The Secret History of the America Empire*, *Confessions of an Economic Hitman*, *Shapeshifting: Techniques for Global and Personal Transformation and others*.

"As a ballet flats kind of gal, I approached this book with more trepidation over the shoe wear than the spirituality. But regardless of your footwear inclinations, Alice puts us all at ease, talking us through the mysteries of the universe as though she was talking us through a particularly entertaining Saturday night.

It's funny, fascinating and inspirational; to the point that I actually began to quote sections to my friends! I feel spiritually richer from the experience so I guess, on a deeper level, I am well heeled after all. Thanks Alice"
Heather Abela, Award winning writer and director of films and television

"Grist explains her work as 'a modern woman's introduction to a world of spirituality and alternative thought'. What it actually does is re-unite the modern, commercially afflicted female with the concepts, ideas, beliefs and practices of the Earth Mother within. Grist clearly explains that there is no need for ditching the comforts of home for a life of solitude in a damp cave, far, far away in order to improve well-being and developing spiritual integrity. It can be as simple as a change of mind or heart, taking on one thing that resonates can lead to a myriad of improvements.

This book goes a long way to bridge the gap between the 'land of confusion' and a place of infinite possibilities."
Kate Osborne, Editor, Kindred Spirit Magazine

'The High Heeled Guide to Enlightenment is a must-have for every modern gal who wants to learn how to 'walk the path' with style, balance and grace. Alice Grist will show you how... with shed-loads of humor and heart.'
Karen Sawyer, author of *'Soul Companions'* and *'The Dangerous Man'*.

"An enjoyable, light-hearted, first-hand account of spiritual experiences, from psychics and shamans, to crystals and Kabbalah. Alice gives us a fun, yet in-depth account of how she combines modern-day life with a spiritual path."
Katy Evans, Editor, Soul & Spirit

Reading The High Heeled Guide to Enlightenment is like embarking on a journey with a close friend you haven't seen for years: a breathless, compelling ride catching up on all aspects of love, work and the meaning of life. With Alice, we journey through the various Wonderlands of New Age philosophies, and not only do we learn about our tour guide, but we are also gently persuaded to go further: to peer through the looking glass and

examine our own beliefs and ideas on some of life's big mysteries.
Frank Clifford Astrologist, Palm Reader & Author, London
School of Astrology and Flare Publications

"The High Heeled Guide to Enlightenment is a must have for
every woman wishing to explore their spirituality but don't know
where to begin their search – ladies, look no further. Alice informs
in a humorous and concise manner that will certainly make you
think about changing your life. Fantastic read – every handbag
should carry a copy!"
Deborah Chamberlain Spiritual Life Coach, Psychic Medium &
Reiki Master
Founder of Inspiration, School of Psychic and Spiritual
Development

Grist's witty and frank take on all things spiritual provided me
with the much-needed 'spiritual cuisine' my hectic work/life
calendar required. Working in the advertising inundated, all
singing, all dancing world of style and lifestyle whilst running
four businesses, the inner me was definitely crying out for a no-
nonsense guide to reassessing my lifestyle and shifting my way of
thinking.

Grist's book is much more than that too, allowing you to dip in
and out, develop as a person, and to do all of that easily and with
enjoyment!
Bethanie Lunn, Entrepreneur and Style Writer

For James,

Your love and support has been one of the most Enlightening things of all. Unconditional love is at the heart of all spirituality, and Darling, you certainly have mine. From the bottom of my heart, Thank You. Always, Alice x

Acknowledgements and thanks

This book was written with the generous help of my parents and the support of my poor, neglected friends! Unending love and gratitude to you all.

About the Author

Alice Grist is the author of The High Heeled Guide to Enlightenment, a practicing Intuitive Tarot Card Advisor, Freelance Writer and Reiki Practitioner.

Alice's father turned Vicar to Witch when she was a young girl and thus her indoctrination into alternative spirituality began. Her interest in Women's issues can be credited to her feminist American Mother and this early learning was followed up by her completion of a degree in Women's Studies. Following university she toyed with a number of intriguing jobs including glamour model, promotions girl and bar manager. Alice has since worked as a freelance writer contributing to a number of websites and magazines. Alice soon decided to combine her passion for writing with her interest in alternative spirituality and women's interests.

She now lives happily with her musician boyfriend James and their cats and chickens. She is currently collating ideas and research for her second book.

http://web.mac.com/alicegrist

Introduction

The High Heeled and Glamorous Guide to Enlightenment is a modern woman's introduction to a world of spirituality and alternative thought. This is no doubt a subject that calls to you, but between work, partners, kids and a hectic social calendar, you rarely find the time to dig that little bit deeper. Unlike some of your contemporaries, you know that enlightenment is not the new blonde shade by L'Oreal. You would love to seek it out, but any attempt at meditation has ended in a mental mediation between plans for supper, sorting out the next crisis in your love life or fretting over the bills/promotion/boss (insert your own personal foible here). You may have toyed with, or even attended a spiritual evening held in the local wine bar, and you are more than likely to consult your horoscope on a daily basis (in several publications). Maybe you have ignored your gut instinct to your distinct disadvantage or had psychic experiences that you cannot explain away. Perhaps you simply feel an overwhelming urge to connect with something other than your Internet provider?

As a modern, no doubt glamorous female, perhaps you feel like you spend all your time in a state of constant physical upkeep. Not necessarily by your own choice, but influenced and encouraged by the society around you, the magazines you read, the celebrities who just will not go away, and the friends who always want to be two pounds lighter? That, it seems to me is the modern woman's burden, and no matter how you scrub up or how high flying, well educated, or career orientated you are, it is likely that these things impinge on you to the extent that you have precious little time for the inner you. And I am not talking about nutrition, stomach flora or the bones of you, I mean your very inner soul, my dear! You are starving, and it is not because of the newest fad diet, but because there is a massive neglect going on within yourself.

You are not alone. Thousands of people are reaching out for

1

some kind of spiritual cuisine to complement or transform their lifestyles. At first you might reach out to externals to help launch this change – recycling, buying fair trade products, becoming a conscious consumer and reading up on the goings on of planet earth. When the organic / free-range veggies no longer suffice it may be because your soul, so busy with the mundane day to day, is neglected, lonesome and stuffed full of empty calories!

I have suffered this hunger myself. Everything in my life was generally pretty good and yet there was something missing, something that a bumper bar of chocolate and a night in front of the box could not touch. At first you may blame the people around you as a sense of general dissatisfaction begins to taint and impinge on your daily routines. Your usual pick me ups, shopping, new shoes, fabulous new lipstick, great sex or girly chats are not hitting the spot. You wonder if you are depressed and a series of 'what ifs?' begin to form in your mind. My suspicion is that you have a case of the spiritual munchies. I strongly suspect that you are in need of some conviction and a search for your spirit that goes on beyond your favorite cocktail.

All the women I know are incredibly busy people. With or without a family, it seems our bums barely skim the sofa before they are back to work to pay off the credit on said settee! Society expects females to look after ourselves, be calm, poised and beautiful, whilst fitting all we humanly can into an increasingly tight schedule. This often involves making time for friends, shopping, preening, seeing one's other half for quality time, going to the gym, cooking, cleaning, carrying, lifting, listening, driving, dating, eating, dining, wining and eventually, if you are lucky, you might grab some alone time to do nothing but switch off. This is commonly referred to as sleeping! On top of this all my girlfriends agree that there is constantly somebody you need to look after, as that is what we girls do best. Those of you with little ones spend an inordinate amount of time caring for them, whilst those of us with big ones often have our work cut out dealing with severe bouts of 'man flu' and/or 'man trouble'. On top of our big and little family members we have pets, parents, depressed pals, poorly houseplants, weeds on the patio and no doubt a huge migraine developing!

Perhaps unsurprisingly, I do not know a woman who does not harbor some interest or belief in the afterlife, spirit and all things otherworldly. Headache and diary permitting she may attempt to indulge this interest, but where to start searching for a light that you cannot see or grasp is often too much to ask. Spiritual pursuit is not something easily undertaken and for today's modern women it may take a near heart attack to slow you down enough to examine your life and your needs closely enough to realize what might be missing.

I had been vaguely playing with the idea of my own spirituality for several years, proclaiming myself spiritual without really knowing what I meant. It was only when my whole life seemingly turned upside down that I sought out the means to repair myself. In doing so I discovered that most of the dramas that I had surrounded myself with were of my own making. I had created my very own devil in the detail, perhaps because I was bored, I needed attention or because somewhere in-between worrying about everyone else I had stopped thinking about myself. It was with a vague sense of me in mind that I started to explore alternative religions, therapies and thought.

I was lucky enough to have a religious upbringing, my dad was a vicar for my first few years of life, and following this he traded in his dog collar for a cauldron and became a witch. It was here that I got my formative spiritual leanings, but in the haze of being a boy-obsessed teenager, a partying student, and then continuing to party as a (still slightly man obsessed) young woman, I forgot all of this. It was only upon my return to these early learnings that I began to resurrect the Alice I was familiar with.

On doing so all the excess and drama dropped away like an

unnecessary cocoon. I was revealed, happier, lighter hearted and healthier. And what had changed? Nothing. My life was the same, my friends were the same (although in fairness some were hastily dropped), my partner was still by my side, and my job still employed me, was not so bad, and above all paid the mortgage. Yet all my negativity had dissipated, it was as though it had never really been there, my forays into my spiritual side had helped make me realize just what was important. I cleared the trash from my mind and in turn I satiated my famished soul. Strangely and wonderfully I became quite content, even, dare I say it.... happy!

Although I am far from perfect, still capable of falling foul of the temptations put in my path, I am significantly happier, and perhaps a teensy bit wiser. I still adore my make up, party frocks and glass of pinot grigio, but these now share a special place in my heart with spiritual loves that include tarot, reiki, crystals, meditation and Buddhist mantras.

As a result, I bring you my high heeled and glamorous guide to all things spiritual. It is my intention that this book will entertain and enliven you; maybe even assist you on your way to a happier existence. And for those who are happy already I hope this book acts as a pointer to those things that call to you, helping you to nurture a blissful spirit well into the future.

Forget about your stereotypes of tree hugging, LSD popping hippies, or fairy loving kooks who offer to read your palm and curse you to hell and back if you refuse. Nor do you need to worry about old wives' tales, folk stories, gypsies and tealeaves.

This book is purely 21st century, matter of fact and without the clutter of fairytales to pad it out. It is researched first hand by me, an utterly modern, glamorous rock chick type. It refers to my experiences, not a friend of a friend or my Aunty Jenny's best friend's second cousin. In doing this I hope you may see how these things can relate to you, I will show you what you need to know, saving you the time consuming work of years worth of spiritual study. This is religious education, amped up, stilettos on and leather gloves off – enjoy!

The High Heeled Content

You might wonder why I have chosen the topics I have. What the High Heeled Guide to Enlightenment aims to do is display the array of alternative spiritual thought that is available for you.

Living in the western 'civilized' world, you are no doubt familiar with the doctrine of the more established World religions such as Christianity, Judaism, Islam or Catholicism. If you aren't then you will at least have a stereotyped view in your head. Many of you will have been raised in or alongside such institutionalized offerings, and are likely trying to escape or find a viable alternative.

Mainstream religion is structured, formatted and condensed to a point that it becomes difficult to make your own mark upon it, and it is near impossible to twist it to fit into your modern, female view of the world. Essentially one faith pretty much reflects another in so many aspects, however an archaic, dogmatic, military style of worship and governed behavior often associated with 'serious' religious practice is far too stifling. What would become of your one lie-in a week if you were to attend 'Sunday Worship', and how would you fit the 'Call to Prayer' into a hectic social timetable and an appointment with the hairdresser? Rigid, prescribed reverence does not suit or flatter the high-heeled believer. Such hardnosed concepts, timetables and rulings are bad enough to swallow at work, so why bring them into your home or your soul?

The faiths and practices I have chosen should help you look inside of yourself for your spiritual truth. Externally you will not need a stone altar, wooden cross or a grand temple to help espouse your commitment. All you will require is an open heart, an interested mind and eyes to see the beauty of nature, our planet and all the things you adore, be they your expensive Jimmy Choos, or your old Moggy cat 'Molly Anna Tallulah Moo'.

We live in an age where choice is paramount. Every day you make a dozen decisions and each one speaks of you and your character. We wear our hearts on our sleeves literally, our choice of lunchtime meal reveals our frame of mind, whilst the subtle pink you choose to paint your nails lets the world know whether you feel kitten soft or vampy. With a billion shades, contexts, textures, styles, shapes and flavors available, there is no urge to conform and there is every reason to create our very own highly individual selves.

The High Heeled Guide to Enlightenment literally aims to enlighten you on your options. You may pick one or you can mix them up and cherry pick your favorite parts. Be assured that every topic I cover is road tested by me for its suitability to the conscious consumer in you. I am personally acquainted with each of the topics and highly recommend them to you.

There are likely dozens of other spiritual beliefs I could have included, but then I would have been writing a compendium without the personal touch. The beliefs I cover are hopefully something to stir your soul, even if some of them sound spectacularly bizarre at first glance, I assure you there is a likelihood they will grow on you. Even if you choose not to incorporate them into your personal beliefs, I am certain they will leave you a better person for having opened yourself to their wonder, albeit briefly.

Buddhism can certainly be classed as one of the larger mainstream religions. Despite this it has incorporated itself very nicely into the western world; it has shown flexibility and adaptability. As a religious system, it is fairly forgiving and you can practice Buddhism quite casually or as a basic way of life, rather than as full on yoga at dawn. Buddhism represents an amazing set of alternative teachings. On the other hand, Buddhism is iconic and fashionable and I admit Buddhism's bright lights and celebrity following wowed me. Beyond the glare of its well-deserved spotlight it offers a remarkable and peaceful truth. Like a superb therapist or exceptional self-help manual, Buddhism gives remarkable answers to our heartaches and pains. Other than that I just like it. It's a big one but it is worth mentioning.

Wicca (White Witches) has featured both amusingly and heavily within my life. As a pagan tradition Wicca is commonly poorly thought of; yet it is so very good, heartfelt and happy. For women it is an empowering and affirming religion. Admit it, as a teenager I am sure you harbored some desire to be a sexy, awe inspiring, all-powerful witch with the power to beguile and influence? Although Wicca cannot give you quite that, it can help you tap into your unique womanliness, helping in turn to boost your ego and self esteem in a truly positive manner. If nothing else, Wiccans worship sex, fertility and femininity, whilst enjoying a massive eight celebrations a year. I felt Wicca was an important one for girls who love to party!

Shamanism was a topic I knew little about, but upon learning about its naturalistic and environmental focus I was hooked. For an exhausted and suffering planet Shamanism offers hope that goes beyond the boundaries of body and mind. It offers up a heady mix of spirit, nature, animals and the environment. It believes in the equality of all things and you cannot say fairer than that! It is particularly relevant to our disillusioned, materialistic lifestyles and offers a breath of fresh air, literally.

Spiritualism embodies a whole world of paranormal intrigues, occult and contacting the dead. It's reminiscent of sleepovers with the girls, ghost stories and Ouija boards! Alongside this, angels, auras, orbs, spirit guides and spiritual development feature heavily. Fluffy paranormalists should apply here! Whilst Spiritualism is often led by men in suits or late-middle-aged ladies who speak with the dead in between having their hair 'set', Kabbalah is followed by Madonna, need I say more? If Madonna worships Kabbalah, then we need to know details! That woman has led trends and fashions for near on 30 years, there must be something worth knowing!

The High Heeled Guide to Enlightenment also features a

selected array of spiritual accessories based around healing and divination subjects. These are chosen for their ability to hasten, improve or accessorize your spiritual urges.

Past Life regression is a psychiatrically influenced and ridiculously fascinating subject. For me personally reading about Past Lives and regression heavily influenced my journey into my own spirituality. Depending on how you look at Past Life Regression it can be a therapy, a belief or an education. Reincarnation is of course common to many Eastern religions such as Buddhism, Hinduism and Sikhism. Yet the western take on it makes it accessible and stunning for people like you and I. Tarot can be a marvelous counseling tool in the right hands. Meditation, yoga, reiki and crystals are all ideal instruments to help you access and deepen your own spirituality.

The High Heeled Guide to Enlightenment is here to help feed your hungry soul and remind you that outside of the daily grind, lovely, warm, fuzzy, interesting spiritual things exist. There are a million handbags or holidays available to give you some pep in your step. But when the buckle has broken and the only thing left of your holidays is sand in your suitcase, then it's time to search within for a feeling of true peace and exhilaration. If you choose to embrace your personal version of a 'religion' then may you develop an inner confidence and glow that comes not from an expensive face cream, but from developing a holistic approach to life. We all want to look and feel good and whilst beauty products, good food, fitness and friendships play a huge part in this, I believe this life has more to offer.

Enlightenment is not something you can purchase or apply, but it is something you can search for, starting here and starting now, and at a bargain price of zilch, nothing but a little faith, ladies. The High Heeled Guide to Enlightenment is your handbag sized, tried and tested introduction to spiritual living, stilettos and all.

A brief note on coincidence....

"A young woman I was treating had, at a critical moment, a dream in which she was given a golden scarab. While she was telling me this dream I sat with my back to the closed window. Suddenly I heard a noise behind me, like a gentle tapping. I turned round and saw a flying insect knocking against the window-pane from outside. I opened the window and caught the creature in the air as it flew in. It was the nearest analogy to a golden scarab that one finds in our latitudes, a scarabaeid beetle, the common rose-chafer (Cetonia aurata), which contrary to its usual habits had evidently felt an urge to get into a dark room at this particular moment." Carl G Jung

Before I begin, I think it is necessary to pre-empt quite a few of my personal little stories with a brief note on coincidence. Coincidence has played a huge and vital role in my own high-heeled path to enlightenment. Coincidences have come in the form of synchronous events, like a friend having the same thoughts as me, at the same time, or the classic example; picking up a phone to find the person you are going to call already at the other end.

Other coincidences that may not be quite as 'psychic' are things such as chance meetings with people who inspire you or help you in some way. Such meetings with people might lead you onto a new path that eventually brings you to a happier place in life. Occasionally the meetings with people would appear to hinder you, cause distress or generally break your heart for a little while. That does not mean that their occurrence in your life has no value. The coincidence that you met a person who then preceded to cheat, philander or wreak havoc in your life, does not make that meeting meaningless. As a wonderful spiritual woman said to me very recently, 'sometimes the biggest arseholes in life are our biggest teachers'.

In my experience, it is the hundreds of coincidences both

noticed and possibly unnoticed that prompted me to write this book. Throughout this book I refer to or touch on coincidences that have affected me, and that have eventually informed my own search for enlightenment. Many a book has been written entirely on this fascinating matter, whilst the great minds of numerous philosophers and scientists have eagerly pondered this subject. Coincidence has, for example, been studied as a stand-alone subject by scientists searching for the secret behind the apparently magical synchronistic flight patterns of birds, whilst other bearded scientific chaps have spent time and government cash searching for an answer to perceived psychic phenomena. I guess that to harness the possibility, potential and power of coincidence would be a real coop for the powers that be.

Deepak Chopra is one of the mega gurus of the mind, body and spirit world. His book 'Synchrodestiny' is a powerful glimpse into the world of coincidence. He asks the reader to think back over their life to try to see the interconnecting random events that led them to where they are today. He prompts you to choose a theme to help specify and pinpoint one precise area. You may choose to think about cash, exercise, diets, religion, education, career or relationships. If you pick one of these topics and trace its path from say, ten years ago, chances are you will see a pattern emerging. You should see that many of the events and decisions that have occurred in your life were pushed, pulled and prompted by people and events around you. An otherwise series of random events will begin to show themselves as 'coincidences' that have actually caused you to be where you are right now.

Having written this book I have had every chance to review and revel in the ridiculous amount of coincidences that have happened to me. These are events that in retrospect suddenly have become clear and make perfect sense. But what about you, what are your head and your heart telling you? When a bizarre coincidence occurs in your life do you exclaim the commonly heard phrase 'oohh what a coincidence!' If you have said this, which I am certain you have, do you really believe that it was a just a coincidence, or does a teensy part of you want to believe that it was meant to be?

'It was meant to be', is that another phrase you have commonly used? Or here is another one you may be familiar with, 'it happened for a reason'. We often express these phrases casually, but the weight and significance behind these words is astounding. If it was meant to be, why was it? And if it happened for a reason, who decided it would happen and what is the reason? Does your logical mind tell you not to be so silly, whilst deep in your heart somewhere a little voice wants to believe that somehow the fates have conspired to bring a person, event or thing into your life at just the exact and perfect moment?

As I continue to develop spiritually and lurch further forward toward some kind of enlightenment, I can look back on my life and see wonderful, crazy patterns. I can see people who I am sure were planted there or strewn across my path to trip me up, counsel me, educate me or just to make me think. I can see catalysts to where I am today, and I am sure that if certain events had not happened I have no idea where my life would be right now – and that includes some of the hardest, most painful events. Indeed it's the painful ones that can make the most difference because those events are the type that get you really thinking!

At the core of every decision I have made there sits a coinci-dence of some sort or other. I no longer believe coincidences to be meaningless, random events. In fact I am certain that coincidence is sent to us to encourage us onto the right path for us. If you embrace coincidence then you are showing that you are willing to start following the direction toward your destiny. By 'showing willing' you are opening up a glut of possibilities that will spread forth causing more and more fabulous coincidences in your life. All it takes is being open to new opportunities, being prepared to go outside your comfort zone, having the confidence to strike up new friendships or being able to start friendly, simple conversations with well meaning strangers. If you can do one or all of these things, then hold on tight, coincidence is a powerful, exciting and life changing force!

I will not speak now too much more about coincidence; I am going to save the rest until the end. I just thought it important to place the concept into your brain, so that you might bear it in mind as you read each chapter. Perhaps you will do me the favor of considering the coincidences in your own life such as, why did you pick up this book, what led you to this very page? Maybe whilst reading this you will begin to notice coincidence differently. I advise you to keep your eyes open, and do not reject things that may have significance, keep an open heart and mind. I will revisit coincidence later on and you can see if you feel any differently toward the subject. For now I will leave you with a very basic and silly coincidence that happened to me today.

For weeks now I have been flailing around, doing bits of writing on this book, but not really getting stuck in. I visited a superb psychic and one thing she told me was that the project I was working on was going at 30 miles per hour, when really I needed to rev it up to 100 mph. As a result I decided to book today off work and get lots done before my summer holiday. Last night, upon leaving work and arriving at the gym I discovered I had left my phone at work, something I have never ever done, especially not when I am going to be away from work for a whole day. All you technologically dependent gals will be sympathizing with me right now, I am sure.

There was no way I was heading back to work, although being without a phone is a nightmare, nothing is ever so bad that I would haul myself back to my desk in my free time, no way missy! On top of the phone disaster, I also have had really bad shoulder ache for a few weeks and decided to book myself a massage on my day off. This was a bit naughty seeing as I was supposed to be writing all day, non-stop.

Anyway, as you may guess, this also failed and the massage

people did not have an appointment for me. It appeared that fates beyond my control were working to ensure that I do what I had set out to do: a whole day of writing, no disturbances, no distractions and no chatting to my mate Roshy for hours at a time whilst filing my nails and drinking too much coffee. As for my painful shoulder, it is likely that a whole day's writing would only make it worse, which means that by the time I do get a massage appointment I will be really incredibly grateful for it! So as you can see coincidence, although sometimes vaguely annoying, always works her magic in the end!

High Heeled Reincarnation and Life Between Lives

I turn to this subject first as it has a huge emotional pull for me. What started out as an excited interest in reincarnation stories set into motion my current path to enlightenment. Let's get straight down to basics. The belief in any religion or faith requires an acceptance of the fact that there is more to life than our human existence. To be religious, or spiritual, or a 'believer' means you believe that something more appealing than eternal darkness occurs when you pop your clogs. I am sure that you have some hope, or inkling or firm belief that life continues after death, otherwise why would you be reading this? Key to my search for enlightenment was this very question, though for me it was more of an answer.

Reincarnation, life after death and near death experiences all make fascinating reading. It is also a growth area in research whereby there is some small chance that life after death can be officially factually proven. It was my fascination with reincarnation and life between lives that grabbed my attention and encouraged me to think of my own spirituality. This is where my high-heeled path to enlightenment really revved up and started to take over!

The question of immortality and spirit is at the essence of everything within this book. It is mind blowing and I love it. So let's start at the heart of the matter, the question your parents dreaded, 'Mummy/Daddy, what happens when you die?'

The question of whether any part of our being continues after death is a question that has consumed philosophers, religious leaders, housewives and High Heeled seekers for thousands of years.

For your every day gal on the street, there are generally 101 other things to contemplate before this one comes to your attention. Inevitably death is something that the majority of us rarely think of, and when we do it is often only because we have been forced to. The concept of death is, for many people, utterly unfathomable. We are all very much aware that death is unavoidable, but we choose to stuff this information to the darkest recess of our minds, along with numerous memories of broken hearts, fashion disasters and public humiliation. All of the aforementioned may be cringeworthy, but death is beyond cringeworthy, it is truly despicable, unbelievable, and frightening... death does not bear thinking about.

To me it is similar to when you think too long and hard about the size of the universe, where it begins and if it ends; the result of this being that my brain refuses to join in and I am left feeling, perplexed, small and chillingly human.

So do you believe in an everlasting soul that upon your death floats into the stratosphere, blinks down at loved ones and is met at the pearly gates by your favorite grandparent, Jesus or your first pet hamster? Maybe you want to but you cannot justify it to yourself. Or perhaps you were raised in a strict religion that you believe solely and to the exception of anything else. Maybe you want to believe in something, but do not know where to start. Or possibly the devastating loss of a loved one has left you cold. Either way, whether you believe, are on the fence, or utterly dispute the fact, there is no way that most people cannot find the question intriguing.

Life after death is not a scientifically endorsed truth and never has been. In saying this I mean that it is something the scientific community has paid little attention to. For a scientist to measure our capacity to live after our body has died, she must first be able to measure what part of us this refers to.

If we call this part of us a 'soul', then any scientist worth their salt would wish to measure this soul, quantify its structure and more importantly pin point which part of us a soul represented. For example, is a soul your personality, or just a small part of your personality? Is it your unconscious, or maybe it's the part of you that perks up every third weekend of the month just after you get paid? As science has never found (or looked for) evidence of 'soul', it becomes near impossible for any religious or spiritual theories to be tested. My suggestion here would be that we lack the capacity or understanding to measure the 'soul'. Maybe in the future this technology will become apparent, but for now I choose to throw myself heart first and believe.

I will never forget my father talking to me about life after death when I was very young. Although it was well intentioned, his explanation left me feeling peculiar for a long time. At that time he believed in a Pagan Qabalistic version of different realms of existence and that we would progress through incarnations on earth, onto higher spiritual realms (a theory common to many religions).

What really tipped me over the edge though was his theory that we are all just energy. Biologically, chemically and physically, he was of course correct. Every atom of our body is at its essence nothing more or less than energy – (see Mum, I did pay attention in science classes!) His explanation boiled down to the fact that we actually do not exist, that we are nothing more than a molecular mass. This seriously upset me.

Having gained a little life experience and had a bit of time to think about it, I agree with him that we are nothing more or less than energy. However, I do not agree that this means that we do not really exist, nor do I agree that less, in this instance means less. It simply means less than physical, but possibly more than a human mind can ever imagine? It means that we may not always exist in a physical, familiar form. The energy we are made up of does have a life expectancy, but just as energy never fully dies (it is merely transformed), the same can be applied to our consciousness.

In short I believe that we exist beyond the boundaries of our flesh and that our spirit or soul exists independently. When the flesh is deceased, the core being within is released to wherever it came from. Therefore I must believe that I am more real than I give myself credit for, and that upon my death I will be really, really real, the real me, not Alice, but an aspect of Alice, an accumulation perhaps of other incarnations and of spiritual energy that in my human state I might only dream of... and indeed did dream of, as you will find out when you read on.

Happily, it is not my job to discuss the scientific proof, or lack of proof for the soul or for life after death. I am lucky enough to be endowed with a deep belief that does not require this kind of evidenced, black and white, proving. Some might say that is foolish, but judging by the many religions, and millions of devotees worldwide, I am pleased to say I am not alone in my foolhardy ways! I do very much believe that some things are set deep within us, and that proof is not always necessary, nor is explanation. Maybe you feel this too? It is true that once our most eminent scientists believed the world to be flat and the earth to be the centre of the universe. Unless someone categorically disproves the existence of life after death, or shows me that my soul does not exist, then I will take my beliefs, bury them deep in my favorite handbag and guard them with my life – and when my life is extinguished I am sure that my newly released soul will have a good old giggle about it all.

Although I do not have proof, I do have my reasons, and these matter more to me than a scientist's approval. I guess that I just simply believe, deep down inside of me, that there is something else beyond this life. I know this is not the 'scientific' or even the 'logical' approach, but to me it feels right, my experience and learning has added to this. There is nothing measurable about this knowing, but even if this 'knowing' were merely a trick of the mind, or my brain's way of coping with life, then at least it would be likely I will never know differently. However, as a result of this unfathomable, unproved, gnawing gut feeling, I am where I am today and I write this book in the hope that women like you will feel the same way.

The event that truly triggered this knowing deep in the pit of my belly occurred whilst I was still a student at university. I was lucky enough to wake one morning in uncontrollable fits of hysterical laughter. I felt ecstatically happy. To this day I am not sure precisely what prompted this laughter, but I am certain that I had been gifted a glimpse, or a reminder of why we are all here. It felt as though somebody had informed me about information I already knew, but had long since forgotten. This information can best be summarized by the quote from the one and only William Shakespeare, 'All the world's a stage, and all the men and women merely players".

I awoke that morning with a sincere, and hugely amused belief that I had been reminded that our lives are a game of learning, and all the serious, dark and deep stuff, (although very important in the now), was little more than a performance. The overwhelming feeling I experienced was that when we wake from our lives, we will look back in astonishment at how seriously we took it all. I felt like I had been reminded of where my true home lies, and that I am merely a visitor here, carving out a meaningful life to report back on, upon my return.

This was such a strong and psychically vivid experience that I knew from that point on that there is a spiritual life after death and that our life on planet earth is temporary. This life is a half way home or a schoolyard where we are sent to learn, to be challenged and to enjoy the benefits and pitfalls of a physical life. Our life after death is a homecoming to our actual reality, to familiarity and to our true selves.

I am not sure I have ever felt more happy or secure than I did upon waking that morning. Of course that feeling fades, and like everyone else I have moments when I fear death, particularly that it may be painful, lengthy or premature. And the thought that my loved ones will die terrifies me to the pit of my stomach, just as it does everyone else. Yet, I am privileged to have a seed of belief sown within me, and the fact that you are reading this shows that you may do too.

So if I have not confused you enough let's move on to try to get a grip on this very confusing and mind boggling matter of life after death. Inevitably this subject is at the very heart of this book, for without a belief in 'the other side' or the 'unknown' how could you possibly waste your hard earned cash on a medium or a tarot reader? Why would you have faith in any spiritual thought? And why on earth would you have bothered to pick up this book?

Reincarnation – Past Lives Revealed

Reincarnation has always fascinated me. As a child, when my peers were telling ghost stories at Brownie camp, I was leafing through pages of case studies on reincarnation. I read them greedily whilst getting myself well and truly freaked out. Reincarnation is in itself an amazing concept; many religions believe in it, many don't. Popular western religions really do not entertain the matter and our understanding of reincarnation in the western world is significantly dampened by that fact. As we have no religion regularly preaching reincarnation, or instilling it into us from a young age, many westerners tend to view this peculiar occurrence as the results of an over active imagination, or perhaps even as superimposed mental suggestions from a too eager hypnotherapist.

So what is reincarnation exactly? Well, it is the belief that once your physical body has passed its use by date and expired, your everlasting soul is released, eventually taking up residence in a new human body. A common addition to this is that upon release, your soul might hang around for a while, perhaps to comfort or connect with grieving friends and relatives. Following this, the soul is led away – toward the light and/or the spiritual embodiment of Jesus, your great granny or Bob your first pet dog.

In this realm, that I will refer to as the 'life between lives', the soul reflects on the human life it has just lived. It may be that the soul connects with people it had known in that lifetime to discuss their influence and effects on one another (a scary thought). The soul can then choose to party, relax, chill, learn and heal for a little or long while before finally beginning preparation for its next life.

My personal favorite parts about reincarnation theories are what I will refer to as the 'warm and fuzzy' aspects. Forget the serious things such as karma, learning and atonement, and think for a moment on some of the following.

First and foremost – soul mates. Much theory about reincarnation allows for the possibility that we all have a 'soul mate' or 'twin flame', one other soul that we reincarnate with time after time, usually as a love partner. Other theories suggest we have a team around us whom we constantly reincarnate with. This is a particular group of soul mates and soul associates that we have with us in our lives. In your life today this team may include relatives, friends, partners or ex-lovers, colleagues and fond acquaintances. It might even be people you have had a fleeting contact with but who have had an intense or hugely influential impact on your life. These could be your favorite teacher at school, a long lost romance, a neighbor or even a stranger who you never really got to know, but who was there to help you when no one else was. We meet our 'team' at different times as our lives progress, some you may have known from birth, others may take half a century to appear, some may never show up at all in this particular innings. Either way your team members don't show up by accident and their appearance in your life is often profound.

The 'warm and fuzzy' aspects of reincarnation are fantastic to bear in mind especially when life in general can be so hard and frustrating. I like to return to this thought when I feel low and lonesome. It essentially reminds me that somewhere, maybe close by, or a phone call away, I have soul mates at my disposal, friends who I have known and loved throughout eternity. Even if we barely speak or have fallen out over the hogging of the remote control or washing up, it's reassuring to know that at the very end of the day, when little me is dead and buried, I will again be with these people, without the day-to-day grind getting in our way, and hopefully in a place of pure love, peace and learning, as is described by much of the reincarnation theory.

I find hope in the idea that people I have lost contact or fallen out with will eventually turn up as a soul group member. Any quarrels will be quickly forgotten and we can reacquaint ourselves in the hereafter. This is a fantastic thought and I will return to the subject of soulmates a little later on...

There is a lot to be said for reincarnation. In my opinion reincarnation theories are only as wacky as any other religious doctrine. If you are going to poo-poo them then you'd better start poo-pooing heaven, angels, Jesus and his miraculous resurrection, alongside Noah's ark, Buddha's nirvana, or the Virgin Mary's virginity.

My point is that most societies are religious, religion is scientifically unproven, yet many of us believe it or would very much like to. And although it still cannot be categorically, undeniably proven, it is equally true that it cannot solidly or irrevocably be disproved. The evidence is there in vast quantities to be scrutinized, and reincarnation is one of the spiritual areas that some scientific factions have started to accept as a potentially viable area of further study. This however proves nothing...yet.

Unless you have been acquainted with it as a concept for a long time, an introduction to the theory of reincarnation can actually be quite intimidating. I believe that the reason why some people get so disturbed by the thought of potential past lives is simple. The belief that you have lived before involves incorporating an understanding that you have not always been you, and that you may have once been somebody else entirely. When you have known nothing but the same old flesh, frustratingly curly/straight hair, gym defying podgy tummy, bad habits, vices, chocolate addiction and personal allergies all your life, this thought can be absolutely terrifying. It shakes your sense of self to the very core, and in doing so some peoples' egos probably reject it, refusing entirely to even entertain the suggestion.

When as a child I read my dad's books on reincarnation, these thoughts all crossed my mind. As a youngster, how could I possibly envision that I had lived before, possibly elsewhere, and indeed that I had been an adult before, had different parents, maybe been a parent, had different hopes, maybe a different personality and an entirely different outlook on life. I can comprehend that this is both disturbing and frightening. It draws your 'uniqueness' into question; it throws the meaning of 'me' into a neon state of glaring, confusion. However, if you view reincarnation in a spiritual or even religious context, this fear of the unknown does lessen somewhat.

Put into a specific framework, reincarnation can be seen as a progression of the soul and the improvement of your essential self. Reincarnation over many different lifetimes improves and polishes your soul's uniqueness. A bit like major plastic surgery, except that you have to die first then mess around in waiting rooms before you come back to earth with a mighty bang, a whole new face and a serious case of amnesia.

The Evidence

The late Dr Ian Stevenson, a physician and psychiatrist, is likely the most famous scientist to really research the truth of reincarnation. His research techniques involved meeting with children who claimed to remember a past life. He would carefully record the details of these lives, asking pertinent questions and establishing a thorough account from the child and the child's family members. He would then set out to verify these facts. This might involve visiting relatives of the deceased person whom the child claimed to be a reincarnation of. In many cases, the children appear to have reincarnated quickly and their previous families were still alive. Alternatively he would check historical, geographical and sociological information for accuracy. This would involve visiting an area to see if it was how the child described it, or at least if it was that way in the past.

Although some people rush to discredit his research, it clearly raises some serious questions regarding the human condition. Even if this were not evidence of reincarnation, some argue it is evidence of a mass telepathy, or that the child had somehow plugged into a universal consciousness. These concepts are equally as peculiar as reincarnation, and to me do little to disprove anything, rather they simply suggest other, similarly crazy possibilities. One way or another, his research proves that there is more to this universe than any of us can currently hope to understand.

Much of Dr Stevenson's work was carried out in Lebanon, a war torn country where many people have in recent decades died young. It also happens to be a country where reincarnation is accepted. None of the families Dr Stevenson met had anything to gain by indulging him. He offered no money, fame or bonuses; indeed some families were reluctant to help his research.

The picture revealed is compelling. The fact that Lebanese people appear to have a high incidence of reincarnation may simply be because they accept it and do not fear it. Families seem willing to listen to and acknowledge or even encourage a child's beliefs, in some instances, helping to find a child's previous family for them so that they can meet again. In some cases the child's bond with their family from a previous lifetime was so strong that they wanted to keep in lifelong contact. One tragic account tells of a young girl who found her husband from a previous life. She was reincarnated quickly and her hubby is still alive, however, he is now shacked up with a new wife. The young girl stays in contact with him, seemingly incapable of moving on and meeting a new husband in her new body.

Dr Stevenson's work brought a strong sense of reality to my belief in reincarnation. Having read many psychiatric / hypnotherapy accounts of reincarnation, it is easy to get carried away with the thought of 'the other side', the romantic thoughts of soul reunions and the possibilities of my own life and what I may be here to learn.

Dr Stevenson does not address immortality, nor does he look into the possibility of a life beyond death, of heaven, hell, karma or even a reason why. He does not try to relate his findings to any kind of religious doctrine or teachings. He simply sets out to establish, scientifically, the claim that a person has lived on earth before but within a different body. It is as simple as that. There is a healthy dose of practicality within his research that brings the question down to that very basic level. He does not try to unfold all the secrets of the universe, just the one, and in doing so the results are focused, single-minded and believable.

Before his death, toward the end of his career, Dr Stevenson stated that he felt it would not be unreasonable, given the evidence, for any sane person to choose to believe in reincarnation. Although, he never stated publicly that he did believe in reincarnation, this statement speaks volumes.

Old Souls is a book written by Tom Shroeder and it records Dr Stevenson's last case studies. Shroeder does this from a cynical reporter's point of view and the result is intriguing. Tom Shroeder, a renowned journalist and clear skeptic, is left struggling with his beliefs by what he observes of Dr Stevenson's work. Shroeder follows Stevenson around the globe, meeting with allegedly reincarnated children, observing and eloquently reporting back in the pages of his book. My hunch is that by the end of his experience, Tom Shroeder is as fascinated, and perhaps as convinced as you and me! Although, like Stevenson, Shroeder does not declare his belief in black and white, the implication is apparent.

Happily, Dr Stevenson's work continues after his death, so hopefully advancements will be made, and perhaps in our lifetimes we will come to have that more definitive answer with which to bolster our own belief systems.

Psychiatry and Hypnotic Regression

Many psychiatrists other than Dr Stephenson use the hypnotic regression into past lives as a valuable therapeutic tool. It is their belief that this helps patients overcome trauma that they have brought with them from a past existence. This is a massively growing area, and you can access hypnotic regression either as a result of on-going treatment for psychiatric issues, or you can book yourself a session from a specially trained Past Life Regression therapist. I would recommend this route if you are merely feeling fascinated and do not need the psychoanalysis!

Several psychiatrists have written intriguing accounts on how their ventures into hypnotic regression accidentally led to the hypnotized person somehow slipping into a past life experience. They note that this was often remarkable in curing phobias, fears or other crippling psychological and physical symptoms. Some claim to have regressed people forward into the future and even to the space 'between lives'. I find many of these accounts pretty convincing and even if you are not convinced, they certainly make spectacular reading.

Thousands of people have been subject to hypnosis, and yet time and time again their accounts of past lives, and the between life state are so very similar. Few of these peoples' past life memories were seemingly influenced by any desire to have been a famous historical figure, and most subjects had tended to lead lowly lives as ordinary folk who were not particularly successful, famous or influential. This is what really hooked me. Particularly as I saw no evidence that the psychiatrists involved prompted their patients or said anything leading or suggestive. They merely acted as objective guides, whilst it was the patients that led the session and determined the direction that the regression took.

Dr Michael Newton – Journey of Souls and Destiny of Souls

Of all of the psychiatrist's accounts that I have read, I highly recommend the books by Dr Michael Newton. He thoroughly explores his patients' past lives and their 'life between lives'. It is his books and theories that gave me a push in the spiritual direction I have since headed in. They answered questions I did not know I had posed, whilst re-enacting the same feeling in my gut that I felt all these years before, upon waking in my university bedroom. It was Dr Newton's work that inspired me to push ahead and go for past life regression, not once, but twice, and eventually to go on to experience for myself 'life between life' regression.

Dr Newton's work is fascinating to me. He, like many other psychiatrists, stumbled into a 'past life' and 'life between lives' via a routine hypnotherapy session. He has since hypnotized thousands of subjects and without asking leading questions, he has discovered that their experience of life following death and reincarnation is remarkably similar. The picture he paints of the afterlife is intriguing. He suggests that we all belong to 'soul groups' and that upon death we are returned to this group. Once we have got over the initial exhilaration of returning home, we undertake intensive studying of the life we have just lived.

For those who hated school, this may sound less than fun. However, the 'school yard' picture painted by Newton is not one of discipline and timetabled structure. Rather it is a willing learning environment, where all manner of educational tools are implemented. The syllabus is far more exciting and interactive than math, science and English! The life between lives classroom is all about self-analysis on a grand scale. A sample lesson might involve reliving certain scenes from our lives, with the relevant people. Or we might swap and share memories with those we have affected, allowing us to see how we made other people feel with our actions and vice versa. This might range from effects you had on the lover you jilted, the stranger you chatted to on the train thirty years previously, or the call centre operator you yelled at in frustration. The suggestion is that our actions ripple out into the world further than we acknowledge or take responsibility for. In our life between lives we all have to face those small or seemingly insignificant acts and see how they truly affected others for better or for worse. I am sure you can think of many people who have affected you, some more obviously, others very subtly, perhaps by a comment or suggestion that really made you think. As a result you may have gone off on a new path that possibly changed your life without you realizing it.

I believe it is interesting to think in negative and positive terms about all these actions. The things that have really hurt you may turn out to be the hinges of your life. Times of pain could have been the points at which you made decisions that were massive, soul enhancing or actively positive for you. I do believe that it is times of struggle that really define your soul's character. How well you coped with trauma, stress, heartbreak or sadness is a good measure of your progression as a soul. That is not to say that you should always handle things well, but the ability to forgive, move on and learn from bad events seems to be an essential part of soul progression. Those souls that harbor bitterness, anger or allow the rubbish that life throws at them to drag them down, and as a result make wrong, harmful choices, are likely to be less developed and will need to do extra work on aspects of themselves.

One major bonus of this interactive soul development, at least for us still living on earth, is that you will be able to tie up some loose ends that you never got a handle on in life. It may turn out that the player who broke your heart was never aware of the damage he caused whilst in life. Or then again, maybe you will realize that you had pre-planned with him that he would break your heart so that you might become a stronger person and move on to the next opportunity to grow. The teacher who you blame for hampering your development was possibly having a bad day and problems at home, yet you resented her for the rest of your days. You may be able to tell that stranger on the bus that her suggestion led to you quitting your job and starting a successful business.

Who knows what will come out in the wash, but I can only imagine what a tremendous learning experience this must be. Without wishing death upon myself I must say that I am quite looking forward to it! There are one or two folks I would like to grill, and am sure there may be a few more who will want answers from me. It gives a whole new meaning to the phrase 'hindsight is a wonderful thing'. Bring it on!

The nicest thing about this chance to probe friends, family, colleagues and acquaintances is that there are no real recriminations or pain carried over to the life between lives. If someone has hurt us terribly in our life, then we may sit down and have a real heart to heart about it, to understand why and how events occurred as they did. However, there is pure forgiveness, because essentially all souls know that human life is incredibly hard. Indeed Newton claims earth is one of the hardest of many planets where souls can reincarnate, due to our intense emotions and physical and mental experience.

What really matters is that we learn from each life, and once we have shed our human feelings of jealousy, anger, hate, frustration etc, then we are left with only joy, love and peace, which makes this learning process easier. By hurting someone, or breaking a heart, or having our heart broken, we can choose to act differently in our next life and become a better soul as a result.

In case you are wondering, Newton even deals with the matter of souls who have committed great atrocities whilst on earth, such as Hitler. Depending on the level of evil they have caused they may be sent away to be purified, or are segregated for personal tutoring for long periods of times. The fact is that most souls, upon death, will realize immediately what they may have done wrong and will quickly be distraught at their behavior and willingly retreat to mend themselves. Newton suggests that one reason for evil is that some souls might not be able to cope with the particular intensity of the human body it has arrived in. He claims that all souls in human bodies are subject to intense human feelings and hormonal influences that we simply do not experience in the life between lives. The soul melds with the human mind and influences it, but occasionally the human state can be more powerful, acting in a way that the soul alone would never dream of.

This is complicated, as is the view of what happens to 'ghosts' and those who commit suicide. Ghosts often choose to hang around, or are simply very confused individuals indeed, the confusion sometimes caused by a chaotic or unexpected death. Suicides often regret their actions immediately and regret the waste of a life that they could have lived differently. In some instances, say if a person is in great physical pain, then suicide is seen as understandable. If however, a person had other options, which they have squandered by killing themselves too soon, then it is seen that lessons were not learned and that person may again reincarnate to a similar situation to see if they cope with it better. The world of the soul is apparently very forgiving and we are given endless second chances to help eliminate our foibles, vices and tardy ways. So whether you have a grumpy streak or you are a completely nasty piece of work, you will be given a million chances at life to sort yourself out, to progress and to live a worthy life. There are no recriminations against a soul that 'done bad', but chances are you will keep living the same lesson in life after life after life until eventually you get it right.

My love of Newton's books is that I found he had an answer to many of the questions commonly posed to religion. For example, if there is a God why do we suffer evil, tragedy, and death? Having read his books I would interpret that mainstream religion simply got it wrong, we are not here to be loved by an all powerful god, we are here to progress and return home to digest what we learned. Pain, death, suffering, tragedy are all part and parcel of that process. But happily our journey here is fleeting, when we return to our true home the pain we suffered or the pain we caused will make more sense.

It is via this playing and learning in our groups that Newton claims we progress as souls. This is shown through the color of our form. Brand new souls are a bright white light, this dulls and turns through yellow to blue as the soul gains more experience and becomes wiser and more experienced at life. With experience we learn from mistakes made in this and other lives and eventually we stop making the same errors. Those of us lucky enough to be 'old souls' are rarely people who you would expect, they tend to blend in with the masses and contribute vastly to society in quiet and non-attention seeking ways. Newton points out that many of the rich, famous and celebrities are often new souls, they are being given a chance to play around with their lives and see what human existence can bring them. Like magpies they hoard glitter, fame and success, possibly to the detriment of relationships, family and friendship. This perhaps explains why they manage to get themselves in such intriguing pickles and constantly need to go to rehab. At least their calamitous lives keep Perez Hilton and the gossip pages in business!

As we progress, we may take on other 'jobs' in the afterlife. These include becoming a guide/teacher to less experienced souls. Other souls might practice with energy to create plants, or living creatures, while others go into soul rehab, helping damaged souls overcome their human life traumas. Each soul group has their own teacher, perhaps somebody who when we are living we would refer to as our spirit guide or angel. These loving beings are more progressed souls, who love us infinitely and try to help us become better. They can tap into us even when we are on earth, placing intuitive thoughts in our minds, warning us of danger or maybe giving us that bright spark of an idea that comes from nowhere and seems to be the thing you were put on this planet to do! Of course we might never recognize that these ideas or warnings come from elsewhere, and yet I am sure you would have examples of times when thoughts or plans have simply popped into your head to protect you, guide you or even change your life.

My personal example of this would be the random thought that I would start to write a spiritual based blog every day before I went to work. As I sat down at the computer and started to type I suddenly realized that I loved what I was writing, that I had a lot to say, and that it felt strangely right. It was then that I suddenly realized and knew that I had to write this book, a thought that seemingly came from nowhere. I had no plans prior to this about writing any kind of book, and was struggling to get my one page of music writing done for a magazine once every three months! But when the thought dropped in it felt perfect. I was at the right stage in my life and there was nothing to hold me back. In many respects, I felt I needed to write the book, that it was part of my personal journey, the progression of myself and the logical result of all my culminate life experience (perhaps in this life and beyond!) It is this experience that I can personally relate to Dr Newton's discoveries and that I like to think was my plan before coming to earth. I assume that on that random morning my guides on the otherside chose to remind or influence me, giving me a kick up the butt to choose or remember the direction I have now taken.

There is so much about Dr Newton's books that I would love to tell you here, however, I might be bordering on plagiarism, so I strongly suggest you read them for yourself. They were comforting, life changing, and life enhancing to me, and because of this I cannot recommend them highly enough.

I would also recommend the writings of Dr Brian Weiss. Weiss claims to have stumbled into a past life regression whilst working with one particular patient – Catherine. Although this was of great benefit to Catherine and her personal problems, it appears to have been more helpful to Dr Weiss, in transforming him from a total cynic, to one of the foremost psychiatrists working in the field of past lives and reincarnation. This is described in his book

Many Lives Many Masters. In this he describes how his client Catherine was a bit of a gibbering wreck, she was afraid of just about everything. By using early life hypnosis (childhood memories) he was able to make some small improvements, however nothing was really getting to the core of the matter and she was still suffering from crippling phobias, fears and massive anxiety. Under hypnosis he requested that she go back to the time that had caused all of these mental problems, and it's then that she clicked into a past life. Working with Catherine over a period of months, he regressed her to a variety of past lives encompassing a startling time frame of thousands of years. The experience had clinical benefits too. As a result of this regression work she swiftly made a significant recovery, becoming a confident, happy and well-functioning person.

Meanwhile, Dr Weiss was uncovering information about reincarnation that he previously would never have believed or taken seriously. This led to him becoming one of the major authorities on hypnosis and regression, and he wrote a number of books documenting his forays into past lives and indeed future lives.

Dr Weiss's books are in some respects similar to Dr Newton's, although his contact with the in between space is not as significant as Newton's, he does have some communication with the other side through Catherine. This acts as verification of what is happening, with voices coming through Catherine and telling him things about his life that Catherine could not possibly know. Both doctors chose to keep their questioning to a minimum and allow the hypnotized subject to lead the conversations. Both claim that they did not go out looking for evidence of reincarnation, or life after death, and as a result, a sense of awe and fascination comes across clearly in their writing. It is as though the universe chose them to be the messengers of this glimpse into something wondrous and inexplicable.

Past Life Regression High Heels to Habits in Ninety Minutes

It was my reading of Dr Michael Newton's books that really set me off wanting to experience this for myself, although it was not something that I actively pursued until sometime after I first read them. A couple of years I was giving them a second reading, when coincidentally a friend asked me to attend Bikram Yoga with her. Bikram is the sweaty kind of yoga done in silly hot conditions. The Bikram Yoga center hired out rooms to all kinds of therapists and I found myself face to face with a leaflet for a young past life regressionist, Ms Lucy Gibbs. As I had been exploring the subject again it occurred to me that this was a great opportunity to indulge in some past life investigation. I was pleased that this would be in familiar surroundings, and I realized that it would be a great compliment to re-reading the books. I embraced this coincidence and figured I would have been a bit mad not to have a go!

I booked myself in and the day approached. I have to be honest and say that I got myself in a real flap in the lead up to my regression. I researched other people's experiences of past lives and became acutely aware that it was likely that I would see my own past death scene, or maybe even multiple death scenes. As a result I got more and more worked up about the whole event. On the day I arrived early and sat in my car ready to fend off parking attendants who appeared to be loitering with intent. I felt positively anxious, if not a little on the terrified side.

Now I can be a skittish rabbit from time to time, but I had truly gotten myself vexed about this situation. I entered that office like a Playboy bunny fresh from a beach blonde bleach that had soaked too far into the scalp, entered the bloodstream and left me ditzy. There was little that the therapist could do to appease my nerves. She was very nice, and of course she said all the right things, but by this point I was pretty convinced I had died a horrible, traumatic and painful death and it was only a matter of minutes before I relived it in surround sound, Technicolor glory.

As a result of my all-encompassing nerves I honestly believe I was only half hypnotized. I am sure that the therapist earned her money with me, as I was pretty hard work. I was scared to death of death, but the more Lucy tried to relax me, the more I felt my conscious mind kicking into gear. I simply could not shut my mind off in the way I wanted to, and instead of allowing the hypnosis to take over, my busy brain kept coming back in and trying to sabotage any images or thoughts with logic. (That's got to be the first time anybody has ever referred to my brain as being logical!) I convinced myself I was not hypnotized, I said to myself I was not relaxed, I thought that anything that came into my head I was simply making up to make the hypnotist feel better. It was ridiculous! But in spite of all this, eventually I had some truly interesting experiences.

Due to my Playboy Bunny brain being on overload, I believe that I felt much of the past life regression in my physical body rather than mentally. So whilst my head was listening out for the yoga class next door finishing, or hearing the noise of cars and caught up in listening to police sirens from the city below, my body had slipped into a state of physical hypnosis, and along with some unconscious part of my brain, I was experiencing some odd sensations.

The first physical 'feeling' came apparent when Lucy took me back into my mother's womb. Whilst my thoughts were racing on how silly this all was I did begin to feel a change in my physical body. My tummy seemed to swell and my hands that rested on it felt as though they were rested on a big round belly, rather than my normal (more or less) flat one. I felt a heartbeat intensely and all around me. Lucy asked me how I felt about coming into the world and I experienced a significant pang of anxiety in my solar plexus. I knew then that physically, if not mentally, I was remembering the womb, and that as a baby about to be born I was nervous, worried and anxious – perhaps a reflection of how easily

I get into a dither about things now (past life regression included)! Despite this worry about my imminent birth, I did feel an immense sense of joy, wellbeing and a peace, calm and innocence that I cannot remember experiencing before.

We moved from here into trying to view my past life or lives. Again I questioned the images coming to me. Lucy asked me to look at my feet and report back what I was wearing. In my mind's eye I thought I could see rags on my feet, and disappointed by this I decided to say I saw nothing. I was still fighting the hypnosis and convincing myself that my brain was making it all up. In many respects it does feel like you are making it up, although not purposefully. It is very difficult to accept that the images you see are not planted there by a desire to see something, rather than because they are actual past life memories.

That said if I was making it up it certainly does not explain the bizarre and extremely non-rock 'n' roll life I appeared to have had as a nun working in an orphanage. Yes, it's true; I was apparently a nun. When I did relax enough to get some images and feelings, I only believed them because they were too damned weird for me to have made up. If I was going to have lived before I was hoping I had been an American Native Indian or at the very least a maid to Cleopatra, something with a bit of 'wow factor', but no apparently not.

The way I discovered this holy role was again through physical symptoms rather than any obvious mental images. It started in my body, I felt my arms curl in on themselves and one side of my body curve over and become useless. I knew this was peculiar and told Lucy, who explored it more. She asked what was wrong with me, and although I could not name it I felt and knew that I was old, arthritic and tired. She asked me why and the answer that seemed to fall out of my mouth was, 'too many babies'. But when questioned I knew these babies were not mine; they had been my job. For year upon long year I had looked after other peoples' very young abandoned babies. I was exhausted from it and my body had become crippled due to the physical demands. I was sad that now after years of being the carer, it was now others who cared for me. I felt useless. I knew that I did not have any friends and that my life had been entirely functional, day in, day out. I did not love babies, nor did I dislike them, I just looked after them. I knew all this without having to be asked, I knew I was frustrated, maybe a little bitter. I knew I had devoted my life to the church, I could feel my background was European, possibly Spanish or French but definitely not British, I knew that my nun's habit was dull gray in color. I did not really get a decent image or feeling for my death scene, but I believe it was in a bed and that the priest was there, maybe with other nuns, and it was a peaceful, welcome death.

That, in essence, was what I learned from this first past life regression. In many respects it makes some sense. I have always been averse to babies and looked at them as extremely hard and slightly intimidating work. I have not generally been a 'children' person, and have in the past sworn that I will never have them. Prior to the past life regression I found babies exhausting and whenever a proud mummy asked me if I wanted to hold her bundle of joy I would cringe inwardly but accept only out of politeness. Even as a child I remember a distinct feeling that I did not want babies, that they were nothing but work and even then I would look at them as little alien beings that might start crying and make me feel on edge.

Since the past life regression I am a lot more relaxed about tiny kiddies, I can appreciate them in a way I certainly did not before the hypnosis. I even occasionally get broody, in spite of my reservations about the work of nappies, vomit and screaming. I see babies now as potential people, rather than as unrelenting graft. I appreciate that having a child might mean being enslaved to it in some respects, but that once the baby phase is over, the real drudgery will be over, and that other phases in the child's life would commence. My own reluctance to have children has become less hardened. Indeed I may have even considered producing a small brood at some stage myself. This for me was an eye opener and represents personal evidence that past life regression works on some levels.

Some might argue that all regression does is tap into your fears or dislikes and conjures up a story to help, and if this is true then at least it helps. However, it does not explain my intense physical feelings of old age, or why I would tap into a dislike of children and 'cure it'. My aversion to babies was far from being a crippling phobia or even a true fear. I personally do not believe that I 'tapped' into this to help with my mild distaste for infants, I just think that it was an interesting side effect of viewing a life that has clearly had some small impact on my current one.

The strangest and best thing about this experience is yet to come. The day after my past life regression I was seriously aggrieved with myself. I felt I had not relaxed properly and as a result had wasted my time, money and effort on something that I had not fully engaged with. That morning I was taking an unexpected trip to the local supermarket. Marching down one of the aisles I rang my boyfriend close to tears to tell him how frustrated I was with myself. I looked to the side for a second, no doubt distracted by chocolate, as I turned back round, right in front of me stood a little old nun, wearing a grey habit and doing her shopping, trolley and all! I nearly fell over in shock. I had not seen a nun in years, nor have I seen once since. Furthermore, she had simply not been there before I had turned away for that split second. However, on my second glance, she was very much there. She did not look at me, and I did not speak to her. But I left the store feeling that if there has ever been a sign sent to a person then that was most certainly one. It was that experience that proved to me that what I had experienced the day before in past life regression was real and was something I was meant to see. I no longer felt angry with myself for not fully relaxing and I left the supermarket beaming inside, knowing that the little nun had been put there by the grace of god knows what, to show me that there was truth in my experience and that I should be glad. And I was....

Second Past Life Experience

My second past life experience was with a lovely woman named Theresa Hincks who runs a hypnotherapy practice in Leicester, England, named En:trance. Now since my first past life regression I've come a long way. I've done lots more spiritual adventuring and am much more in touch with that side of me. I have almost completed this book and things like meditation, relaxation and going with the flow of information sent to my brain are now far easier for me to do. Through my own spiritual development I have become used to receiving messages from 'above', and I can recognize them as separate from an overactive imagination or my own thoughts. I guess I am now better attuned to my subconscious, or to anything that my guides/angels or spiritual self has to say.

Because of this I walked into Theresa's home free of the fear I felt last time and got on with the job in hand. I experienced two lives, both of which I believe are relevant for me to see at this stage of my life. I do believe that we have probably lived hundreds, so the ones we are shown in regression are the ones that make a difference to us in the here and now. If I return in ten years time, it is likely I will have other matters that need sorting out, and I would probably see totally different lives that relate to my problems at that stage of my life.

In this instance I saw two vastly different lives, but ones that I could see linked together. And indeed I believe they link with the previous life I had experienced as a nun. Rather than go through what happened with Theresa I will simply show you the lives I have experienced and explain how and why they may be relevant to me today.

The earliest life I remembered was that of a Hindu male in the

17th Century. He was a real smart arse, cocky, patronizing, misogynistic and rude. I found myself horrified by the way he/I responded to Theresa's questions. I tried to cool his attitude down, but to no avail. Every time she asked me a question, I answered with a smirk and a supremely condescending tone. I was quite embarrassed but also amused by this. My conscious mind was cringing and giggling in the background, whilst this subconscious Hindu persona was coming out with a real attitude problem that I would never consider to be a part of my character as Alice. Luckily Theresa is used to this kind of thing and I could hear the amusement in her voice. It must have been a comical sight to have little blonde me in my heels and pink lip-gloss speaking the most dreadful patriarchal and self-righteous nonsense!

This life had been one of great wealth and esteem. This man had a family around him, but his attitude toward his wife and children was appalling. He was not cruel or violent, but he simply was not interested. His concerns lay solely in expanding his wealth and power. He sorely lacked the need for human relationships and seemed happy that people feared him. He thought little about his family, and at his daughter's wedding his biggest concern was that he source the largest goat possible to sacrifice, in doing so ensuring his wealth was widely known.

His attitude, however, was not to last. As he became older his wife died and I felt a great sadness on his part, although he certainly did not share his feelings of despair with anyone. Upon his death I was overcome with his mind-numbing sadness as he realized how much he had taken his family for granted. His words upon leaving his body were 'my family were beautiful' and as he said this with such deep regret, I felt myself sobbing on the inside. I felt a great yearning to return to the life and be with that family, but of course it was too late. It was a life spent playing to other's view of him and neglecting the love of the people around him.

Another valuable insight he gave me when he left his body was that 'appearances really do not matter'. I felt that he grieved for all the lost time he had spent building his reputation and his empire, only to realize that this should have been the least of his worries. I think this well reflects the tendency of the modern world to become obsessed with the tiny details, the hair, the nails, the matching handbag, and the expensive jeweler. As a result I have let myself go a little, not entirely of course, but I have loosened some of the edges and instead I give that extra time and energy to my boyfriend James, my cats, my friends and occasionally to the weeds in the garden. So far it's working a treat and I feel happier in my own skin than I did when my nails were more perfectly manicured!

I believe that the lifetime I experienced in my first regression, as a nun in the orphanage came next. Perhaps living as a nun who was responsible for the care and welfare of countless young children was my penance for the previous life of familial neglect. As the nun I was not particularly emotionally close to anybody, but I was devoted to the children's wellbeing, albeit in a regimented fashion. This was a stark and meaningful contrast from the Hindu who had everything but did not appreciate it.

The next life that Theresa accessed was much more recent. It appeared to be in the 1950's and I was an American woman named Emily Johnson. Emily had a fairly insignificant life. She lived with her mother, worked as a receptionist and later had a short stint working in a bar. She never married or had children. She did not seem to be particularly close to anybody in her life. I wonder if the closeted life as a nun had an effect on Emily's psyche that perhaps made her uncertain of men, relationships, children and people in general. Although there was some regret on Emily's part for her wasted life, I also felt she was largely unaffected by her uneventful existence. When I left that body I felt a relief to be going home, as though that life had been one of servitude to existence itself. Emily did not love, she merely breathed and continued. Sad.

As I look across these three very different lives I can see many patterns. Most dominant is the lack of close family or friendships. Very little appeared to be achieved by the three characters, or at least very little out of the ordinary or of any meaning. Recently in my life as Alice I have given much thought to family and friendships and it seems that these days I like to surround myself with both, alongside keeping myself busy and interested in life. I believe I was shown these lives so that I can see how much better I am doing, and that any tendency I might have toward complete independence should be swiftly quashed. In my life today I appreciate the value of people, and I see this past life regression as a stark reminder of that, at a time when so many other things often take precedence, life, work, writing, reruns of Sex and the City.

Strangely enough as a young girl I was always deeply concerned for lonely people, the very thought of Eleanor Rigby in the Beatles' song by that name made me want to weep. I also had an innate fear of being alone and that one day I might find myself all alone in a strange town, with no friends and nothing but a light bulb and crackly old TV for company. I have lived through that now, not only as Emily, but also as Alice. When I first moved to the town I live in now I knew no one, I had one friend who I lived with, but she was away on business frequently. My family were far away and my friends were dotted all over the country consumed with their post university job hunts and new beginnings. I had just split from my first serious boyfriend and the grief and loneliness was immense. All my plans were completely awry and I found myself in the midst of an enforced and frightening fresh start. My house was rented and empty, the television did not work and I felt truly alone. I remember walking down the street and wondering if anybody would notice if I went missing. I feared that should something happen it would be days before anyone realized anything was amiss. I now believe I was purposefully put in that position again; I had to deal with what Emily could not deal with and move on from it. It was a hard lesson, but one that had to be learned.

Instead of curling in on myself, and living a lonely existence, I went out, got jobs and made friends. I was tossed a few lifelines in the form of a lovely next-door neighbor and a first job full of youngsters just like myself. I soon started a significant love relationship with my James and moved on with my life. I can see now that what I did not learn in three whole lives I have finally achieved this time round. The lessons I faced three times over, and did not succeed with are, I hope, now accomplished, or at least in the progress of being so. I guess I have to keep the good work up for the next 50 or so years, and only then will I know if I got it right. That said, me thinks I am on the right path – finally!

What my three or four lives (including this one) have really taught me, and that I think is worthwhile passing on, is that it is unconditional love and kindness that really matter. A life spent pursuing material success, awards or recognition is worthless entirely if you do not share yourself, your possessions and your love with others. One thing that seems to cross all faiths, beliefs and spiritualities is the idea of love and that love is a universal energy. I do believe that once we tap into our own love and pass it about unselfishly then we are moving so much closer to enlightenment. Our world of chocolate bars, weekend city breaks, divine silk dresses and Dior lip-gloss is so full of distractions that it is becoming easier to live life without expressing or even truly feeling our love. Fame, acclaim, cash and shiny rings replace love these days. However, should we choose the fast, easy, purchasable, credit crunching route then, yes we might look good, and yes we may feel amazing (soft skin, glossy hair) but, if that is all we have, then we have nothing except our body. In the end the body will crumble and we will have forgotten how to love. And when we die I reckon you'll be gutted for the waste, and the waste of yourself and your time and your energy.

My thought is this. We are all human, we are all vulnerable from hurts we have carried with us from the past and the unknown hurts that have yet to occur. Our egos boost us up and insist that we act, look or react a certain way, to keep people out, to keep them guessing or to protect our selves. We believe that we are valued upon the appearance and personality that we put across. I know I have done this, the false belief that the correct dress, beaming smile and perfectly applied make up will truly represent your inner being and make people admire you, respect you, envy you...The list goes on. What I believe I am learning now is that appearances really actually do not matter. What does matter is the hearts of the people we love, and even the hearts of those that we do not. What is sacred is not a spa day or a facial, but compassion, acceptance and the gift of our precious time.

Love is the only thing with any true value. In the literal end it is all we have and it is all we leave with. If we do not have it, or we do not give it, then our lives are pretty futile. How we act as a result of our love is key to our souls' progression. You can win an Oscar, a Nobel prize, the lottery and a top modeling contract all in one day, yet none of these achievements mean diddly squat when paraded next to the achievements of the heart, forgiveness, kindness, generosity and all those other big, lovely words. Anyway lecture over; I will leave you to think about it...

Life Between Life Regression

Now in all honesty most of my Life Between Life (LBL) session was far too personal and private to reveal. As you flick through the preceding pages of this book you will notice that I have revealed a great deal about myself. I am sure you will understand that I have to save something for the next book! Yet despite my willingness to lay my soul bare, to go into too much detail about my Life Between Life Regression would be a literal and precise baring of my soul. If what I do say intrigues you, I suggest you get your own LBL done. Because intriguing as my soul may be, it will be meaningless and dreary compared to learning all about your own!

I will start this section with something intriguing I learned about soul mates and love. Leading on nicely from my last rant, here I go again…

Within my Life Between Life I was lucky enough to meet with my soul group. This is the special group of people I have been with since my creation, and with whom I have spent thousands of years and countless lives. Altogether there were six of us. Of these six I recognized two as people that I know. Happily, one of them is my current boyfriend. The other is… well that would be telling! I will not be naming names as it really is that person's journey to figure out on their own, if they want to. My influence might be both unwanted and possibly terrifying.

I will tell you something utterly brilliant about the two people I recognized. I already kind of knew they would be in my group. Have you ever met someone and nearly fallen over backward because you seem to recognize, know and understand that person without ever having met them? Have you felt an instant click and been able to pass hours, or days in their company enjoying a deep and unexplained sense of comfort, peace, ease or bliss? If you have, then I believe there is a good chance you have met one of your soul mates. Perhaps, if you are very lucky one or two of your soul mates have always been around perhaps in the form of your annoying but adorable younger brother or a childhood best friend?

Soul mates are of course a lovely concept, laden with overtones of perfection; happiness and an elephant sized load of expectation. I have to say that given my Life Between Life experience, the idea of a 'perfect' soul mate is rather unrealistic and misleading. Having met a couple of my soul mates, I know that it is not so simple as meeting Mr or Miss Charming and living happily ever after. Soul mates are literally a team; they are the ones we grow with. Yes, we may become entangled in Romeo and

Juliet style romances with them, but there is every chance that your relationships with these people will be fraught, educational, intriguing and often stressful. Living with or knowing our soul mates on earth can be more of a challenge than dealing with complete strangers. In spite of any problems, you will still feel deeply drawn to them. This is fine, however, you could have a whole heap of disillusion or disappointment in store for you if that person lets you down, deceives you or cannot match your heavy expectations. It is through pre-planned agreements with our soul mates that we suffer, that we feel pain, and that as a result we become more experienced and grow.

In some instances a 'soul mate' on earth will make your life easier, although for souls intent on progressing further with their 'soul lessons' some of these soul mates might be present in your life to stir things up incessantly, giving you plenty of juicy material to learn from. It may be a soul mates pre-agreed role to appear in your life and cause all kinds of untold difficulty and damage. In the name of soul progression we might plan all kinds of awful stuff to happen to us. We may agree to rejection and clandestine affairs. We may agree to hurt and tears and heartfelt sadness. Sometimes that is just what a developing soul needs. The nice thing is that we will not hold it against our soul mate once we return to them after our life is over. Once we get over any initial disorientation we will no doubt shake their hand and thank them for playing such a dastardly villain and in doing so teaching us so much about our own selves and our inner strengths.

Have you ever cared for someone despite his or her inability to treat you nicely? Have you ever forgiven someone after your friends tell you not to? Have you ever loved someone so deeply that any wound they inflict does not even dent your feeling for them? If you say yes to any of these then maybe you met a soul group member teaching you something valuable. This is not of course a reason to be a victim, nor am I suggesting you should put up with bad treatment, however, sometimes, in retrospect, we can see that the friend who hurt you, was actually enacting a valuable lesson for you both. All you need to do is take the lesson to heart and move on.

I am currently very happy with my partner, though in the past we have certainly had our ups and downs. As a result of the Life Between Life regression, I can see that we are supposed to be together, and that we will always be together for eternity because we are members of the same soul group. This is such a lovely thought and has lent a new sense of comfort and happiness to how I feel about him. But I can also see why things did not always go smoothly, or why we rubbed each other up the wrong way, and why arguments started over nothing. This was all part of our growth and learning. It is a sad but true fact that soul mates when in human bodies are not perfect beings, they are only human, and no matter how much we love them they are just as liable to mess up as anyone else.

Another thing I realized from my Life Between Life regression is that when we are not inhabitants of human bodies, love is a very different thing indeed. On earth we enjoy and bask in all the trappings of romantic, sensual and sexual love. In the spirit world these perky peculiarities of love do not exist. As a result we do not feel the counterpart emotions such as jealousy, anger or bitterness. Instead what we have is vast amounts of unconditional, passionately felt love for our entire group and other groups beyond that. Once we are out of our human skin, love becomes less picky and of course less physical. Attraction is different. I am not sure that souls feel attraction in the way humans do. Passion exists in bucket loads, but it is more equally shared. Although we may relate to one soul more than other souls, we do not require their undivided attention in the same way that we do here on earth. This has the result of making soul life so much easier. No wonder some people call the life between human incarnations, heaven!

As souls I do not think that we are always faithful to one particular soul mate. I believe we reincarnate with a soul that suits that lifetime. I also think that after a certain point, say several hundred thousand years, you really are going to want a change of partner, no matter how much you adore the original one! This change is not because you 'split up' with a soul mate, but enables you to learn new and different lessons with someone who you are perhaps not so comfortable with.

I am also sure that you can be perfectly happy in a relationship or deep friendship with somebody not of your soul group. Dr Newton tells us that it is rare for a person's parents to be in their soul group. It may be that we choose parents from closely related soul groups. Think how much you love your parents (or your children) and that will show you very clearly how love and learning comes not just from our own special posse, but from other posses too. It may be inconceivable to some that their parents or kids are not bonded to them in that way, but it also shows that love is not limited in any way by barriers, cliques or inner circles.

When I met with my soul group, the vibe I got from each and every soul was very different. The ones I recognized were so happy to see me, but in very different ways. I was spun around, danced with, embraced and kissed. Other souls placed thoughts of love into my mind mentally, or did some kind of fancy energy transfer tricks that made me feel warm and fuzzy inside. Not one of them did I want to strip naked and make sweet passionate love to. Not one of them did I fancy or even have the slightest crush on. I just felt a huge degree of respect, admiration and adoration for them all. Yes, I agree that it is a bit weird that souls do not jump each other's bones, or have a cheeky snog after one too many Flirtini's at their local cocktail bar. I would say it is a shame that souls miss out on that very human behavior! But the thing is, it is not a shame.

It is easy to think that what humans have is the paramount experience of sensation. But maybe that is because when we are here on earth we do not know any different. What souls do experience is a thousand times different from what we on earth can comprehend. The life of our soul is even more powerful and awe inspiring than multiple orgasms with somebody you truly love, in an exotic location and high on pure ecstasy. Yes that might touch the edges, but the life of the soul goes far deeper than the ecstatic pleasures of the human body. Do not worry, great sex, great food, the agony of teenage crushes, the ecstasy of the perfect first kiss, and all of that other 'human' stuff is not gone forever once you return to your Life Between Lives. There are umpteen more human lives you can live in the future where all your saucy fantasies can come true and where you can sample every single delight that a human body can revel in.

My LBL experience was special. It showed me that I had made certain plans before I came to earth, and that thankfully these plans are currently being enacted very nicely. It was great to see that I am on the right path and it was spectacular to know that James is coming along for the ride. As I did not recognize half of my soul group, I also have their presences to look forward to in the future.

Life Between Life regression is certainly an eye opener, and it has totally transformed the way I see my world. It has been the cherry on my enlightenment cupcake. I cannot really explain in words just how precious this experience has been, so I say you should do it yourself. If you are looking for eye watering, near immediate enlightenment, then this is the way to go. Life Between Life regression can literally change your life, I kid you not, what are you waiting for?

Past Life Conclusion

Coincidentally, in between a spot of editing and proofreading I was checking my Facebook, yes sad I know, I am too old for all that malarkey! A Facebook friend of mine had sent me a message saying 'What was your past life, click here to discover'. Well apparently Facebook is now scrolling into the past, no doubt using an automated system to second-guess one of several likely options. This got me thinking about the sheer amount of rubbish that abounds relating to past lives and spirituality in general. There is no regulatory body to safeguard areas such as this, it is easy to get sucked in, taken advantage of or plain and simple lied to.

Example: Recently following a tarot reading on Spitalfields Market in London I was told I had lived as a witch and an Egyptian priestess. 'Rock on', I thought. But on second thoughts 'Jog on love', and 'please tell me how you know that?' The overpriced tarot reading was fairly inaccurate and now she expected me to believe that, as well as her promise to shoot some Reiki energy up my spine, I think not! As I am now a fully fledged Reiki practitioner I know that Reiki will not be shot anywhere that it does not want to go. Basically there are a lot of Charlatans about, so tread carefully. If someone in the back of a magazine tells you that for £1.60 a minute you can phone her up and she will tell you all about your past lives, be suspicious, ideally rip the page out and stick it in the recycling! I have had enough experience of these dodgy distant readings to know they are not worth paying for and are not worth even contemplating.

Hypnosis is of course a vulnerable state to get yourself into, so make sure that if you do go in for a regression you check carefully who it is with. If possible go by recommendation or valid certification. Dr Newton has a website listing all his trained hypnotherapists, (see the recommended section), so that is a great place to start. Dr Weiss has his own CDs so you can do regression self-hypnosis at home. Whatever you were in a past life and whoever you are now, do not be a fool, and do not let your quest for spiritual paths in life lead you down the wrong one.

Oh and in case you were wondering, according to Facebook, I was quite unsurprisingly Teddy Roosevelt the 26th President of the United States of America. I cannot imagine why that one did not come up in the regression sessions…hmmm

So they say that you only live once? Interesting theory that! I guess in some respects it is true, you only live once in this body, with your name, your face and your flesh. But beyond that I reckon it could get a lot more exciting than the atheist theory of eternal nothingness. From my own experiences, I am inclined, no, I am obliged to think differently.

The theory about past lives and living as a soul has rocked my world, the knowledge I have of my own past has changed this life. All of what you have read in this chapter is what got me started on the high-heeled path to enlightenment. It is because of this that the rest of this book exists. I have covered this early on as it is so darned important to the rest of everything else I have to say. I hope it may affect your life as radically as it has done mine. If not I hope it has at the least made you raise your perfectly plucked eyebrows in astonishment, intrigue or amazement?

Back to that whole thing about 'You only live once...' That, my dear, is what parents would say to try to get you to do your homework. It is what your ex-boyfriend said to try to lure you into a threesome with his ex-girlfriend. It is what maniacs say to try to get you to jump out of planes for fun. People only ever say 'you only live once' to try to make you do things. They say it to scare you, or to make you feel guilty; it is a manipulation tactic extraordinaire! Next time someone dares utter those words to you, tell that cunning person that you happen to know better. In fact, even better, scoff in their face and tell them to blooming well bugger off and take their veiled threats with them! You only live once? I have never heard such nonsense in all my days!

The High Heeled Buddha

"All Happiness in the world arises from wishing others to
be happy"
– Chanti Deva

I turn to Buddhism next because I truly believe that had I been a serious Buddhist all of my life then many of the conundrums and catastrophes I have encountered may have been avoided, or would have had significantly less impact. I am in no doubt that I would be a happier, kinder, more generous, tolerant, and highly cherished member of society. This is of course conjecture and I am sure many a fine Buddhist has fallen foul of the various temptations and delusions they are supposed to avoid.

However, the wonder of Buddhism is that the principles are so heart-achingly simple. The general gist of Buddhism is as follows: be a good, caring, unselfish person and do not allow the unpleasant details and/or valueless temptations of life drag you down. If you can get this right you are on a one-way course to a future life in a higher realm, or at the very least a better position in the food chain. Let's explore...

Buddhism is infinitely sensible, it tells you what you already kind of know, but it does so in a way that makes you want to commit to it. Apart from the threat that if you do not attempt to adhere to the philosophy you might come back as a baser creature (think slug, spider, lame calf) it all makes perfect sense! Although you may not want to adopt a rigid Buddhist lifestyle, Buddhist thought certainly contains some tips and hints on general living that will suit and assist anybody. Similarly to most religions, it has 'rules' on behavior, but rather than simply dictating these rules Buddhism gives you reason to wish to follow them as an inherent part of becoming and developing your true self. This guidance when followed will advance you as a person and bring about a better sense of well being with oneself and the world around you.

Before you embark on your Buddhist journey be warned, being a good person is so much harder than you might at first imagine. The Buddhist version of a good person is far more complex and mentally taxing than other approaches. In most religions if you are generous, caring and do not kill or harm living things, you are generally set up for a nice life and a cozy little set up in the afterlife. With Buddhism, not only are you required to be wonderful to everyone else, but you also have to deal with being wonderful to yourself.

Now I always thought I was pretty nice, and generally a kind, thoughtful and loving young woman. That is, until I studied Buddhism and realized that in fact thinking so highly of myself was 'delusional'. To counter this severe delusion I must think highly of others – all others – even the ones I detest. I must also think only modestly of myself, which of course is not a problem as I am possibly one of the most modest people in the world, ever so modest I am! If I choose not to follow this path I would develop a state of mind referred to as 'self grasping ignorance' and I would then end up being reborn as a Christmas Turkey. Oh dear. So you can see it's not as straightforward as 'Alice play nicely'.

Indeed when committing to a Buddhist path, or when looking to Buddhism for guidance, you might not realize at first how inherently bad (or at least mischievous) you are! I am not for one second suggesting you are evil incarnate, daughter of the devil or even a good friend of sin, however I bet you are worse than you realized! I certainly am.

Buddhism requires at its highest level, a true purging of one's own moral character. In the 21st Century many of our sins, delusions and temptations are part and parcel of everyday life. Our moral and ethical compass is seriously out of whack and things that Buddhism says are bad may be things that you and I enjoy on a daily basis. For example gossip. We all love a good gossip, or 'idle chatter'. Well, straight away that is not allowed, it is banned and you should not do it, no way Missy. From harsh experience I can tell you that stopping the chatter is not without exceptional effort.

I have in the recent past found myself drawn into idle chitchat. The idle chatter had proven most painful when the person the chatter was about, found out. Although we had honestly not said anything malicious, she was understandably upset to learn that in her absence she had been a topic of our conversation. This situation then spiraled out of all proportion and became a seething bed of suspicion, distrust and general misery. We all felt aggrieved, wondering who had chatted what about whom. Stories became confused and what was initially little more than a touch of talk came more to resemble the evil cursing of three malignant hags. It took almost five months for things to straighten out and for the underlying problems caused by all of this to smooth themselves out, indeed I'm not convinced that things will ever be quite the same again in that particular friendship. However, we all learned a great deal despite it being a painful lesson. As a result I approve heartily of the Buddha's stance on such things. This is not to say you can never mention other people in their absence, for example you could get away with saying, 'Reina got engaged, she looks so happy' or 'Roisin is taking her kids to the cinema tonight, she is a great mum'. However, if Buddhism is to be followed you had better keep it constructive, upbeat and clear from any ill feeling.

Furthermore, just because an individual about whom you regularly deposit the poisonous lashings of a venom filled tongue does not know about your consistent bitching, this does not make it better. Although in some instances you may feel quite justified in giving out a frequent verbal battering, you must resist. By harboring a dislike or hatred you are damaging yourself and the people around you. You are allowing negative feelings to consume you at the expense of your good, naturally kind and loving heart. If you are to avoid a future incarnation as a small diseased ant, then you must learn to overlook others' perceived faults and look upon any enemy as a loving mother might look upon her cherished child.

Other hot tips on how to be a Buddhist would be to avoid temptation and self-seeking desire. This one is a bit of a bugger. If you feel desire it is generally down to hyped up hormones. Temptation is what the western world is built on. However, that does not mean we cannot break from that cycle and take fuller responsibility for our actions. Inevitably we are not Tibetan monks and nobody expects us to behave to that rigorous level of sacrifice. If we did, the human race would come to a standstill and eventually go extinct. So I do believe that a little modernism and moderation can be injected into Buddhism to ensure the continuation of mankind, and to allow for a meaningful life.

Once you have invoked the Buddhist rules and are satisfactorily abiding by them, you must also remember not to be too pleased with yourself. According to Buddhism, to cherish one's own self highly is pretty much a cardinal sin of the Buddhist variety. So to put it as simply as possible, be modest (just like me). Thus far, Buddhism consists of modesty, impeccable morals, self-control and the unrequited love of all other beings.

I never said it was going to be easy now ladies!

Who was Buddha? – in a Teeny Tiny Nutshell

Buddha was a living human being. His name was Prince Gautama Siddhartha and he was born in Nepal, Tibet. He lived an easy life of pleasure and frolics as the son of Royalty. He never left the palace or saw anything of real life until he was 29 years old. At this time he did eventually persuade his parents to allow him to leave the palace and what he saw distressed him deeply. All around him he viewed suffering, illness, poverty and death, concepts he had not considered.

Following this he left his wife Yashodhara and their child while they slept (charming!) and went off to find answers. His mission was to accomplish a way by which suffering and pain could be stopped or reversed. Through various arduous tasks such as month long meditations and trips to the wilderness, Buddha gained enlightenment by the young age of 35 and he spent the rest of his life disseminating this learning. I am sure his wife forgave him, as we long suffering women tend to do. These lessons came to be known as 'Dharma' and are used by Buddhists to this day in their search for enlightenment.

Principles and Teachings – the Basics

Buddhism is at its essence the teachings of Buddha. The term 'Buddhism' came about over time and at first Buddha's teachings were simply referred to as 'Dharma' or 'Buddha Dharma' – Buddha's teachings. The term Dharma is one of the most important ones to understand as it basically incorporates every-thing that you must learn and do if you wish to follow the Buddhist path. Dharma means teachings/practice; Buddha taught Dharma and we practice Dharma. For a Buddhist, Dharma is their homework, their lesson, their school and their life, Dharma is a Buddhist's bread and butter.

The people who follow the Dharma, are known as the 'Sangha'. The Sangha can refer to a collective group of Buddhists or all Buddhists worldwide. Together these three terms, Buddha, Dharma and Sangha are referred to as 'The Three Jewels'. The Three Jewels are essential as tools to help us escape the sufferings of 'Samsara'. Samsara is not just a perfume by Givenchy, but in this instance it refers to the state of misery we are all placed in as life forms upon earth. To escape Samsara is pretty much akin to a mass departure from the perfumery that is our planet, onward and upward to the next level of being.

Enclosed within the very pretty sounding 'Three Jewels' there lays a complicated set of beliefs, teachings and practices. These are further confused by the fact that there are three different styles of Buddhist belief. These are Tibetan Buddhism, East Asian Buddhism and Theravada Buddhism. Alongside this there are no doubt hundreds of thousands of different interpretations of Buddhism making their way around the western world. If you want to become a fully-fledged Buddhist then hopefully I can point you in the right direction. But, if like me you are more a 'do it yourself' kind of chick, then perhaps you can amalgamate some of the Buddhist teachings into your own version of the world.

The first thing we need to know about Buddhism, is that the meaning of the word Buddha is 'awakened one', or simply 'awake'. By becoming a Buddhist your main end goal is to achieve a heightened state of enlightenment. Once in this place you will have relieved yourself of all human suffering. By following the Dharma, you start by practicing 'mindfulness'. This is pretty much like 'minding your manners' but on a more significant, life altering kind of level. Mindfulness is a key word when thinking of Buddhism, because much of the Dharma is about keeping control of your thoughts, and in turn your actions. To become 'awake' you must start by growing alert to your own self. Your perceptions feature highly in all this, and some soul searching is going to be essential. Inevitably you will aim to alter your perceptions so they are more realistic rather than a result of how you have imagined things to be.

Unfortunately, simply becoming a Buddhist does not immediately make you a Buddha-like being, nor in fact are you in any way guaranteed to reach a state of 'awakening' in this lifetime. Thankfully Buddhism allows for reincarnation, and therefore you have infinite chances to move to the blissful state of becoming enlightened. Anybody, given time and good practice, can eventually become a Buddha, even if it does take you through to the next millennium. Unlike Christianity, where there was only one Jesus Christ, in Buddhism we all have a shot at being top dog. Just bear in mind that it is not all Nirvana and inner peace. Like most religions there is a flip side and hard work will be expected. If you are naughty you risk affecting your karma, by this I mean your bad behavior will come back to bite you in the ass, ouch. If you are really, really bad then there is a chance that when you are reincarnated you will come back as an animal. As an animal lover I do not see the problem myself, I get ever so jealous of my cats who get to sleep and eat all day long as they please. However Buddhists see animals as lower beings and believe that they live frustrated existences. Once you are an animal you will have to claw your way back up to the elevated status of a human being before you can even begin to understand Buddhist philosophy and try again. You have been warned!

The path to the awakened state of becoming a Buddha is evidently a treacherous one, requiring commitment, self-control, sheer bloody mindfulness, masses of meditation and absolute mental perseverance. That said, once you do gain the elusive state of becoming a Buddha, you will be free from all human faults and pain, so really it is worth a shot! Those things which worry everyone else (laddered tights, expensive phone bills, bitchy mates, death, destruction and misery) will have no effect on you, indeed you will mentally have raised yourself above any everyday gripes – sounds good? Then keep reading.

The Buddhist Precepts

Precepts are very much like the rules of Buddhism, although they are not necessarily commandments per se. They are more like recommendations that followers of Buddhism agree to abide by. Many of them make perfect sense and are reflected in the laws of the land (do not murder) or most people's ethical stance (do not bonk your mate's husband). Although some are infinitely sensible, others may cause a few raised eyebrows such as 'refrain from getting intoxicated'. This may prove harder for us in the west to abide by – 'what no more wine Wednesdays!', I hear you cry! I personally choose to interpret that one loosely; have a drink but stop before losing control and/or before vomiting. Whilst refraining from 'unchastity' is all very well and good, we do like to continue the human species; so I take that rule in terms of sexual misconduct such as adultery and abuse.

1. Refrain from killing living things.
2. Refrain from stealing.
3. Refrain from un-chastity (sensuality, sexuality, lust).
4. Refrain from lying.
5. Refrain from taking intoxicants.

These five precepts are the main guidelines for all Buddhists and are helpful when trying to establish a good moral code. Indeed these are essential in the conscious avoidance of negative states of mind and the cultivating of good karma. I believe we are big enough and bad enough to interpret these in our own very sensible and responsible ways.

Karma

Buddhists believe that all actions are connected so it therefore makes utter sense that all actions will have their eventual results. Cause and effect so to speak. So just as what you ate last week may affect your body's fat content today, the exercise you do this day will affect your fitness and fat content next week. Karma translated literally means 'action'. The concerns around karma in Buddhist terms are similar to the repercussions of eating three slices of gooey chocolate cake. They taste fabulous at the time, but afterward you feel a little sick, in a weeks' time you have gained two pounds, you no longer fit your favorite jeans and you want to cry, then maybe you do cry a little bit. Similarly the repercussions of your thoughts, deeds and intentions will be felt in those things that occur to you later in this life, and possibly through to the next life, they too may make you cry.

Basically the theories around karma make it worth your while to be on your best behavior. Not just for purely selfish reasons either. Yes, you may not wish to be reincarnated as a blind donkey, but surely you do not wish sadness to befall others as a result of your actions?

The Buddhist law of Karma asks you to be totally conscious of all you do, whilst bearing in mind that your actions today, be they good or bad, may come back to haunt or help you. In his very easy to understand book, the Introduction to Buddhism, Geshe Kelsang Kyatso puts this quite simply, "Virtuous actions sow seeds of future happiness and non-virtuous actions sow seeds of future suffering". This furthers the point somewhat as rather than simply avoiding bad actions, it shows that purposefully committing good deeds, kind actions or simply 'doing the right thing' is sufficient to help create a happier future. Selfishly speaking, if you do the right thing today, great things will happen tomorrow. But if you do the wrong thing today, even if it feels amazing right now, it will sure as hell feel downright awful eventually!

The crux with karma is that it is not just what you do that counts, it can be what you think and what you *intend* in whatever you say or do.

Buddhists believe that karma originates in the mind. At the highest level your best bet is to be a completely pure soul whose mind is in utter focus, who never thinks a sly thought and is certainly never secretly happy at the woes of her enemies. All actions are thought up before they occur, in this respect certain excuses 'I didn't mean to' or 'I just didn't think' become somewhat redundant. If a person is not thinking their actions through, then they are not behaving like a good Buddhist. If they want to be a good Buddhist then they should start examining their own brain before leaving their bed each morning.

Buddhists believe that when you die, if you have outstanding bad karma, this will affect your next reincarnation, although those with good karma and a clear pure mind will experience a fortunate reincarnation. An unfortunate reincarnation would be in what is deemed as the lower realms. These lower realms are the animal realm (think donkey, bug, bear, fish, bird), the hungry spirit realm and the hell realm (eek, say no more). Alternatively for those cashing in on a life full of good karma, the realms potentially open to them are the 'human' realm, the 'demi-god' realm and the 'god' realm – hmmm that sounds better.

Obviously, we are currently in the human realm, as are all other people on the planet earth, including those blessed with good looks, fame and fortune such as Mr Pitt and Ms Jolie. We can all presume that we did OK last time round.

If you are having a particularly hard or tragic life, Buddhists would believe that you were carrying some residual karmic baggage that you brought over from a previous life. For those of you lucky beggars, living lives of luxury and general comfort, do not rest on your laurels. If you take it for granted and do not keep up the good karmic work, you could slip backward and be reincarnated into a harsher human life, or potentially one of the other more scary options.

For a determined Buddhist there are meditations and practices that can help purify bad karma. Although for most of us, not yet ready to commit to a full on version of Buddhism, you may want to purify your own karma by making sure you do not veer from your good intentions. Occasionally go out of your way to do good or even great things for other people. Be good to all creatures and to our environment, do not squash bugs, not even spiders. Think positive thoughts for other people and give out the kindness you would hope to receive. If all else fails, examine your actions and seriously contemplate the following... what harm can it do? On a day-to-day basis I reckon it is noteworthy if you just do your best. Good karma, good intentions, pure thought and general loveliness are certainly conducts worth striving for.

Delusion

Buddhism is anger management with bells on! Many of us are used to living on an emotional tightrope. Even the calmest most serene people may be covering for a great deal of turmoil that they simply do not display outwardly. Buddha, like any good counselor, wants you to let go of all negative emotions and attachments that are disturbing you and standing in your way to accomplishing inner peace. It may be you are too attached to your material objects, unhealthy relationship or business reputation. You may worry unnecessarily, fear the worst or desire new things that you believe will make everything better. Many of us are craving the next thing to make us happy, always believing that things external to us will make the difference. We are like children with toys, we adore our new things but that soon wears off and we get sad, angry, frustrated and depressed, until that is, we get the thrill of the next novelty. We can never just be happy with what we have and who we are.

Delusion is seen in Buddhism to exclude inner peace. If you allow delusions into your mind, no matter what shape or form they take, you will not experience inner peace and your life will be characterized by negativity and foul emotions. Buddha taught that much of our misery is visited on us by our own mind, its wants, needs, imagined perceptions and desires – or its delusions. Dharma practice will steer you clear of many delusions, however first of all it is important to figure out exactly what it is we are steering clear of. Delusion is a Buddhist's foe, so let's get to know the enemy so we can see who or what it is we are avoiding....

All human suffering is viewed as coming from our 'delusions' – in other words, from your own deluded state of mind. This refers to the day-to-day rubbish that we all get mired in and occasionally lose our mind to. A delusion might be something that you attribute significance to that does not really deserve such a high standing. For example, 'If I purchase a lipstick in the 'Pussycat Bows' shade of red then Friday night will be perfect'. Or the belief we have all encountered that another piece of cheesecake is definitely, without a doubt, the right way to go.

Delusion informs you that you will be happy when you have your next car, holiday, man, job, kitchen, etc. It is the material things through which we define ourselves. It is all those things that we mistakenly believe make us happy, but that only make us happy temporarily. It is the person we fell in love with who one year down the line cannot live up to our expectations, but we blame that person rather than looking at our unrealistic perception of them. It is our vivid imagination that imagines goodness where there is none only to be let down time and time again. It is when we mistake lust for love, alcohol for confidence and jealousy for caring.

Delusion is a tricky scoundrel and often we use/abuse our minds to justify our behavior. In doing this we mire ourselves down in negativity and immoral actions. We lose our sense of self and our perceptions become warped and unreliable. We suffer a broken heart constantly as nothing makes us as happy as we think we deserve to be. We do not realize that our own feral and abandoned selves cause all of the misery we are suffering.

All things that lurk and stagnate around the fringes of our society are likely to result from somebody's delusions. Greed, intolerance, addiction, prejudice, crime, cruelty, and violence are without doubt attributable to delusions gone crazy. Whatever form it appears in, delusion is ghastly, it is ultimately destructive and something that Buddhists aim to purge from their lives.

Before you can fully eliminate these emotions or attachments you have to recognize them, how they specifically affect you, or where they might catch you unawares. It may be that a sexy body or delicious ice cream is in your grasp, your mind might desire these things, and you may feel that you need them, one or both, even simultaneously. In some instances this desire may be harmless, healthy, normal. In others it is delusion acting up, for the married woman or obese dieter this delusion becomes a form of self-sabotage. To believe that these things will give us the happiness we crave is liable to lead to abstract misery. Delusion is a drug, we cannot get enough and alas we are our own dealer!

Delusion may not always be something you see in front of you that you can touch or possess; it will come from your own mind, your insecurities and messed up view of the world. You may be prone to jealousy, inappropriate crushes, paranoia, insecurity, emotional outbursts or possessiveness. Maybe you fall head over heels for every guy or gal who looks your way, only to get hurt time and time again. You might feel a deep sense of incompleteness unless you have the newest phone, ring tones, bed linen, or handbag. Maybe you look for self worth by being desired by others or via the buzz that booze, sex, chocolate, cocaine or cigarettes give you.

These are all things that a good dose of counseling could help with, but for Buddhist purposes you must aim to eliminate these negative states of mind completely and utterly. These are not things to be managed or dealt with; they are seen as damaging, mentally exhausting delusions that should eventually be extinguished. Once these are removed, you will find your joy, pleasure and self worth will come from within, no person can then take that away or destroy it. It is an ambitious course of action for many of us, but the long-term benefits are reputed to be immense.

There are of course different levels of behavior depending on what you are aiming for. A Buddhist monk may be aiming for ascension to the higher realm and to totally avoid reincarnation as a human. They will abstain from just about everything. You and I are no doubt happy to reincarnate as a human a few more times, and therefore some management of delusions would be acceptable. In Buddhism it can be satisfactory just to lead a good life, we need not all be Buddha. (Thank Buddha for that! I think I had my work cut out!)

In today's world we do tend to look for happiness in other people, objects, possessions and achievements. If someone writes off your brand new car or you catch your boyfriend in bed with the neighbor it is natural that you react badly, your friends and family would expect it. A Buddhist temperament would require you to attempt to rise above the hurt, forgive them and offer unconditional love to them and all beings. Realistically, I am sure you can do your forgiving from a distance, and nobody is saying you have to take the womanizing scoundrel back!

Alternatively, say you fell in love with somebody who was already taken, or felt compelled to trample over a colleague to get an overdue promotion; Buddha's teachings would want you to recognize that neither of these things would truly make you happy. Buddha taught that it is solely you and your mind that controls and creates your happiness. Any negative emotion you feel is the result of your mind, and of those naughty delusions creeping in.

Inevitably a fully-fledged Buddha would have sympathy and love for all people, rather than anger, hate or emotional turmoil. A Buddha would maintain a sunny and calm disposition no matter what the circumstances. It may sound a little like you should shut yourself off from all human experience, but this is not the case. Indeed it is only the harmful and delusional experiences you should choose to avoid. This cultivates an inner peace that will see you through whatever malevolent events life has in store for you.

It is fair to say that Buddha never married Mick Jagger nor did he have his brand new VW Beetle totaled by a drunken idiot. And do not for a second think that if I caught my man in bed with another lady I would not go anything other than completely crazy. Quite frankly I am not convinced I will always be able to say no to that last piece of pizza, or refuse to listen to the remarkable gossip in celebrity magazines. However, given a few lifetimes of Buddhist practice you and I may just about be getting there. If you can control your delusions you are certainly well on your way to enlightenment. Of course nobody expects you to be rid of delusion overnight, and for now, seeing as we are merely beginners still, I suggest we aim for a 'best endeavors' approach to get us started.

Meditation

Ongoing meditation is essential to Dharma. It is one of the main tools through which you might eventually rid yourself of these delusions, improve your karma and prevent your rebirth as a cockroach.

Meditation is a form of mind control or gentle self-hypnosis. It is a tool that Buddhists use to get to know and then control their own minds. As a result of daily meditation followers are better placed to tackle the problems of delusion and karma. By meditating Buddhists aim to create a space of perfect clarity in which they can be peaceful. In this wondrous inner space the stresses and strains of the world external to them will not affect them. Over time this leads to a perfect and happy state of mind that is accessible at any time, transferable skills, so to speak.

Through the regular practice of meditation a person is essentially manufacturing their own happiness, a happiness that stems from inside, and does not require possessions, partners, friends or other outside influences to maintain. Of course, hopefully you would still have all of those things; however, the enduring source of your happiness and peace would not be reliant on others. The end result of this is to achieve 'Nirvana'.

I am sure you are aware that Nirvana is so much more than a fabulous grunge rock band with a now deceased lead singer and a drummer who currently heads up the Foo Fighters? Nirvana is a perfect state of being, a state that clearly Kurt Cobain never reached, if he had, then perhaps he would not have taken a gun to his own head. On a positive note, if Kurt had reached Nirvana his music may have taken a twist for the cheerful, and his legions of teenage fans (including me once upon a time) would have nothing to turn up to high volume and vent their angst upon. Once a Buddhist has reached Nirvana it is said that she will be happy and peaceful for eternity.

For everyday use meditation will help you to maintain a calm and relaxed attitude to life. It helps strip away the unnecessary stress that you pick up as you go about your daily life. Although you may never reach the blissful state of Nirvana, meditation can help manage and maintain your lifestyle in a comfortable manner. It can assist you in dealing with delusions, contemplating life choices and karmic responsibilities or simply as a means to relax. At a basic level it will help you achieve a balanced mind and prevent your thoughts rattling round your skull, making things worse than they actually are – or is that just me?

For those serious about following a Buddhist path, earnest Dharma is the way forward. Dharma consists of the Buddha's teachings, and is practiced by the conscious meditation on Buddha's various teachings.

The first steps of Dharma involve the serious and prolonged contemplation of death. This includes repeating the thought 'I may die today', frequently during the meditative state. The point being, that if a Buddhist is severely aware of the potential of their imminent demise, they have a heightened awareness of their behavior and their own mind. This ensures that they are more likely to live their lives as though they may die at any moment. This of course does not mean that they go on a mad spending spree, drunken bender or throw themselves into numerous passionate flings. What it does mean is that they choose to live in a manner that is constantly good and respectful of Buddhist precepts. This ensures that on their death their rebirth into the higher realms is assured. Ladies, this means consistent, unfailing good behavior – you got that sweetheart?

Although this might sound somewhat depressing, it is clearly an extremely mindful way to go about your life. As much of Buddhism is based around the concept of being mindful, the ultimate way to respect this is by being mindful of the very end consequences (death), at all times. This seems fairly miserable, and I am not going to argue that fact.

We must remember that Buddhists have their eye on the goal, which is not just a decent rebirth, but also the end of all their suffering and eventually the accomplishment of full enlightenment. Put like that it makes sense, we can see that the seemingly morose contemplation of death is in fact a step toward a richer reward. The price being to put up, shut up and love, love, love.

Antidotes

Buddhist practice teaches that by implementing certain mindsets we can defy those thoughts that drag us down, thus circumnavigating delusion and negativity. Buddhism identifies that there are 26 negative mindsets and only eleven positive and virtuous mindsets. Luckily, however, the positive ones are pretty powerful and like any good multipurpose cleaner, singular positive mindsets can be implemented to wipe out a multitude of nastiness.

Non-hatred is an opponent to anger, as is patience. Renunciation is the opponent of attachment. This means letting go of emotions, or possessions or whatever it is that has a hold on you and is preventing your happiness. You might try giving things away rather than letting them fester unused in your cupboards. Or you could practice non-hatred by actively making an effort with people who you think you dislike, you never know, you may make a new friend.

Like much of Buddhist theory this implementation of antidotes to negativity is simply another way to tackle your wayward mind. Buddha in his lifetime taught around 80,000 lessons, and what I have touched upon here is only the very general gist of these. The intention, of course, is to develop a peaceful, contented and spiritual mind. This, in theory, is wonderful, but the only person who can choose to do it is you. There is no priest to baptize you and cleanse your sins, there is no

67

confessional box whereby your history will be forgiven and erased. Buddhism is a hard mental slog. Read on to see how I coped with my few days as a wannabe Buddha in training!

Buddhism and Me

I have been ringing the Buddhist bell pretty loudly throughout this chapter, but could I cope with the reality? I decided to put my money where my mouth is, attend a Buddhist school for the day, pick up some tips and practice a little Dharma for myself. I attended a Buddhist center in the leafy outskirts of Nottingham a city in central England. This center houses several resident Buddhist workers and a handful of ordained Buddhist monks, both male and female. I was surprised to see that these were proper monks with impressive robes and shaved heads – even the females.

Upon entering the building I was immediately greeted by several people who were all keen to drag me in every direction, show me about and sign me in. I settled on a friendly female who tentatively took me to the café and ladies restroom. I had a peek into the meditation room, but could not enter straight away as I had to remove my shoes first. Shoes off, I had a wander round the little shop with its honesty box for payments. Then I was off outside to the courtyard, in the midst of winter, to find the free tea and coffee counter. I returned back inside, with a steaming mug in hand, which was not of much use to my freezing toes, only to discover that we did not need to enter the meditation room for another twenty minutes and my shoeless state was at that stage entirely unwarranted. The only purpose it was serving was putting me on a fast track to pneumonia. Shoes back on I wandered round trying to kill time.

I was frequented by several of the residents who were keen to have a little chat and let me know what lay in store. One of my main thoughts was how dreadfully friendly everybody was. Of course, there is nothing wrong with friendliness, however, it was a little like the Stepford Buddhists. Smiles permanently plastered on, ready and willing to help me at my every literal turn. These people are seriously practicing their Dharma and respect goes out for the extreme level of friendliness I encountered. One poor man tripped up, nearly lost his teacup and dropped his sugar on the floor in his efforts to grin happily and greet me as I passed by. Or maybe that was just because of my low cut top and mini skirt? I am of course joking; it was far too cold for such frivolous clothing!

However the friendliness was astounding, slightly intimidating and I am sure it's hardwired into the residents as their way of living the Buddhist dream and recruiting new mini Buddha's in training. I hate to be cynical or critical, but in some small respects it reminded me of those smart suited young Mormons or Jehovah's Witnesses who come to the door with a massive smile and perfect manners. The Buddhists had that same googly-eyed, startled look of awe accompanied by a profoundly childlike desire to please. Although maybe that's just what people look like who have found a semblance of inner peace.

The meditation room was so peaceful. The front housed an altar with a variety of Buddhas. These ranged in size and were decorated with gold leaf, some of them had cute little yellow jackets with pointy hoods on – adorable – Buddha is a hoody! Each Buddha had himself some dried spaghetti and what looked like orange juice. Many people offer their Buddha statues gifts, and I deduced that this is what the pasta and squash represented.

The teachings were interesting and confirmed my understanding of Buddhism. Each session began and ended with the singing of prayers. To be quite honest I almost got the giggles the first time as the singing went on for about ten minutes without warning or explanation. Bear in mind that it was a beginner's course and you might get an idea of the confusion abounding around the room. Not to mention the two teenagers who had clearly been dragged along by their parents. They were sat directly behind me and did not even attempt to stifle their hilarity. Part of me wanted to shoot them a dirty look, except that would not have been very Buddhist of me. The other more youthful half of me wanted to up sticks and join them on the back row and have a right lark around with them. Luckily their dad did the dirty look for me, and I sat there, hand over mouth, being very grown up and taking it all very seriously.

As the day went by I found the singing less amusing and more pleasurable. I did not join in as there were too many strange words that were hard to fit into the rhythm and timing. Not that I cannot sing or anything like that.

After hearing each prayer/song several times, the beauty of it really did sink in, even after I got home that night the echo of the sound and sentiment stayed with me. Indeed I awoke the following morning having heard the prayer all night long in my sleep. I cannot explain why or what I mean by that, but I know that all night long those songs had been with me. Not in a tiresome way, but on some deep level that did not disturb what was a great night's sleep. The best part of the day for me was the meditations. Until recently I very rarely meditated, though I always intend to. Being forced to was a welcome opportunity and also a great way to consolidate what I had learned. The last meditation of the day left me absolutely exhausted. Afterwards, I drove home in a peaceful daze contemplating everything I had learned. The next few days I was pooped and I do believe it was in no small part due to the meditation and my active assimilation of Buddhist practices.

I subsequently found that just a few days Dharma practice caused me to take a long hard look at myself, whilst attempting to break some lifetime habits. My conclusions were truthfully not what I expected. Chilled out from the meditations at my Buddhism course, I was utterly taken with the idea of Buddhism and raring to bring a little peace into my life. Although sadly by the end of the week I felt Buddhism may be a little too peaceful for me. What I have learned will certainly be absorbed into my version of enlightenment. Should I ever need him again I will happily return to Uncle Buddha for some more of his life enhancing, wise talking counsel.

My first action in my Buddhist week was to try to minimize the distractions of the world so that I could focus on the internal. Distractions, much like delusions, take up huge amounts of our time, indeed in our fast paced world it is not often that we are without one distraction or another. Some of these seemingly harmless distractions are just that, harmless. But mixed with a day full of them there is precious little time to be alone with your thoughts. We are well practiced at keeping so utterly busy that a few moments alone with our minds will lead swiftly to abject boredom, confusion or the active seeking of entertainment to fill the void.

The distractions I am referring to are varied but some of the worst culprits are televisions, films, music, radio, computers, internet, games, mobile phones, magazines, the list goes on and on. Not only do these things divert you from time alone with you, they can also lead directly to delusions. A mobile phone begets a new mobile phone that is smarter, smaller, and sexier. The television submerges you in images of female perfection until you are drowning in a sea of personal discontent. In all of this madness the 'little me' inside of us goes into hiding and our mind becomes too easily influenced by the barrage of information, commotion and desires.

My first day without such distractions was an eye opener. Not listening to music on the drive to work was a daunting venture. I always listen to music and I always listen to it loudly. Without it I thought my journey would be lonesome and boring. In fact it was the opposite. I kept myself company very nicely and had some intriguing thoughts. I realized how the music I choose to listen to has a habit of leading my thoughts in certain directions, occasionally unhealthy directions. It occurred to me how I use music to reflect or exacerbate my mood, only to wallow in states of fantasy, sadness or anger. I realized that these moods or thoughts would be curtailed abruptly by not listening to the music that makes it worse.

How many of you have been dumped and purposefully listened to some miserable love song incessantly? Have you ever felt angry and played a CD which pumps you up, gets the adrenaline going and in some perverse way makes you feel justified and powerful in your anger? I am sure you have, many times. In some respects this can be cathartic, in other ways it can be damaging. Music (like other external forces) can be far too influential if we let it. Check out Michael Moore's film 'Fahrenheit 9/11' to see the devastating ramifications of allowing emotions influenced by music to take control. Watch the good looking and wholesome young American soldier talk about shooting the shit out of the poor Iraqis, then singing 'burn motherfucker burn' with a satisfied smile on his face.

That's not to say you would let music take hold of you in such a violent way, but why let music (or anything else) dictate to you, make you feel worse, or feel and do things you would not normally feel or do. Maybe you should occasionally turn the noise off, give your brain a breather and examine what you are left with?

Having spent a forty-minute journey with nothing but my brain for company I did not drift off to Wonderland. Instead I enjoyed constructive thoughts about my life, my day and even this book. I felt very independent, free from the shackles of an ever-changing mood brought on by whatever the radio was playing at that moment. I was shocked then that within two minutes of leaving my car and entering a shop the first song I heard had an enormous emotional effect on me. I was wandering round with my shopping basket looking for a suitable breakfast, when some warbling lady in the background managed to make me feel terribly glum. It was only after several minutes that I realized this effect. The saddest thing about this was I had nothing to be sad about. The music was a typical bleeding heart love song, and I was perfectly loved up and satisfied, yet, there I was wandering the aisles like a bereft widow.

The distraction of music is a powerful one, and not one I would choose to give up. However, with these thoughts in mind I will use music more carefully in future. If I need to think about something important then I will drive to work in silence, or refrain from sticking the television on or logging onto the internet as soon as I get home. If I'm feeling sad I may try sticking on something upbeat and happy rather than something that makes me feel worse.

I will be taking Buddha's teachings on such external things in moderation, however I will attempt to utilize my distractions carefully and mindfully, rather than removing them altogether. That said, I am currently writing this with the Red Hot Chilli Peppers as accompaniment – will I never learn – OK, OK I am going to turn them off now!

Now that I can concentrate properly, let's move on to everything else I learned about distractions. The same day as the one where I temporarily liberated myself from music, I also had the luck to observe an entire group of people consumed by distractions. James and I went to an afternoon party that consisted of adults and their kids. We were there for a couple of hours and in this time not a subject of conversation was raised that was not about computers, Nintendo Wii's, TV's, or mobile phones. It was the phones that took up the most time, with the youngest generation comparing them, showing me ring tones, discussing the facilities of the newest models and generally conducting their lives through these small communication devices. The baby of the family was in on it too, holding her mum's phone; she danced along, miming the words and shaking her tiny baby ass. She had great taste in music, but that aside I had to wonder what is becoming of the world! This revealed to me the huge extent to which people are dependent on their technology. Not just as labor saving, convenience devices, but as focal points of their existence. It was frightening.

Like most other people in the western world I have a mobile phone, but ask me what it's capable of and I will giggle nervously. To live your life through a phone is incomprehensible to me, yet so many people live via their gadgets, possessions and perceived achievements. What would happen if these things were taken away and it was just you? Strip us of our youth, luxuries, technology, anti wrinkle cream, fake tan, favorite shoes, exam results and career titles and what is truly left?

I like to think that I have enough about me that I would still have a life without these things. But would you? And if you fear that you would not then I suggest you do something about it, quickly. Western civilized society has our heads stuck in the latest trend to the extent that we lose ourselves and have no idea what is happening two steps away. In this respect I believe the Buddhist precept of renunciation is spot on. If you cannot give stuff up because it has become a part of your soul, then something is gravely wrong.

Of course I have no intention of giving up all my stuff, but like the distractions, I intend to use things more wisely. Do I need the newest phone? Hell no. Do I define my well being or status via my job title? Goddamit no! Will I be happier when I understand what the heck is going on in 'Lost'? Hell, yes, but only for a few moments, then I will be back to the old grind; a litany of emotions will need processing, the dinner will need cooking and the floor will always and forever need cleaning.

Buddhism teaches the importance of the internal as opposed to the external. If happiness comes from within then devoting our lives to the things we possess is the highest kind of folly. My take on this is that if we want to value ourselves, then we must do just that. Valuing ourselves does not mean purchasing the perfect coffee table, it means being happy in our own skin irrespective of furniture,. We must exist apart from our possessions and try to cultivate some confidence and peace of mind that stems wholly from our sense of self. Once you have done that, feel free to dig out the killer heels. Until then maybe a little karma busting meditation would not go amiss!

My following of the general rules went pretty well and as yet this week I have not killed anybody or committed sexual misconduct. The refraining from idle chatter is a little trickier. That said neither was it such a hardship. I found myself steering talk in a positive way to influence conversations away from 'bitching' for want of a better word. I did slip a few times and chattered about a few unnamed individuals but I am a work in progress. Idle chatter was not too hard to avoid and is definitely a valuable exercise in self-restraint and habit breaking. Indeed when you practice the art of loving everybody such restraint becomes much easier. Idle chatter is a bit of a habit I have been trying to kick for a while and is in my experience one of the more damaging things you can do. It is well worth packing it in, Buddhist or not, for anybody on a spiritual path I believe there is no reason to hate, and if you do not hate then why talk about people or things as if you do hate them?

I do think we are naturally gossipy creatures; we get bored too easily, suffer paranoia about people's intentions and have a tendency to think the worst. This is advice for life that I find to be undeniably shrewd – stop the idle chatter. I shall take that one and run with it.

A major thing that has been liberating about my Buddhism practice is the notion of loving everybody. The thought of treating everybody like they are your 'kind and loving mother' is quite out of character for most human beings. This is particularly true if you believe otherwise of that person, or have a controversial past with them to contend with.

To suddenly remove negative feelings toward my fellow mankind was in fact a lovely feeling. It was not a hard state of mind to conjure up and I discovered that by doing this you are forced to think the best of people, and to look on everyone as a friend. As a result I started to look at things from other people's perspectives for once. Rather than blame people for their behavior, I considered what had happened to them, or what I might have done to provoke the way they acted. It was a much more conscious way to go about my daily business and resulted in learning about myself, as well as getting on agreeably with all and sundry.

I also found I was more honest and would tackle issues head on rather than going away seething and developing bad feeling toward a person. It became surprisingly easy to look on people with love, even those I was not so keen on. In fact the less I liked someone the more easily I looked at them with love. I became aware that the people I currently disliked are people I do not know very well. Any feeling I had for them was not representative of who that person really is, it was merely my perception. Realizing this made me much better disposed toward others. It made me question why I had allowed myself to dislike them in the first place. The reason was often so vastly important that I could not remember what it was.

As humans we all like to have a common enemy to keep us motivated and to give us something to talk about. I realized that by extending love toward everyone it was far nicer to have no enemies. Hey, maybe if this mood continues I will make myself some new friends! Love, apparently, changes everything. It was empowering. Try it!

Buddhism is very cool; whether I could fully implement it in my life I am not so sure. I am certainly no nun, in any sense of the word, nor do I want to be (been there, done that – see reincarnation chapter!). In my week of Buddhism practice I did find it hard to reconcile some of the teachings to my modern day life and I felt that although I wanted to embrace Buddhism, I had difficulty with the extreme examples of it. The people I met at the

Buddhism course had been very much immersed in Buddha's teachings. They did little but work, whether that is in their jobs at the Buddhist center or working at their Buddhist practice. It seemed to me it was a very passive existence. And although they spread the word of Buddhism and were likeable people, I felt their version of inner peace did not transfer entirely comfortably to mine.

Firstly I cannot give up my emotions. Not that Buddha says to give them up entirely, but I am not sure I want to be in control all the time. Sometimes people do hurt me, and although Buddha would say that it is their problem, I am not convinced. If somebody hurt my cat or stole my hat, I may well feel angry, I would feel entitled to be so. I really do not want to not feel angry with those people. I know I will not be angry forever and I will likely forgive them in time, I may even sympathize with them and consider their terrible upbringing or lack of education. But at the end of the day, hurt my cat and I am going to be pissed, that is that! Nor do I wish to shade my eyes from the rainbow of emotions and feelings that I am capable of. I do not always want to distract myself from other people's suffering, or my own. I believe I function better to help others if I can empathize with their pain. That is just me, I am touchy-feely. I certainly believe there is a place for calm, moderated, prescribed emotion, but it sits better on a Tibetan monk than it does on blonde little me!

I know that by embracing Buddha's teaching I could probably heal any hurt another person makes me feel, but I am not ready to give up my natural responses. Admittedly I can be a drama queen and quite frankly I like feeling love, I love a bit of lust and I am quite attached to my boyfriend, our house, my books and my computer. I believe that in modest doses some of our negative emotions can help us evolve and get through life. You know what, sometimes I love putting on a soppy film and crying for no reason. I get pleasure from dwelling on past events or fantasizing about things that would make me happy in the future. I am just not fully ready to give all of that up yet. I am not so unhappy that I constantly seek happiness from external things, although I do like a nice meal or the occasional new outfit. I am sure that naturally I am fairly well intentioned and of a sunny disposition. As a Libran I have to get the balance right, Buddhism for me is a little too far the other way.

There is, of course, a huge amount of good that can come from some Buddhist self regulation and mindfulness. My personal feeling is that some people would thrive in that environment whilst seeking the kind of peace and contentment that comes purely from within.

Buddhism is beautiful; I am glad I made its acquaintance and like any good friend I intend to take Buddha's advice to heart. In that respect I am on my way, I am practicing and essentially that is all that Dharma is – a practice. Through the practices of Buddhism, dharma and meditation you can (probably) discover that true, lasting happiness can only come from one place, and that place is deep within you. And if that is all you take from this chapter then it's a hell of a fact worth remembering!

As a thoroughly modern lady I am currently on earth to revel in life with the best of them. There is so much to experience and I believe I can try my hardest to experience it with a pure mind and loving heart. However, for me Buddhahood may have to wait a few dozen lifetimes yet.

The High Heeled Shaman

What do I know about Shamanism? Good question! At the start of my quest into Shamanism I was aware that a music group called The Shamen produced some wicked techno rave style dance hits back in the early nineties. Sadly I was too young to go to a rave or even fully understand the rather overt subtext of 'E's are good', but I could dance like a mad girl and I did own the album on cassette! Man I was cool. Other than that my knowledge of shamanistic ritual, religion and practice was sadly lacking before I decided to research it for this book.

Perhaps you, like me, considered a Shaman to be an odd middle-aged white bloke from somewhere as utterly average as Wolverhampton, in England. He has too much feathery facial hair and a variety of bizarre sloganed T-shirts (possibly tie dye), potential feathers in hair and a slight tic from a past history of too many hallucinogens? Not that I wish to stereotype, but there is not a huge amount of obvious information out there. Shamanism is hardly a belief system that you see advertised alongside the 'You can be a Teacher' adverts on the bus. So before I perpetuate any more slightly unhelpful stereotypes shall we dive right in?

Although I started out a little ignorant on the whole Shamanism topic, I am now an avid fan. My trip into shamanistic culture and beliefs has been one of the highlights of writing this book for me. Shamanism grabbed my interest in a way that other subjects simply did not. I felt intimately drawn into and fascinated by everything I learned. At some stage of human evolution all of our ancestors would have held some kind of similar shamanistic beliefs, and perhaps my genetics were harping back to that olden time. The environmental focus on animals and the planet, was also a big winner for me.

Shamanism made me think differently, it made me think outside of the human world and extend my spiritual belief throughout all of creation. Whatever it was that got my attention is irrelevant now; Shamanism was a big and valuable education. This journey culminated in me undertaking a Native American style Sweatlodge I write about that in detail towards the end of the chapter.

Shamanism is the belief in the teachings, ritual, magic and medicine of tribal indigenous groups. These include the fundamental religious thoughts of groups such as the Aborigines of Australia, the various native tribes of North America, tribes that still exist deep in the Amazon, even cultures in remote parts of Siberia and tribes in deepest Africa. There are dozens of indigenous, shamanistic groups still existing, that currently live in tribal societies and help contribute to the beliefs of the modern day western Shaman. Their knowledge sits alongside a wealth of history from semi extinct groups who have retained some of their ancient beliefs, medicine and thinking.

One thing that many of these diverse tribes have in common is their profound love for the earth and her nature. This is particularly poignant in comparison to the larger Western, Eastern and Middle Eastern societies who have made it their business (literally) to go about destroying the earth with bulldozers, skyscrapers and a super sized lust for everything to be bigger, better, faster.

In comparison shamanic indigenous groups live in perfect harmony with the planet, utilizing its natural resources for the good of the group, but never abusing or butchering the environment for short term, selfish, personal, business minded gains. It is core to shamanic beliefs that all living things – even rocks – possess a spirit, a spirit that is equal or superior to our own. Shamans endeavor to contact these spirits, and when contact is established a Shaman will learn from the spirits and commune with them for the good of their people, to invoke healing and to become wiser.

Such audiences with the spirits might be gained in a variety of ways. Amazonians take a mind altering plant concoction known as Ayahuasca that stimulates awe inspiring journeys into the spirit world. Native Americans may indulge in a sweat lodge ceremony. This means they sit in the equivalent of a super hot sauna till they start to hallucinate and/or enter another spiritual reality.

Drums, dancing and music are also pathways to the spirit and to gaining access to alternative realms where a Shaman can cure disease, learn from the spirits of nature and gain knowledge invaluable to their tribes or individuals.

This of course sounds akin to many people's Saturday night in a hot sweaty club, high on Ecstasy and dancing with crazed zeal to drum 'n' bass music. That said, I am sure many of those clubbers could report back on evocative, spiritual experiences brought about by the circumstances in a club, which are inevitably quite similar to those induced by Shamans. Just because you are in a club in Manchester, pumped up on pills, rather than in the Amazonian jungle out of your face on jungle juice whilst flipping about to a handmade drum, does not necessarily make the experience less valid. The main question is how do you bring that connection to spirit that you experienced in the moment of ecstasy, back to your community? The clubber whose reasons are comparatively shallow probably won't even consider using this experience for their own or other's benefit. But the Shaman who is consciously tripping to another level of existence does so purposefully and for the greater good.

Shamans abide by a natural empathy with nature that we all possessed as children, but that many of us have now forgotten. This idea really grasped me. As a child I earnestly believed in magic, miracles and the fairies at the bottom of the garden. I imagined that prayer could shape my life and that some higher power was guarding me, guiding me, and thinking of me always. At a young age I felt certain that I was never alone as I made my way through sunny days talking to bees and dancing with butterflies.

Shamans practice the natural magic of 'medicine men' to overcome ills or to create good fortune. They look inside themselves and into different states of consciousness to promote good health or discover the answer to their woes. This is all done in harmony with nature whilst heralding nature as a provider, a mother figure and our sacred home. Indeed Shamans see that we are nature, nature is us, and that all aspects of nature must be respected and held as sacrosanct.

We westerner's destructive tendencies and monopolistic reign over our world is viewed with abhorrence. Shamanism is the ecological warrior's godsend. If we were all to follow the Shamanic path then hopes for the survival of planet earth against the modern influx of destruction and pollution would be far more positive.

Shamans believe in the power of the dream, both daydreams and nighttime dreams. They believe that dreams have the power to change the world, and perhaps that is becoming a more common theme in our society with an influx of ideas on things such as cosmic ordering, or positive thinking. Shamans see that the consumerism dream of the western world is warped, unholy and is inevitably quickly killing off our planet. Our society's goal to possess more, earn more and have bigger everything is pivotal to this destruction. If our desire for status continues to be fully flexed the result could be catastrophic. Shamans want us to change our dreams, individual, corporate, social and societal. Shamans wish us to be more shamanic in our ways, we must learn to give a little more back to the planet and take a lot less from her natural resources. Shamans believe that we are all naturally shamanic, but that time, culture and societal pressure have made us forget this. Looking back on my childhood, I think that I agree. As a youngster I resided in this world in a very different way from how I live in it now. My curiosity was constantly piqued and my respect and devotion to all things natural was immense.

My study of Shamanism has made me remember vividly the

nighttime terrors of my youth that gripped my mind in fear at the state of the planet. I would have sleepless nights over pollution, the destruction of the rainforest and the extinction of beautiful wild animals. It broke my heart into pieces and I owned several T-shirts emblazoned with slogans such as 'Save the Whales', 'Save British Wildlife' or 'I love Squirrels'. My bedroom window was decorated with World Wildlife Fund stickers and my thoughts would worry and fidget over the potential demise of our wondrous Mother Earth.

My small trip into Shamanism has taught me that we must all try to relearn this innocent love for the planet. While drafting this chapter I have felt sickened by the concrete jungle that continues to spring up around me. Only today I went out for Sunday lunch and sights that are normally quite benign took on a powerful significance. Housing estates seemed to be springing up at every corner. Peoples' conversations in the pub seemed ignorant and clumsily safe in their reliance on the tabloids for facts. I felt despair for a desperate looking tramp drinking liquor with nothing but a bin bag for company. All of these things left me feeling so poignantly sad. I longed for a return to something more natural; to get away from a society that rates success as profit, bankability and ultimately destruction. Western society with its business minded aspirations and goals seemed suddenly very trivial and empty.

Consumerism and progress occur to me as empty promises that only serve a very few people, whilst the rest of us sit in those people's pockets, slaves to their dreams. We are very much pawns in a richer person's games. We are duped into this position by the millions of distractions and the need to make money and spend, spend, spend our cash or credit.

We build our personal dreams on top of other people's advertising visions. We do not consider how we would really like things to be if we had the choice. Our lives are dictated by somebody else's terms, our options are limited by what we can buy, and what is produced for us. We measure our success by our own interpretation of what the media manufacture as the 'ideal'.

We follow the crowd, even when we are being quirky and original. My 'quirky' kitchen wallpaper was bought at a well known DIY branded superstore. Come to think of it, my dream of being 'different' is very much informed by home decorating television shows.

It has become easier to tag onto the bigger scheme than to think for ourselves. Imagine for a second a planet entirely devoid of history, vision and invention. Imagine a world where we are not encumbered by pre-fabricated lives designed by companies for us to purchase and adhere to for 60-90 years. Imagine the freedom you would have to be yourself. That freedom is so far removed from anything we can conceive of right now that is frightening.

Do we have that choice, the choice to think for ourselves and change our dreams? I think that maybe we do, but sometimes it is easier to ignore it. Our planet depends on our ability to recognize our choices and use them more wisely. Shamans certainly think we have that choice, they think we must change our collective plans, schemes and dreams or else we are all screwed. I know it is easy to get happily lost in a world of convenience fast food, medication, mass media, cosmetics, fashion, gadgets and cash.

I am not so sure about all these things any more, I am beginning to think the expense is too much, and I do not mean my personal bank balance, I mean the expense for my children, for your children, for the sake of bluebells, clean water and blossoming forests. I can see that it is literally my children that might suffer, which means that it could all go pear shaped anytime between now and the next eighty years. Either way someone I care about and love is going to have it hard as a result of the choices we make today, unless...

Unless... we recognize our innate spirituality and our true independence as living, breathing, conscious individuals who are able to bring about miraculous change. We have lost our natural rhythm and now everything beats to the pulse of the all-powerful dollar.

Shamanism may give us an opportunity to rediscover a drumbeat that suits the planet better. It might allow us to recognize our spiritual selves, whilst also recognizing the spirit of the planet, her moods and her shifts and the plants and creatures living alongside us.

Shamanism could contribute to a better society in a way few belief systems have ever done. If we listen to the spirit of the earth as the Shamans do, maybe, just maybe we will not all die in a catastrophic global meltdown brought on by our societies' greed and lusts. Today I wanted to stop the world and get off. But maybe there's another way....

My Shamanic Life so far...

It was musing on this that made me realize that my life has been punctuated by glimpses of a shamanic and natural world. My great grandmother many times removed was a Cherokee Indian named Fanny (it's not funny!). My bone structure and my mother's family tree testify to this as fact. As a child I spent time with my adventurous wildman Uncle Bobby and my brothers in the raised fields of Kentucky hunting for ancient arrowheads. We found many of these and saved them before the builders covered them forever with housing estates and shopping malls. Bobby gave me two impressive specimens from his own collection and I still carry these today when I feel I need to be brave.

As a very young child I have a memory of envisaging a beautiful American Indian male standing on a plain with a burning ochre sunset behind him. This image was not one I was familiar with and looked nothing like the archetypal cowboys and Indians of the westerns. It also pre-empted the more finely tuned and sensitive representation of American Indians in recent films such as *Dances with Wolves*. I felt great adoration and love for this man and at the tender age of five wished to have him as an older brother or a husband. I do not know where this image came from, but my first sight of Anthony Kiedis from the Red Hot Chilli Peppers evoked it again. Needless to say, like many a good woman before me, I have had a crush on Anthony Kiedis ever since.

I had relatives in America who bought jeweler from tribal groups. I still own some delightful mother of pearl rings and cannot help digging them out occasionally. Other pieces crafted from turquoise and silver I have somehow managed to 'borrow' from my mum, I guess she must wonder where they have gone! As a child I housed a small box of 'worry dolls' in my bedroom; I was told that such teeny tiny dolls were used all over the Americas by the native people to attempt to keep bad thoughts and nightmares at bay. You pop the dolls under your pillow at night or carry them in your pocket and they protect you from all things mentally creepy and bad.

As a teenager I wrote a performance piece for my college drama studies group based on the lives of Native American women whose husbands had gone into battle with white men, never to return. We learned native chants and unearthed traditional symbolism whilst trying to make relatively accurate costumes and make up. Later that year I went on a girls' holiday to Tenerife, but it was not all booze and boys, and I got myself a tattoo of one of those tribal symbols. My boyfriend constantly refers to it as a blobby duck of some sort – what would he know! This blurry duck is now permanently emblazoned to my right hip, right where the fat tends to gather after Christmas. A tattoo on holiday at age 18 is of course never a good idea, but I can rest assured that I do not possess a Chinese Symbol that reads 'Supermarket', 'Tinned Fish' or 'Chicken Chow Mein'.

Shamans believe that much of our power can be wielded through dreams or daydreams. I have personally always been very good at both. A grouchy newspaper shop owner once told me that I was a dreamer. She was my employer and I was sweeping the floor at the time. She said this with derision and disgust, but maybe she saw me as a young student who would not be sweeping floors forever. Inevitably all that lay between her and the broom was me, it was not my dream to be her cleaner. In the light that Shamanism has shed on daydreaming, I will now choose to think of her comments as a compliment!

One of the most heart breaking things I have witnessed was a Native American standing by the roadside, in full tribal clothing, feathered headdress, the lot. He stood beside a cage in which was captured an enormous live grizzly bear. I am not sure which of the two souls was more bereft: the bear or the man. The man's only role was to stand by the bear with a tray into which white tourists such as me would toss the odd dime.

In Native American tradition each feather on a headdress represents a brave act that man has committed. What brave acts had this disenfranchised soul performed to be stood by the roadside touting one of nature's wonders for mere dollars? I wonder now if he mourned the ancient traditions as obese pedestrians, on their way to the next 'all you can eat' diner, launched their spare change his way. Two magnificent beings rendered to nothing more than a sidewalk circus act in fancy dress, my heart bleeds.

I have always been lucky enough to be surrounded by nature. My maternal grandparents had a farm with a lake in Kentucky, USA. The farm was nearly self sufficient with home grown vegetables and the lake full of good sized, healthy, organic fish. We would sit for hours on the porch shelling peas, so simple; yet looking back it is like another life. Occasionally things would go a bit wild at the farm and we would be ushered in away from a stray snake or snapping turtle. The weather could be phenomenal, the lightning storms, watched from the patio would barely touch the heat of the day, but would light up the sky like the Goddesses' own birthday party. At night the crickets would croak and rattle into the silence, it was simply amazing.

My grandparents in England also owned a farm, full of home grown goods, a field of sheep and racing horses housed in Kent. Slightly more civilized than the American equivalent but just as spectacular to a growing girl. My home growing up near Bolton, in the north of England, had a perfect view of Winter Hill and the Pennines started a mile up the road. At night I would hear the owls hooting and the fields and river behind my house was my playground.

I was lucky to be born into these things; many people grow up in areas considered leafy because the city council has chosen to plant a few conifers on the corners. Many people may barely or rarely know such natural beauty until they are old enough to find it themselves; even then they may choose the familiarity of concrete or a computer screen to spend their down time.

But for anyone who has experienced nature, you must know it is magical, it soothes the soul, and it reminds you of your place. You are not an office worker, you are a little piece of a giant miracle. You do not sit and type all day, you daydream wonderful things and glimpse infinity. Whatever you dream, you can be. This is true whether your personal piece of Shaman comes from growing up under a waterfall, or being caught in the rain.

Shamanism recognizes the beauty and spirit in everything, from preparing a meal to watching a sunset. The beauty in these things had evaded my appreciation in the past ten years or so, but I feel this returning and I am likely to find a way to honor it. I am already a slightly loopy green goddess wannabe, but from here on in I may feel obliged by the Spirit to play my part in helping our tired, over-exhausted world to find her feet and regain her former glory.

Through Shamanism all is not lost. Shamanic belief might be buried, marginalized, demonized and stereotyped, but is it lost entirely to history? No, it is not. Shamans exist from the ashes of proud and magical societies, they learn from the knowledge that these societies held before they were trampled over by western explorers and white scientists.

I like to think my cheekbones are a result of genetic Cherokee history, but what about my heart, my soul, my longings and my desires. What about yours – it is true that we all descend from some tribe somewhere, therefore it is in all our hearts and genetics.

Through the precious shamanic traditions of the world, we can learn more about ourselves, the Great Spirit, and our intimate ties to nature. The Great Spirit might be you or I, or an old weathered tree, a lost goat or a crow picking the remains of a chicken that tried to cross the road. Why would a chicken do that? The magic might be in a baby's laugh or a herb that fixes a wound quicker than a stitch.

A Shaman recognizes the magic in nature and the nature in miracle. Above all a Shaman sees that the Great Spirit links us all. In western terms, the Great Spirit might be akin to a god, or many gods and goddesses, angels, spirit guides, sprites and fairy folk. A little bit of Shaman is desperately needed. It's time for a reality check and a gentle reminder of where we all came from, before where we came from is no more.

On my desk at work I coincidentally have a pack of Native American Medicine Cards. These depict different animals and their meaning. You pick one card a day and let its mantra style meaning influence your actions.

Today's card happens to be a bat. The bat's meaning is the following –

"Be flexible, prepare for rebirth, the time is NOW, the power is YOU."

These are positive and inspiring words indeed. Perhaps my rebirth will be as a little high-heeled Shaman. So I will fix my cute little dream catcher above my bed and see where this journey takes me.

Shamanism, Sexism and the Ladies

One amazing book that helped prompt all I have written above is by a man named John Perkins, and is called *The World Is As You Dream It*. Mr Perkins had been a successful businessman, in part responsible for some Amazonian destruction. He eventually turned his back on big business and formed a business harnessing ecological powers. Following this he packed in business altogether and went to the Amazon to learn from the lifestyles and religion of the Shuar people. Check out this website to see even more about some of the incredible projects he is involved in www.dreamchange.org. Since then Mr Perkins has written many books on the shamanic traditions of existing tribes and how these can be incorporated into our western world for the sake of our souls, our planet and everything else that lives here.

Shortly after beginning his book I am sure I felt the animal spirits coming to me, reminding me of my love for them and the planet. In a meditation I clearly saw a big brown loving horse's eye. In the past week I have seen a baby cow galloping by the side of the road, escaped from its man made jail in a field. Only this morning I was enchanted to see two stunning deer munching the grass along the A50 between Leicester and Coalville. I have taken that road every day for nearly four years and prior to this the only animal I have seen has been road kill, so an escaped calf and two beautiful Bambis in the space of a week is impressive.

Most peculiarly, I spent a night tossing and turning having nightmarish dreams about turtles – a bit weird I know. Yet dreams are supremely important to shamanistic cultures, and so it makes sense to examine my dreams here. In one dream a horrid warped man had crushed and boiled his wife's pet turtle as some kind of cruel psychological and controlling torture. It was awful. I awoke breathless and totally freaked out. Later that night I dreamt I had four pet turtles that I kept in a fish bowl, but because I did not know how to look after them I changed their water too often and two of them died.

The next day, following these stressful dreams, I picked up John Perkin's book again. He was talking of his first visit with the Shuar people of the Amazon. What was particularly moving was his reference of the water goddess 'Tsunkqui' who rides on the back of a giant Turtle.

I took this to be more than a coincidence in the light of my vivid dreams. The Shuar people worship gods and goddesses and firmly believe in the equality of the sexes, and look highly upon women. This, of course, is very different to western society where laws are needed to protect against discrimination and where women, in the recent past, have been thought of as lower class citizens, unable to vote and worthy only as housewives, baby makers, sex objects and cleaners. In our society it is sadly not uncommon to find men who hate women, who are imprisoned for assaulting, raping and murdering women, or who simply believe that women are inferior. I hope I am not referring to any men that you or I personally know, but if you can't imagine what I mean then all you need do is pick up a couple of newspapers and see what tragic stuff you can find. Sadly I don't think that this will be a difficult task. This of course only refers to our 'civilized' countries, if you dare look further, or perhaps take a glimpse onto Amnesty International's website then the worldwide degradation of women comes into shocking, depressing and frightening focus. We have a long way to go ladies.

The Shuar appreciate the qualities of men and women, recognizing that the two genders are lost without each other and that both are truly precious. Perhaps the turtles in my dreams were meant to remind me of the damage that mankind has done to our planet. The feminine aspects of nurture, sensitivity and intuition are all trampled to make way for more concrete, competitive masculine traits. In my dream the man cruelly destroyed the woman by killing and maiming her turtle, so I believe the turtle in my dream represented the wild and wondrous feminine, spiritual side of our world that has been trampled to make way for technology, machines and architecture.

The dreams of our society, which have mainly come from male thinkers, have destroyed that mythical turtle, just like the cruel man in my dream who destroyed his wife's pet turtle as she watched, helpless and heartbroken. My guess is that we need to reclaim all of the feminine attributes and give them the status they deserve. They may not make a short-term buck but they are sure to make the world a better place.

I do not believe that women share the same dreams as men. We are life giving, nurturing beings. We do not generally invoke war or violence, and yet we are subjected to it and dragged into it by the men around us. This is not to say that all men are made this way, many men are pulled into war, just as women have been implicit in terrible and cruel acts.

But historically speaking we have been more timid and repressed. Our power as individuals or as a unit has only just, in the past century, been allowed to co-exist alongside the dreams of men. Our dreams in past centuries were mainly of marriage and babies, and even now for many women, they still are. By nature, though, we tend to create rather than destroy, and to nurture rather than dream great monuments. This is of course, a massive and complicated can of worms. But very broadly speaking women are the peacemakers, the life givers, the carers, the nurturers, and the homemakers of this planet. Very few women will start a war or become involved in genocide. Sadly we are more than likely to be the victims of such things, alongside the men sent into war. Women did not create the mass business or media circus that prevails in the world today, it was created initially by a masculine dream. Historically men have shaped the world. If it could be different what would you change?

These days we accept and enjoy the world as we have come to know it. However, I believe that women, in particular, are not as far removed from nature as we pretend to be. Indeed how can we be when it is via our bodies that new life comes? In spite of our technology and gadgetry, and despite the 'progress' in cloning', no man (or woman) can yet reproduce the miracle of birth. So no matter how sophisticated we may believe ourselves to be, we will still have to double over in agony, rip, tear and bleed the next generation out of our wombs.

Rather than be disgusted, as admittedly in the past I have been, we should embrace it. I have spent a good deal of my life aghast that one day I may have to give birth. I have been horrified that in the 21st century somebody has not found a way to form a baby outside of the body, in a slinky silver machine. But today I am glad of birth, yes I may get a big tummy (temporarily I do hope) I may well waddle and lose some of my bladder control, but that I am afraid, is the way things ought to be.

As humans we are all capable of being shamanic, but for women our links to nature are entirely inescapable. For that reason alone our shamanic side deserves some exploration. We owe it to ourselves, and our sisters, to make the planet a little safer for our daughters and more soulful for our sons. Plus if nothing else, with the exception of John Travolta and very few others, men can't really dance can they? Bring on those shamanic drums honey, Woo Ha!

Amazonian Shamans

It is South American Shamans (of the Amazon, Peru, Mexico, Ecuador, Inca, or Mayan) that appear to heavily influence the western interpretation of Shamanism. Many western groups offer regular trips to the Amazon to join in traditional shamanic customs. The more I learned about this the more my interest expanded. Soon all I could think about was the Amazon. Indeed I was contemplating how I personally could get there to take part in the plant medicine rites whilst exploring the undergrowth, waterfalls and wildlife.

The main drive many westerners seem to exhibit when wishing to visit Amazonian Shamans is to sample their medicinal herbs and plants whilst exploring a wholly alternative way to exist. The resident Shamans believe that the plants and animals of the jungle have much to teach us about life, spirit, love and our own nature. Their faith revolves around living as one with the foliage, butterflies, insects and elements.

These days there is a huge focus by the Amazonian Shamans to re-educate the westerners who visit them. Happy in their simple spiritual lives, they view western life as destructive, shallow and unhappy. Many of the westerners who visit are looking for answers, they hope to discover a slice of life that western society has kept hidden from them. This is increasingly true now that the damage done to the Earth by westerners, or northerners as we are to the Amazonian Shamans, is becoming achingly apparent.

Amazonian Shamans see time, space and religion very differently from us. All time is seen to run simultaneously, so what happened now and what occurred ten years ago or ten hundred years in the future is still happening now. Time to them is an irrelevance.

Shamans claim to easily access different times, often practicing healing exercises through this 'time traveling'. One such example is that of 'soul retrieval'. Soul retrieval allows a Shaman to reach back into the heart of somebody's problem, no matter how old that problem is and cure them. John Perkins gives an example of a woman who was afraid of heights, in particular of crossing bridges. This debilitating problem was preventing from her joining Perkins on one of his Amazonian trips due to one particularly frightful bridge over an Amazonian river gulley.

Using soul retrieval, Perkins, who has trained with Shamans and learned their techniques, took the woman back in time to when she first developed this fear of heights and falling. This journey led them on a conjoined mental and spiritual journey back in time to a previous life where the woman was sacrificed by being thrown from a cliff. Perkins then manipulated, negotiated and re-wrote the woman's experience. He asked her to speak with her killers and suggest that they need not sacrifice her, but that they should throw flowers from the cliff instead. Eventually this was agreed and the woman was saved from being a sacrificial lamb in her previous incarnation. Needless to say the woman's fear of heights has evaporated. When faced with the scary bridge in the Amazon she can now trot over it happily, then back again, as her companions watch in awe.

How this works is anybody's guess, whether they have really taken an actual journey back in time, or accessed past life memories, or simply in a shamanic version of a psychological therapeutic technique imagined the whole scenario, is debatable. However, what is stunning is that they appear to access another time, another life previously unknown to the woman. What they find there gives them an opportunity to fix the current problem, and it apparently works. Shamans have been using this technique to cure their people for millennia.

Shamans believe that they can travel out of their body to different parallel existences, perhaps as an eagle flying high, or pay a visit to the spirit realm, and by doing so they can learn a great deal about our world.

This fits in with the core belief that time and space are only separated by a veil of consciousness. And that in actuality time and space do not exist in the strict confines that we attribute to them. Shamans know how to access any time or any space and when they have accessed another time or space they can then go about healing and curing problems that originate in that dimension. One way this is achieved is via the use of a mind-bending mixture named 'Ayahuasca'. Ayahuasca is a medicine made from a variety of psychotropic Amazonian plants. It is used by Shamans to gain insight into other realms and to generally hang out with the Great Spirit. Translated the meaning of Ayahuasca varies from 'Vine of Death' to 'Vine of Enlightenment'. It is reputed to give the drinker one on one access to 'Pachamama' – the world of animals, nature and the supernatural.

Many places in the Amazon now offer retreat style getaways where you or I can go and take part in a ritual that involves ingesting Ayahuasca. Ingesting is apparently pretty difficult as it is reputed to taste foul, with bitterness parallel to the stuff they put in bleach to stop children drinking it. Drinking it is followed by retching and vomiting, before the hallucinations of the 'trip' begins.

This particular blend of psychotropic plants is said to cure a range of debilitating mental and physical problems. Not necessarily because of the traditional medicinal properties, but because of the crazy mental places it takes you to. Whether this is simply tripping/hallucinating, or you do in fact leave your body and experience other realms is obviously a cause for some contention. However, people who have tried Ayahuasca speak highly of it. Indeed a whole religion named 'Santo Daime, the rainforest's doctrine' has grown out of the use of Ayahuasca for spiritual purposes. As this is separate from Shamanism I will not go into it here, but feel free to Google 'Santo Daime' and see for yourself.

Claims have been made that the Ayahuasca experience can lift severe depression, with long term effects, others say that it has gifted them insights into their character so as to become better, happier people. Some proponents even claim that Ayahuasca can cure mental illness, and physical disease – even cancer. Though Carlos Casteneda, whose adventures with Ayahuasca have been given something of a cult status, stands as a warning that it is also rumored to leave some people's mind well outside of their bodies.

Indeed Ayahuasca's alleged benefits and reputed vivacity as a drug calls into question the very nature of the western understanding of hallucinations, tripping, or being completely out of one's head. Maybe, and I am sure many Shamans would agree with me, the western perception of hallucinogenic experiences being 'imaginary' is incorrect. Maybe when you have a fever and you see or experience peculiar things, you have actually slipped into another level of consciousness, maybe such imagined events are not imagined at all?

Ayahuasca may just sound like another drug, and in some respects I guess it is. Drugs are very much demonized in the UK, USA, Europe and Australia. But they are prolifically used by a huge number of people throughout these countries. Maybe the reason for their extensive use is because they do actually bring you a little closer to God? Isn't it understandable that in a fairly soulless society that thrives on industry and commercialism we are bound to be a little enthralled by something that makes it all go away. Cocaine, Ecstasy and other Class A drugs are now used widely as a form of social lubrication. They break down the barriers of class and race that inhibit us from being a true representation of ourselves. Under the twisted guise of a cocaine high we can chat to that guy we have fancied for months, or dance like J-Lo all night long, in between frequent trips to the toilet to shove a dirty rolled up note up your nostril.

We are all walking round in a fog of pretence, clutching our handbags and constantly checking our lipstick, perish the thought our lips become dry or we misplace our nail file! Drugs make the mundane day-to-day working existence go away; they make the weekend exciting and create an alternative universe in your hometown, in a grotty club. Under the influence of drugs you can be best friends with everyone, you believe you are hilariously good company and you fall deeply in love with life. It's sad that we cannot be like that all the time, but the rigorous codes of conduct keep us all caged up in our little fake worlds desperately waving our designer labels and new haircuts around as though they give us the keys to the kingdom. The thing about western illegal drugs is that, even if they do bring about a long lost tribal mentality, they are abused and they fund terrible crimes. Furthermore I defy you to pop or snort your way through even a small amount and awake with more than a tired hazy memory of what occurred the night before.

Ayahuasca and other hallucinogens (magic mushrooms,

peyote cactus etc), however, are not party drugs. Ayahusaca is taken as a serious shamanic rite that has a status as a highly revered miracle mix. It's not to be toyed with and it is certainly not taken for a laugh and a lark. It is taken as a crash course in self-improvement; it is taken to remember about you rather than to forget.

Ayahuasca is always taken under the guardianship of a Shaman who will be with you both physically and psychically throughout your experience. No matter what happens, the Shaman will be there to help you battle demons and make the most of your experience. One fascinating point about Ayahuasca is that people do seem to have group experiences whilst Shamans appear to have intimate knowledge of a person's journey without being told.

When I tried to explain Ayahuasca to James I did not do a very good job. James told me he would save me the airfare to Peru and just get some LSD in; and once I had totally freaked out he would talk me down. What a kind offer! In spite of that I did politely decline. I totally understand where he is coming from; however, I also see what the Shamans are touting too.

The testimonials from people who have experienced this rite are so glowingly positive it made me very tempted. One girl claims she overcame her lifelong depression and banished migraines. Others attest to being cradled in the arms of God, experiencing flying or direct communication with loving spirits.

A female journalist reporting for the National Geographic experienced devils flying out of her body along with all manner of other evil and atrocious sights. Eventually on her fifth or sixth attempt she did actually have a good experience. Once her issues had been resolved she was free to be with the gentle spirits, and as an end result she was cured of her foibles, insecurities and personal issues. From what I have read it takes a brave soul to exorcise her demons in this dramatic manner, not one for a Saturday night up town then!

I was seriously considering finding a way to get myself to Peru to have a go at this myself. It sounded like a hard fought journey into my inner psyche whilst taking active learning from the heart of the jungle and the living essence of the earth. I felt this particularly strongly and I found it hard to tear my thoughts from this goal once I had set it.

What did snatch me away eventually was one bad dream and a weird meditative experience that made me question why I would want to put myself through such an intensely 'bad trip'. The dream I do not actually remember but I know it was influenced by the thought of taking Ayahuasca and I know that I woke up terrified.

The meditation was during one of my Reiki training sessions and my Reiki teacher informed me it was likely to be visions of past lives or repressed fears. The images I saw in my mind were of warped, deformed, mummified dead and rotting children – not nice. They were right there in my head and it took a few minutes to shake them. Putting two and two together I realized that if I were to take Ayahuasca, this is what I could expect, but in 3D and for six hours, alongside ridiculous physical sickness. I decided against it, South America is a very long way to go and a lot of money to spend for a potentially ghastly experience. I am not digging my passport out on that one in any hurry. It is a plucky person who can handle the vivid and glaring depiction of what's in the murkiest corners of the mind.

I guess at its best, Ayahuasca can be a fast track to almost immediate spiritual awakening, however for most people I think a gentle introduction and steady progression is the best way to go.

What Ayahuasca does for the mind and body, however, is recently becoming of interest to medical science. I hope that they may find in it a wonder drug, a cure for depression, or serious diseases such as Aids or cancer. Maybe a way to take the drug in a more mild mannered way will come about, allowing us all to taste its spiritual and heart lifting properties without being pursued by devils or drowning in snake pits as a side effect.

It occurred to me that my personal desire to take Ayahuasca was in fact a symptom of western need and greed. In our society everything has its price; anything can be done, used and experienced. My short obsession over Ayahuasca was in fact masking the true face and facets of Shamanism. There is more to it than meets an under the influence psyche!

Ayahuasca is one of many ways to alter your state of consciousness. Slightly tamer options are available such as drumming, fasting, dreaming or other Native American options that I explore in the next section. If you or I were to adopt a shamanic lifestyle, it means more than going on an amazing holiday, tasting a concoction of plants and experiencing great highs and lows. Shamanism runs parallel with the need to transform our grasping, materialistic society into a society that loves and respects the earth as much as we love our dearest friends. Yes, you may take Ayahuasca to enhance this and to connect to spirit, but the journey does not begin and end there.

The Amazonian Shamans are trying to show us the errors of our ways and that the world exists far beyond the boundaries set for it by western science, maps and reason. To our minds Shamanism might seem like a lot of smoke, illusion, magic and miracles. But to the people who practice Shamanism it is a way of life, it is normal, natural and satisfying. To them it is us who live under illusion, with our grand dreams of retirement homes, 'enhanced' breasts, more beautiful clothes, the latest sports car or dining in the finest restaurants. We define ourselves by our small plastic miracles, by what we create and the physical objects we collect.

As a whole we tend to shun what we do not see or understand. Because something cannot be touched, or valued, we find it quite sensible that it does not exist. So whilst we marvel over a psychic's ability, we go home to our purpose built houses, slurp our instant hot chocolate, slip into imported silk pajamas and suppose that we live a contented life. Yet every aspect of our lives comes from the dream of materialism, every small part of our life is lining somebody else's pocket with gold and diamonds. Whilst the smallest percentage of people live with plenty of money in the bank, the planet and we as individuals suffer because of this dream.

In our desperate need to cope, we subscribe to that dream wholeheartedly. We aspire to be wealthy and have more, more, more. Yet all of the material goods that we desire are literally inconsequential – you cannot take them with you. The Shamans know that, their children know that. Our children grow up glued to a fake televised world, living life through boxes and screens and buttons. Our children's worth is measured not by their mind or ability but by their clothing and possessions.

The Amazonian Shamans want us to realize that what we desire and lust after are all false gods, and that we are all suffering and miserable because of this. Worse than this, we jeopardize the future of the planet due to our insatiable lusts. If we take this on board then all our actions must be weighed against the damage they do. Amazonian Shamanism asks us to tread lightly on the earth, putting more into the planet than we take from it. By embracing the world of Shamans we can learn to heal ourselves, all of our hurts and the hurts of our beautiful Mother Earth.

Native American Shamanism

Native Americans, like many other shamanic people, believe in the ultimate magnificence and spirituality of the earth and all of her life forms. They access the 'dreamtime' (dreams) and the subconscious mind to bring about a better future, for individuals and for the planet and to connect them to the universal consciousness of every living thing both spiritual and physical – aka the 'Great Spirit'. The human body is pushed to a variety of extremes to draw on a person's inner resources and to call on the powers of their spiritual guides. Active movement meditation through long walks or protracted dance sessions feature highly as a form of communion with spirit and self-healing. Tobacco, a plant indigenous to the Americas, is revered highly and used often in healing and magic or as a gift to the Great Spirit to say thank you for good times and positive happenings. In common with any other form of Shamanism, animal helpers feature highly in both symbols and as active helping guides.

Native American Medicine Men (mystics and healers as some prefer to be called rather than Shamans) are not like traditional doctors, they do not attempt to make you better. Rather they kick-start a journey of you learning to make yourself well.

Marsha Scarborough beautifully demonstrates this in her book 'Medicine Dance'. Marsha worked with mystic Native American Healer Joseph Rael aka 'Beautiful Painted Arrow'. Upon learning that she had a potential cancer, and being shoved around by the institutionalized medical profession, she sought help from Joseph Rael. Marsha's extraordinary journey clearly demonstrates how knowledge of Native American healing practices can bring great change to a person's spiritual health and physical vitality.

With great awe and a tinge of envy, I learned how Marsha endured sweat lodges, 50-mile silent meditation walks and marathon dance meditations.

The sweat lodge is particularly fascinating and involves a group of people literally sweating it out in a tepee style sauna in pitch-blackness for hour after hour. The purpose is to force the participants to face their deepest fears whilst eventually succumbing to those fears and becoming one with the immense heat and claustrophobic conditions. Whilst undergoing a sweat lodge, prayers are made out loud asking for the healing of the lodgers and others.

The end result is apparently akin to being reborn. Having soaked the heat into your very core, the eventual return to a normal environment is said to be very much like reliving your birth. Emotional outpourings or the finding of some spiritual truth about oneself and the surrounding world often accompanies this.

For some crazy reason this really appeals to me. It is essentially a similar practice to the Amazonian rite of taking Ayahuasca, except you can end it if you need to by leaving the sweat lodge and you aren't opening yourself in the same way to frightening or possible demonic hallucinations via a toxic mix of plant juices. Now I have of course considered sweating it out at the gym and attempting to get the same effect in the sauna. However certain parts of the sweat lodge ritual don't fit so neatly at the public leisure center or members only club. If I started wailing, praying or hallucinating there is a good chance I would be removed from the premises for frightening the other clients, or I might be carted off in a straitjacket. Either way is a pretty damning occurrence for my street credibility! Plus I pay way too much for that gym to have to endure the embarrassment this would likely cause. Then again I have been trying to think of a way to wriggle out of my gym contract...

The prolonged dance sessions are feats of courage that pitch mind over body, they are said to provoke a greater experience of Spirit and of self. Marsha took part in a four-day dance, at first glance this might appeal to you as it does sound quite fun, a bit like partying it up at a festival for a long weekend. But it is not quite that straightforward. During these dances Marsha was not allowed to eat or drink anything, including water. Now that might sound infinitely ridiculous, however, Marsha survived whilst apparently sustaining no long-term or short-term health problems. Indeed her health soared as she learned more about her inner being and her connection with the universe. This is clearly pretty serious stuff and I would advise you not to attempt this without proper supervision, and, no, attending Glastonbury festival does not count! During the entire dance you are aiming to be completely silent and there is no copping out if a beat you don't like comes on. The music is likely to be just drums and singing, so very primal, no electric guitars or synthesizers allowed.

Drumming is a tool used across most shamanic traditions as a way of inducing trance or spiritual self-hypnosis. So whilst it might not be the same as catching your favorite DJ or band in action, it does have other far-reaching benefits. Anyone who has truly lost herself in dance should have some small inkling of these benefits. In my experience on the dance floor dancing has always accompanied a complete lack of other thought. I have never found myself dancing whilst worrying about what I will eat for dinner or whether I have paid my gas bill.

It is in the nature of dance and rhythm that once you get past any self-consciousness you can truly be at one with your mind and body. It makes sense that in this kind of continual and intensive musical movement; the rest of the brain shuts down, allowing for a higher level of communication with self and spirit. Four days of dancing on nothing but oxygen is a whole other level. Though it certainly sounds like a near impossible task, it is one that you could relish for the rest of your life. It is an extreme, belief based sport, and one that would test your every nerve and eventually show you the color of your soul.

Until reading Marsha's book I had little knowledge of my Native American heritage or its customs. It was not long after gaining this information that I stumbled upon an actual Native American person. A recent holiday in Memphis saw me on Beale Street, the home of the Blues and searching for a bar with live music. Not a difficult task, I must add. This is when I fell upon meeting my first Native American person, as opposed to their legend, image or a book on their history. The man in question was on the stage playing an amazing live music set to a crowd of about four people. James and myself were lucky enough to have him come and sit with us on his break and we listened enthralled as he recounted glimpses of his life in the blues and in his Native

American religion. He has taken part in all of the things that Marsha describes and some. Indeed his briefly recounted religious exploits would bring tears to the eyes of most western folk, who practice a safety conscious version of the ancient traditions.

In many respects this chance meeting brought the idea of Shamanism down to a very understandable level to me. Prior to this I believed Shamans and those that follow shamanistic beliefs and cultures were pure souls and I never considered them to be members of modern day society as I know it to be. My new acquaintance was certainly that. Of course, he is not a Shaman himself, he is a musician, and what a talent he had. I have never seen anyone suck and blow on a harmonica with such intensity or manage to smile his way through a set so fiercely. And yet speaking with him at the bar I realized that Shamans are not some far-flung tribe with a perfect ethical stance.

This guy alluded to his rough and tumble youth, this was the reason for him not drinking alcohol when James offered him a drink. He spoke briefly of his experiences in dance sessions that lasted four days without water. He also told me that at some of these sessions animals are killed as part of the ritual. These animals are not chickens, or mice, or goats, they are cute little puppies, and afterward their bodies are chopped up with parts being distributed to the dancers. Their death is not swift, and they are killed via strangulation so as not to drop their blood. He told us that they would joke about which part of the slaughtered dog they might receive; use your imagination ladies.... He laughed and joked constantly, his jokes particularly aimed at other Indian tribes. He told us how in one dance he was engulfed by a vision of being pierced through the skin painfully by an eagle's talons, he looked down to see that he had indeed been pierced through the chest as part of the ceremony, and yet it did not hurt. He continued to dance without water and with his blood dripping down and drying on his flesh.

The shamanic path encountered by Marsha, is, it seems, a westernized and sanitized version that keeps the basis of a ritual, whilst removing the more full-on tribal, bloodletting parts. I personally do not believe that a ritual loses anything by not killing animals or inflicting wounds on each other. But neither can I say categorically that the version practiced by the man that I met was wrong, although his of course would likely fail any health and safety test that came its way. Yes, the bit about the puppies is distressing, but I believe far worse animal atrocities are committed daily in the name of the meat industry and or to make the leather for your new sofa. This chance and fateful meeting showed to me that followers of shamanic based faiths are just like us, they may drink too much, they may fight, they might tell naughty jokes and flirt with young women.

We are all human, and being a human is a fantastic starting point for becoming a little bit Shaman, and if you want to be a little bit rock 'n' roll on the side, then so be it. Indeed through this small glimpse I saw it was perfectly acceptable to live your life how you desire, travel the world, meet new people and laugh and joke in bars. All of this is great as long as you honor yourself and other people. Unlike dogmatic religions that prescribe good and bad behavior, shamanistic faiths do not seem to do this. Instead they send you into battle and they test you, and when the purpose of the battle is fulfilled, they bring you into direct consultation with the gods.

Dreams

Dreams are vastly important to Native American people. Their content is thought to guide us and shape our lives. By paying attention to our dreams, recalling them and analyzing them, we may solve problems or even foresee forthcoming events.

In her book 'Medicine Dance', Marsha describes how she had a vivid dream that appeared to predict the arrival of two very different lovers in her life. It was not until she met both men that she realized how she had conjured each of them months earlier, during a vivid and thought-provoking night's sleep!

In one prophetic instance, I dreamt of a young man who I went to school with. It was a vivid dream that I reported back to my partner at the time. The day after the dream, just as I was leaving work, the young man I'd dreamt about was walking into my work building. It turns out that he worked there too. We were both far from the area we had grown up in and we had not been in contact since school, nor did we have any friends of friends in common. This was a striking occurrence, perhaps brought about by his close proximity or simply a glimpse of the future. Nothing more occurred in this chance meeting and there did not appear to be an underlying reason for it, though in retrospect, perhaps there did not need to be. Maybe the reason was simply so that at some point in the future, I would be able to report this occurrence to you!

Dreams may well be excellent indicators of our thoughts and feelings for very straightforward reasons. Scientifically it makes perfect sense that at times of stress you might have bizarre or frightening dreams. But how about when you are happy, or when you are enjoying periods of success. Maybe the dreams are not as noticeable as their content may not be disturbing or profound. However, maybe if we were to notice the content of our dreams on all occasions, be they happy or sad, we would be able to better glimpse our inner selves, harness our inner sight, become more attuned to our needs and possibly help strengthen our spiritual development.

As my spiritual development has grown I have had bundles of intriguing, vivid, disturbing and wonderful dreams. I often use dream books to try and interpret the snippets I remember; and what the books tell me it is about usually reflects my state of mind accurately. When I look up the meanings in one of the many dream books I have at home and at work, they are often very significant and relevant to my life at that time.

Many people from all walks of life and belief systems recommend keeping a dream journal, which is a great idea if you are very organized. I have never done this, although I do make a point of talking about my dreams with like-minded friends. Sometimes the very act of speaking about what went on in your mind overnight can help you realize a dream's meaning and relevance to you. Your friend may be able to offer a deeper insight.

Dreams are hugely important across all shamanic paths and are certainly worthy of your inspection. On any spiritual path you are likely to be encouraged to remember your dreams, so why not sleep like the shamanic dreamtime experts and purchase yourself a dream catcher. Native Americans use dream catchers to help grasp hold of their most meaningful dreams and to help the memory retain them. Dream catchers look a bit like spider's webs, woven of fabric (often suede). You hang the dream catcher above your bed to catch your dreams! I have used dream catchers on and off for years. An ex-boyfriend once bought me a gigantic one at the start of our relationship. I now own a much smaller one that I place above my head at night. I must say that size, in this instance, does not matter. The huge one did not help me foretell the messy ending of that particular relationship, whilst at least the small one I now own is discreet and does not require my bedroom to be themed around it My dreams are just as vivid as they have always been, whilst some nights I do not remember dreaming at all. Without fail, the ones I do remember are often fraught with meaning and once interpreted they can certainly add value to my understanding of my needs.

Illness

One of the messages from the topic of Shamanism to really grab my attention is the belief that we can make ourselves ill. We all know that too many late nights, going outside with wet hair or working too hard can all be potentially hazardous to our health, as can the repercussions of casual sex, illicit drugs, broken hearts, and falling over.

However, the illness referred to by shamanic thought is the illness brought about by a lifetime of stress, unhappiness, bitterness or anger. This might be something as simple as being ungrateful, negative or defensive. Such ways of being could permeate through your life, eventually accumulating in a physical disease. In the book Medicine Dance, Marsha Scarborough's extreme example is the illness of cancer, which she believed her friend contracted as a result of living unhappily. Despite one remission, her friend became ill a second time and eventually died. On her deathbed this friend seemed to realize that she had led a selfish life, one that had pushed others away and not recognized the great bounty of love she had access to. It was a sad lesson to learn, particularly as it was so late in the day. Had Marsha's friend been happier, more open and optimistic, it is suggested that she may not have become ill in the first place.

I am sure it is a theory that will have medical doctors utterly appalled, and yet somehow it still rings true.

This goes hand in hand with other Native American and spiritual theories such as the fact that we may have chosen to become ill before we were even born. The belief is that in choosing to be ill we might gain insight into our very souls. This may seem a somewhat callous statement to those born with a debilitating illness or disability. Yet spiritually one of the greatest paths to enlightenment is through suffering and hardship of one kind or another. It is a spiritual truism and every day truth that all hardships, if we handle them well, make us stronger.

I am so lucky that in my life disability and illness has not thus far been visited upon me. However, I have seen it close up and I know the struggles that people are faced with. My mother developed polio as a baby. She was lucky to survive and has suffered greatly with the repercussions of this illness all her life. She has always had to wear a brace on her leg, and her movement and energy has been limited because of the brace and the pain she endures. Yet in spite of this 'disability' she has always lived a full and interesting life. As a young girl growing up in America, sports were a big thing. Because she could not run as freely and as fast as the other kids she became a fantastic baseball pitcher. At the tender age of 21 she ventured across the pond, away from the small town she grew up in, making herself a new home in the city of London, England. There she met my father and proceeded to get married and knock out three lively children whom she needed a great deal of energy to keep up with!

Having sprouted three children, she went on to study psychology, gaining a first class honors degree in her forties. She did this whilst my brothers and I were teenagers, I find this amazing, as I only managed to get a 2:2 despite having great health, and no dependents to worry about. She then got herself a full time career for the first time in her life, working as an advocate for people with mental health problems. Her health has not improved, and sadly she has now had to give up this hard fought for working career. She now suffers a condition called post-polio, and despite its many symptoms and negative effects, she never complains. She is still active and often absolutely exhausts herself to the point of dropping. She does loads of voluntary work and plays the piano at her church. She keeps herself busier than I do and gives a great deal of herself to others. She is a hugely impressive, generous and caring woman.

My thought is that perhaps my wonderful mummy chose to come to Earth and undergo the physical suffering that she has encountered. Her challenge, I imagine would be to deal with it and get on with life as best she can. If indeed this was her plan, then she is certainly winning, indeed she is way ahead of her game, and next time I see her I will have to insist she chills out for a week or two and puts her tired feet up for a bit. Looking at my mum's life I can certainly see how certain difficulties in life may be pre-planned as a way to progress and gain more kudos upon return to the Great Spirit.

In terms of living a sad life and becoming ill, some people may have chosen to become ill as an opportunity to cure not only the illness, but also the personality traits or habits that might have caused the illness in the first place. Two birds with one almighty healing stone! Marsha believes that her friend eventually failed in both respects, yet she did learn eventually even if it was too late. I am not suggesting that bouts of depression or consistent negativity will make you prone to terminal illnesses. However, it is an interesting and in some respects a heart-warming theory. If you consider that you choose illness for yourself, then you must assume it is not a random or unfair happening. Instead it is seen as a passage to growth and a possible opportunity for spiritual awakening.

When we are ill, the shamanic view goes as far as to say that we are occasionally given the chance to cure ourselves. Whether you employ a Shaman to assist you in your healing, or you simply scour the library and see holistic therapists to help you bring about your own cure, the fact is that you have that power of healing within you.

For those of us lucky enough to be in good health, such a theory is a stark warning about how to live our lives. Whilst Christians say bad behavior will make you go to hell, and Buddhists see you reincarnated as a greenfly, Shamans see that your actions may be revisited on you in the here and now through disease, disability, bruises and broken bones.

Alice does a Sweatlodge

Oh yes I did! This particular piece of journalistic reporting went past mere curiosity, and 'book research' and sat firmly on the list of things I needed to do. Having Native American ancestors and feeling so drawn to this culture I felt it was ready to get my feet wet, well, my whole body, totally skin soaking, sweat drenching wet. It was time I challenged myself to some real, full on Shaman style spiritual development. And my word, what a development it was!

I booked myself in with a small but seemingly modern 'self development' outfit named Continuum based in the stunning scenery of the Lake District, among the mountains in northern England. It was a long way to drive but boy was I glad I did it. Not only was the sweatlodge a truly crazy and valuable experience, but I also threw myself into communing with nature in a way I had not expected. It was a solo girly road trip, a weekend in the country, just nature and me… Shamanism as it suits me!

Driving up to Ambleside was quite an experience in itself. I was wary as my past whizzed by on the side of the motorway. The places I had visited as a child were still signposted. These were followed by the foreboding shadow of Lancaster University, a place of much learning for me, though not necessarily related to my degree! It appeared to have sprouted weird green alien-looking buildings all down the side, though to be fair that place never really did have a sense of style and tended to go in for archi-tecture of the vile and depressing sort. I was barraged by the past and memories of ex-boyfriends, crazy student antics and friends I no longer speak to. Unsurprisingly following this assault on my memory, I had quite a headache by the time I reached Lake Windermere. The sheer breathtaking beauty of the Lakes and the clean fresh air soon cleared up that potential migraine.

My hotel was out in the sticks, with no mobile phone reception, except in one dark corner of the car park. I was to be out of touch with everyone. Not that it felt that way, it did not feel like isolation, rather it became a re-acquaintance with myself. It is not often in this busy day and age that we are left alone to dwell with our own thoughts. The remote broadband-free area of Rydal ensured I would not be in excessive contact with anyone but the inner me.

This gave me two choices: stay in my hotel room and read a book, or pluck up my courage and explore the local flora and fauna. I chose the second option; the area was too beautiful to not give it my full attention. I started off with a gentle stroll round Rydal Water. I was a little afraid to venture too far around the lake on my own (due to a yucky teenage experience a friend and I had with a perverted flasher at a similarly secluded spot many moons ago) so I cut through the bushes and sat by the waterside, not too far from a bunch of burly blokes playing football. A few people passed me by in their green and brown walking clothes and clunky waterproof hiking boots. I am sure I blended in well in my magenta city girl jacket with its useless three quarter length sleeves insufficient to protect my poor forearms from the significant gusts that blew round the valleys, and my redundant mobile phone and cutesy little handbag!

As I sat by the lake, I noticed how acute my senses had become. I was overwhelmed by the numerous tiny phenomena that occurred around me and that seemed so spectacular. A leaf falling from a tree to the water put shame to high definition TV, whilst a scurrying squirrel managed to make me jump round and grab my handbag as though I might be mugged any moment! When I returned to my hotel I could feel my whole body buzzing and vibrating, as though the energy of the lake and the stones I had sat upon had transferred their vital essence into me.

I felt a surge of rejuvenation that the natural world always tends to bring. My mother reminded me how as I child I would spend hours in fields befriending cows (it was one particular cow actually). But maybe this amazing buzzing energy sensation had something to do with my love of the bovine!

On the day of the sweatlodge some people fast. I however do not go in for self-denial. There is no way I cannot eat breakfast, especially not when I am staying and paying for bed and breakfast! To me the idea of purposely skipping a meal borders on the ridiculous, particularly a meal that is already paid for. I did however fill right up and then skip lunch. I thought that was a fair compromise, and believe me I enjoyed a hearty breakfast.

So with my belly pleasantly full of vegetarian delights I set off.

The Great Spirit was not too keen to see me go in the right direction and my satellite navigation pointed me toward a road that did not exist. There were two other roads either side, one of which threatened that there were dangerous trees and I should turn back immediately. Not wishing to upset a cantankerous cedar or incur the wrath of an alpine with attitude, I duly backed off. It's amazing the fear a piece of paper can bring about! I parked up in somebody's drive and made friends with their skinny ginger tomcat whilst I called Matt France, the organizer, to come to my rescue. It appears that I did have to take my life into my hands and brave the dangerous trees. This was the first of many grueling events of the day, though I am happy to say it was nothing like the nasty trees on the Wizard of Oz and not once did I get an apple chucked at my head!

I was the first to arrive and had the chance to watch Matt build the lodge. It was much smaller than I expected, probably the size of a round two- or three-man dome tent with a deep hole in the middle. It was constructed entirely of trees that Matt had cut down for this very purpose. These were presumably nice trees that gave their lives for our benefit. I did a small amount of helping, generally holding things in place and throwing sticks for Pips the dog, whilst chattering away and no doubt holding things up. Matt was very gracious and allowed me to twitter away whilst he got on with the hard work. Not long after my arrival others started to turn up and the day soon got into full swing.

The new arrivals were a mixed bunch, though there seemed to be tendency towards working in health and healing. There were two yoga teachers whilst others worked in nutrition, health and alternative therapies. Most unusual background award went to an ex-fireman who was now training in Alexander Technique. The reasons for doing the sweat lodge seemed to be fairly varied. The ex-fireman had done it before and said that following the last one he had been euphoric for days afterwards and that it had helped purge memories from his days in the fire service. One lovely woman, was brought there via images she received in a meditation, whilst others wanted to connect with spirit, detoxify their bodies or just challenge themselves and see what happened.

We all worked together to decide which jobs we would undertake, either building a fire or sweeping clear the floor of the lodge so that no leaves would get in it and smoke us out. Matt ensured we used our intuition to do the jobs we felt called too, and at first it appeared we split into traditional roles by gender, with the men building the fire and the women sweeping the floor. Another two women joined us and soon shook us out of our gender conformity when they quickly got stuck in building the tremendous fire.

Within the wood fire many large rocks were placed, these are referred to as 'Grandfathers'. It was these blazing beauties that would heat up in the fire until they glowed, then they would be placed in the middle of the sweat lodge, glowing and wonderful, and their heat would provide the sweat lodge experience.

We all helped with placing many blankets over the lodge to ensure that no heat escaped, and we placed personal power items upon a small altar outside the lodge. My items were the silver cuff that rarely leaves my wrist, and my two arrowheads given to me as a young girl by my uncle. In respect of my American side I also placed a dime amongst these things. The idea is that our power items will get charged up with the energy from the fire and the lodge. As we waited for the fire to heat up the stones, we got to know each other better. It seemed that the intimate nature of what we were about to do meant that people were very open with one another very quickly. We talked about our lives, our beliefs and our fears and concerns for what we were about to do. It was fantastic to be with a bunch of such diverse strangers and yet feel so at home and so welcome.

And so the sweating begins…

It all starts, like any good regime with a few warm ups and a good cleansing. The warm ups came in the form of stretches and gentle jogging to help prepare our bodies not only for the heat, but for the fact we would be sat in cramped conditions for a prolonged period. The cleansing involved very little on my part, I simply stood there over exposed in my white bikini (it was very cold, think nipples and goose pimples, argh!) as Matt and Gabby wafted sage smoke over me with a condor feather. Sage is famous in all manner of spiritual circles as a great cleanser, and similar things can be done with it to cleanse homes, tarot cards and your own body.

Once in the sweatlodge, Matt talked us through what seemed to be a gentle meditation. Within this he had us picture ourselves up above the earth, far into the sky, looking as our blue and green planet got smaller and smaller. In doing this we merged with the universe, becoming one with all creation. This was a pleasant introduction, and now that our minds were drifting in outer space, the real physical stuff could begin.

The sweatlodge is divided into four sections called rounds, with a break in-between each round. I was under the mistaken impression that between each round we would leave the lodge to stretch our legs and cool down. That was not the case, in fact all that did happen was the door was opened to allow some cool air in for a short time. Each round was themed according to the Native American Mexican tradition Matt had been taught by a Mexican Shaman. This format would be likely to differ slightly across the various tribes. Generally the rounds represent a circle, and as a whole they represent the circle of life.

The first round was for the East and concentrated on birth and beginnings. We passed a large feather around, first in silence and then people spoke. This round started off easily. It took a while for the heat to build up, and I was under the false impression that the lodge experience might be quite easy. How wrong I was!

The second round was dedicated to the South and was for healing. We passed sage to chew on and people asked for healing for themselves and for people they knew. Speaking up in the ever-growing heat is in itself quite a task. I did in the end manage to request healing for some people I know, but it is quite shocking how the mere opening of one's mouth in such extreme temperatures can take a serious toll on the body.

The second round was for me the most difficult. It seemed to go on forever and left me exhausted, stressed and with a fear for my ability to cope.

A sweat lodge is not an easy thing. If you cannot stand saunas for more than two minutes, then it may not be for you. Not only is the heat immense, but so are the highs and the lows. The fear and the bliss slide so easily into and up against one another it is almost impossible at times to disseminate one from another. I will tell you this, at one point during the second round I did not think I could stay in. The heat was stifling, claustrophobic and frightening, my head was light and my heart was beating so quickly. My breaths were constantly coming out as impassioned, frustrated sighs, the supportive kindness of others washed off me with the sweat, and I sat in my own flesh, panicky, nauseous and fearful. This thankfully, did not last. As the fear began to subside I was overcome by what I can only describe as utter serenity. I lay on the sweat soaked earth in the womb like darkness and realized that I felt something so indescribable and powerful. It was the most amazing high I think I have ever experienced, so peaceful and yet so raw.

Perhaps I was connected to the earth, or to the Great Spirit or to my own inner strength. I really do not know what it was, but it was immense. I felt on the verge of tears, but not tears of sadness. I just wanted to stay like that for all eternity, I did not want to move, I felt that I could drift off into a wonderful sleep. Imagine the best orgasm you have ever had and the feeling of release you experience afterward. That dull sleepy calmness that washes over you and makes you feel blissful. It was like that but more magnificent and of course without the sexual element. I would do it all again, the pain, the heat, the fear and the claustrophobia for another slice of that euphoric bliss.

Following my little slice of heaven I felt stronger to continue with the next two rounds. I knew by this point I would not pass out or have an embarrassing panic attack.

The third round represented the West was aptly dedicated to 'death and dying', this was a round to release and let things slip away from us. The heat was intense and was of the flesh-burning, searing kind. This is also known as the Warrior round. Matt encouraged us to indulge in lots of chanting, whooping and hollering as a means to cope. The heat seemed to singe your skin, nose and lungs as you breathed it in.

The final round was for the North and we invoked the spirit world and our ancestors. We all offered our thanks or requests to the heavens aloud. Although it was still darned hot, the fear factor had subsided and I for one certainly felt very relaxed.

This was much calmer and I could feel the relief as we moved toward the end. Perhaps as we called on the spirits for clarity they came to us to buoy us through those last few minutes. Though it was still hot, it certainly felt sweeter, more relaxed and clearer. By the very end, when the door was opened for the final time, I was in the beginnings of a drunken euphoric state. Knowing it was over was so wonderful, knowing that all that was left to do was to cool down felt like an amazing treat.

The whole event is now a bit of a blur. During the sweat it is impossible to think of anything but the present moment, time loses its meaning and nothing seems to exist beyond your crowded eight-person womb. I did not find myself contemplating recent events, or indeed thinking about whether to have a glass of red or white wine later in the evening. During a sweat, for me at least, the only thing that was relevant was my body, my thirst and my breath.

Two things I particularly remember are the torture and the bliss. I remember the kind acts of others, moving out of my way, or placing parts of my body onto theirs so that I might be more comfortable. I remember the relief when the door was opened for the final time and we could relax into the warmth rather than riling around in the stifling angry heat. I remember how amazing it felt to have just a few sips of water as the bottle was passed around. I remember the chants, the singing and the tears that fell at the end as people embraced their need to release emotions.

As we crawled out into what seemed to be the brightest light I have ever seen, I made my way to the nearest tree to be near its roots and feel its grounding presence. I initially felt disappointed in myself that I had struggled to cope, and yet I did cope. Had I found it easy I am sure my disappointment would be greater. We had been in the infernal sweat for near on three hours, though it only seemed like one or two.

I was weak from water loss and when we could find our feet again we all splashed and cleaned our muddied, sweaty skin in the glorious Lake Windermere. I can say in all honesty that water never, ever felt so good, refreshing and pure. It was as though I had never met water before and had been thirsty and dirty all my life. I do not think I would be going too far to say that it felt like a baptism. Rinsing away the past, washing away doubt and embracing the world with new eyes, eyes that see things brighter and clearer.

The lake was filled with grown adults whooping and hollering like teenagers released onto spring break! Yet inherent to it all was innocence and a wild abandonment of our constraints and self imposed 'proper' behaviors. We were all freedom loving kiddies again and it felt great. Another thing that truly rocked was how great the food tasted. I got stuck into some grapes and they tasted like grapes grown by the angels! All of my senses were heightened, a weight was gone from my shoulders and I found I could laugh easier. In my post sweatlodge eyes, the world was a beautiful place, everything was how it should be and my new friends and I would all be just fine.

Afterthoughts

A few days after my sweatlodge experience I feel much closer to nature, and certainly closer to my own nature. I am more myself than I have been for a very long time, and my mind is settled and happy. I am convinced that my intuition has been hyped up, possibly along with any psychic ability I might have. I am sure that if I were to perform Reiki healing on somebody right now the energy would shoot through me as though I were a lightening conductor. Whenever somebody asks me about my weekend I gush on and on about how amazing it was, energy courses through me and it seems to be infectious as they grin back at me, perhaps being polite, or perhaps intrigued.

This supportive atmosphere that developed was key to the sweat. People who were complete strangers with little in common, became somewhat fused by the heat, the sweat and the fear. This bonding seemed to form part of the spiritual backbone to the situation; in many respects it made it all the more wonderful. There was a connection between the group that I am not sure can be established in many other circumstances and later that day I was sad to see them go. As I skipped off to my car in a state of mellow happiness, I did hope that I may see them all again.

Although I had hoped for some grand spiritual enlightenment or crazy visual vision, none of this occurred. It did not need to. My challenge was mainly physical, though the bliss I felt came from deep within and maybe from elsewhere too.

I will definitely do a sweatlodge again. The whole weekend for me was absolutely perfect. I spent so much time in nature, exploring and taking in the everyday miracles that us city girls tend to forget. I yearned to live amongst this foliage and greenery. I felt the energy lift me up and sustain me in a way the concrete and computers of town life never ever could. I believe I started to really, deeply understand what it meant to be a Shaman; to be in love with the earth, to wish to heal and to speak with the Great Spirit as though she were your ever-present sister.

The High Heeled Shamanistic Conclusion

Shamanism is very much about healing and the importance of connecting to nature. Be this healing the earth, our pets, our partners and friends or, if you have time after all of that, healing yourself. Women, I believe are natural healers, for thousands of years we have consistently been the ones to 'kiss things better'. Because of this our shamanic tendencies are more fertile and easily groomed than perhaps a man who has never had to look after himself or others in the way that women end up looking after whole family units and friend groups.

Shamanism is magical. The ways and the rites of the Shaman are so natural and involve taking account of the whole planet and all the varying realms within it and around it. Shamanism is reflected in so many other religions in this book, although perhaps that is because Shamanism as a basic wilderness based belief is what all of our societies once sprang from. But whilst we have gone on to complete complex tomes of literature, music and philosophical theory based around religions, the Shamans keep it simple. They do not need complex diagrams to say something very similar to what a Kabbalist might say about illness or alternative dimensions. Shamans do not require a church or a table upon which to commune with the deceased as a Spiritual Church may do. Shamans find their wisdom in nature, spirit and humanity, all it requires is being willing to surrender yourself to your grass roots.

For Shamans there are no compromises, there is no halfway house that involves sitting in classrooms studying flora and fauna and religious theory. You must forsake your body and hand it over to the drums, the sweat and the pain. You must get tired and uncomfortable, you will see your fears and you will match them. To be a Shaman means to experience, touch, taste, smell and feel the Great Spirit. In doing so you could glimpse eternity or view life through the eyes of an eagle. You must live simply, proudly and in total harmony with the planet. You will be equal to all things and show your reverence not through bible study, but through being a work in progress and a happy vessel for Mother Nature's whims.

To follow the shamanic way of life you must be willing to get up and dance with Spirit, to ingest and digest and fall over yourself until you and spirit are a whirling dervish of mind, body and soul.

In all good writing guides they advise you to start your chapter with a quirky catch point. Stem from this and discuss all the relevant points, but somehow at the end work your way back to that original point. The thought being that in doing this you tie your piece together nicely and make it rounded and complete for the reader. The circle for Native Americans is a powerful shape and is of great importance in their lives, their worship and also in a sweatlodge. I had no intention of making this chapter such a perfectly crafted circle, however it appears the Great Spirit did!

You may remember that at the very start of this chapter I made a passing remark regarding the techno wizards of the 1990s, the Shamen. Well as I was driving back from my sweatlodge I grew tired of the CD I was listening to and switched on the radio. As I did so the radio presenter was introducing the next song, this was, of course, by the Shamen. No it was not the infamous 'Ebenezer Good' track; it was something far more pertinent. I could not help but to whoop out my glee and give a massive grin toward the Great Spirit as it had not only generously gifted me with a closing paragraph, but mainly it had gifted me a song laden with deeply meaningful lyrics. These are lyrics that seemingly echo the shamanistic principles and that capture the feeling that comes with a three-hour session of profuse sweating. Thanks to divine radio intervention, and another brilliant example of coincidence, this chapter's circle is now perfectly, powerfully complete. Glow sticks at the ready ladies; check this cheesy and fabulous rave hit out. The almighty Shamen's classic track 'Move Any Mountain'. Perfect.

The High Heeled Spiritualist

Spiritualism is probably one of the most abused set of beliefs in this book. It is under the guise of 'spirituality' that so many con-artists make their living, be this as clairvoyants, mediums, phoney preachers, ghostbusters or fake healers. We have all heard or read the horror stories of some poor woman who is down on her luck getting addicted to psychic chat lines and landing herself in a whole load of debt as a result. The idea of phoney psychics should be very firmly ingrained into all our minds, and believe me, it is a real danger. Popular television trickster Derren Brown has shown how very easily psychic abilities can be faked, and in light of this we must all, including myself, be a little more cynical.

Because of this I investigated this topic with great caution. Spiritualism comes wrapped in a very familiar format, similar to Church of England but with television host Yvette Fielding and media friendly psychic Jonathon Edwards holding things together around the edges. As a result of famous psychic faces, popular culture has to an extent embraced spiritual pursuits. Séances, mediums and hauntings are familiar territory to anyone with a television or love of films.

However these rogue elements of Spiritualism do not by any means reflect the core faith or meaning of this faith. Although Spiritualism as we know it may well have started with haunted houses, it has progressed to become a meaningful belief in an afterlife, and a heartfelt understanding of the meaning of life as influenced by communication with angels, spirit guides and those who have passed over.

Spiritualism has churches and congregations that gather to form a Spiritualist community. Circles or services are no longer the reign of Victorian style parlor games, or after dinner hocus pocus to entertain an enthralled and slightly drunken party of friends. It is important to separate such occult loving thrill seekers, from those who commit to Spiritualism as a lifestyle and core faith. Those who are interested in the occult are like joy riders; they 'borrow' Spiritualist ideas and play with spirit, either out of curiosity, or occasionally for darker purposes. The Spiritualist folk I have met are not part of this group. Playing with the Ouija board is not part of the Spiritualist faith. Ouija boards, or other random contact with the deceased, can possibly be fun or scary, but serious Spiritualists are not in it for the fun or fear factor. Spiritualists are likely to be actively seeking meaning to their lives, in a way that accepts life beyond death. Though life beyond death is central to their beliefs, it is not something they would toy with, or use as a party trick to freak out unbelievers.

Spiritualist churches are more than a junction to meet your passed away loved ones. They hold worship or circles in a manner similar to traditional churches, with prayers, hymns and readings. They often hold spiritual development groups and provide house-clearing services for those unlucky enough to be stuck with an earthbound spirit that's 'going bump in the night'. This is all taken very seriously and is for the highest benefit of those present. Unlike the televised versions we see so often, Spiritualism goes beyond entertainment and acts as a communication tool to our immortal souls.

My experience of this has until recently only ever involved visiting a 'circle' at the local Spiritualist Church. I made visits to the circle several times and was occasionally vaguely impressed and other times thoroughly disappointed.

My local spiritualist church is run down and staffed by old age pensioners, not that there is anything wrong with that, but it seems their PR people (if they have any) have been unable to introduce many from the younger generations to their ranks. So when someone like me turns up with a glamorous friend in tow there is immediately a generational gap, a social gap and an inability to fully understand one another's perspectives. Outside the main church hall they have a little stand selling paperback books. I noticed a glut of 'Mills and Boon' romances amongst other titles favored by ladies of a certain age. I could not help feeling I had stumbled into a charity shop as opposed to the hub of spiritual manifestation and joy I was hoping for.

The circle I visited was run by a father and daughter duo, they were pretty good. They never had a message for me, but I am lucky enough to have very few dearly departed. They did, however, deliver pertinent and moving messages to my friends and to many other people in the room.

That said, I could not help but notice that many people in the room seemed extremely vulnerable. Many were desperate to contact a particular person, whereas I was merely there out of curiosity. Some were so keen to reach a loved one that they would desperately try to make every message fit their circumstances, even when it was patently obvious it was not a message for them. My only hope is that the Spiritualist Church treats these people with kindness. Their openness and susceptibility was palpable and I felt lucky that I was attending simply for the experience and not because of the pain that so many of them bore etched deep into their faces. I guess this exposes the high likelihood of defenseless, grieving people being taken for a cruel ride. If you have lost a loved one, tread carefully. A Spiritualist Church would be preferable to an overpriced premium rate psychic phone line, but do not expect miracles.

One poor woman had lost her very young daughter in a tragic household accident. She had been attending the Spiritualist Church for several years and was yet to have any contact with her beloved child. In spite of the time delay, she still grasped at every single message as though it may be a message especially for her. In the meantime she had developed her own psychic abilities and interest in Spiritualism, which was some small comfort to her, but essentially this was not what she was truly longing for.

Given my fortunate lack of deceased friends and family, I did not have an entirely wasted journey. On one occasion the father of the double act leading this circle, told me to pay attention that evening as I was falling asleep; he was going to send me something. Apart from being a slightly disturbing proposition, this is a contradiction in itself. Falling asleep and paying attention rarely go hand in hand. That night I got into bed, and was drifting off, absolutely paying attention to nothing, when suddenly I heard my name called as clear as a bell right next to my ear. Well that certainly made me wake up and take notice! I was alone in the room and my boyfriend denied all knowledge. The following week I informed the father of the circle about this. He looked incredibly happy and smug in a cute old spiritual guy way – a bit like Santa after a glass of sherry. I am not entirely sure what his point was in doing, or arranging with spirit to do this. Maybe he just realized I needed something from the circle so he sent one of his spirit mates to spook me. Whatever his reason, I must say it was just that little something that I wanted, a little bit of personal proof.

On another occasion I took along my Native American arrow-heads with me. Each circle began with a meditation and my aim was to meditate on the arrowheads and see if I got anything interesting in terms of thoughts or mental images. I got nothing. However, one of the other women in the group apparently saw very vivid images of tee pees and a Native American village. She looked quite surprised and so I confessed that I had brought some relevant artifacts. The daughter fondled my arrowheads for quite some time and told me they exuded a strong energy. I have never had anyone fondle my arrowheads, or say such lovely things about them before, so I was pleased.

I stopped going to the Spiritualist Church after a few visits. It was not really of any great help to me, and if I felt so compelled I could watch bereaved people suffering on Living TV any day of the week. I have, however, enrolled in spiritual development classes recently, and these are fantastic. Indeed I have dedicated a whole section to them later on in this chapter. I have also explained some of the more important elements of Spiritualism, as

I see them, for you here.

What is Spiritualism?

Spiritualism came about when a haunting situation in New York became a communication between a spirit and two sisters, Margaretta and Catherine Fox. The spirit had been responsible for noisy rapping in their house, which they eventually used to make intelligent contact. This developed into the famous *'knock once for Yes, twice for No'*, style of contact you will have seen in films. These events with the Fox sisters allowed mediumship to move into the public arena, causing many people to set up their own circles for psychic experimentation and communication with spirits. Since this event in 1848, Spiritualism and the Spiritualist Church has massively grown and now has established churches, unions and some basic spiritual guidelines.

These guidelines summarize the belief of Spiritualism, without going into a massive amount of detail. They are known as The Seven Principles of Spiritualism. These consist of seven statements that guard the work of Spiritualists. The renowned Spiritualist, Emma Hardinge Britten developed these statements and they go as follows:

"The Fatherhood of God;
The Brotherhood of man;
The Communion of Spirits and the Ministry of Angels;
The Continuous existence of the human soul;
Personal Responsibility;
Compensation and retribution hereafter for all the good and evil
    deeds done on Earth;
Eternal progression is open to every human soul."

These appear to be a series of blasé and random statements, so I will read into them a little deeper for you here. The general gist of Spiritualism is that once you have died your spirit lives on.

Spiritualists believe that a person's spirit continues to live in a spiritual world, but they appreciate that most of us have little concept or understanding of this premise. At the heart or head of Spiritualism lies the figurehead known as God, though God's manifestation is not dictated. You may like to imagine God as a manifestation of energy, as a friendly old guy, or as an amalgamation of Gods and Goddesses. Your view of God is not told or taught to you; however the existence of a God as the focal centre point is important to Spiritualism.

Also important in Spiritualism is an acknowledgement of the community around you aka the Brotherhood of Man. Indeed, the Brotherhood of Man, the communion of spirits and the ministry of angels work together to progress humankind and to prove the continuous existence of the human soul after death. In essence these four groups of beings, God, humans, angels and spirits make up the 'gang', whilst the next four statements cover goals, aspirations and rules of that gang.

'Personal Responsibility' speaks for itself and is a shorthand way of warning you to be on your best behavior and take responsibility for your actions. 'Compensation and Retribution' takes this a bit further as it makes you consider that any naughty sins you may commit will need to be atoned for, whether now or in the future (it's the Spiritualist version of karma). Much like any other religious belief, it is a gentle reminder that you shall reap what you sow. The final principle reminds us that we can all advance our souls, become better people and that such self-improvement can be sought through seeking spiritual development.

Unlike more formalized religions, Spiritualism does not dictate in any way how you should behave or what specifics you should believe. So rather than sign up to a set of Spiritualist concepts, you are welcome to attend a church, have a chat and make your own mind up. All of the principles are up for discussion and individual interpretation. Spiritualism is in this respect more like a social club than a religious institution. As a result beliefs will vary from church to church or individual to individual.

The main purpose of Spiritualism is to acknowledge and prove the fact that our immortal soul lives on beyond death. Often this is done via the contacting of a dead person known to you, or in my case being visited by night time spooks who whisper sweet nothings into your ear! Once this is proven to you, how you choose to alter your life, or whether you desire to become a better person, is entirely up to you. No baptism or indoctrination is required; however you might expect that once you have proof of an immortal soul you will be more open to self-improvement and more likely to open your heart to a faith system of some description.

Spiritualism is a very relaxed religion, and is ideal for those who want to dabble, or those who want to have a belief in something beyond life without committing to a new lifestyle system. Because Spiritualism is so very open it is also a fabulous addition to any other belief system you may already have. It is also notable for basic spiritual growth and honing your own intuition and psychic skills. If you feel you may be sensitive to spirits and 'the òther side' then Spiritualism may be able to help you develop and manage your skill.

I personally thought I had no sensitivity before; indeed I was pretty terrified of any bizarre or psychic phenomena. I have since learned that people who are naturally sensitive to phenomena tend to be terrified because of the fact they are sensitive to such things. They are more likely to pick up on other people's emotions and unconsciously feel bad vibes, spirits or psychic messages. Once you are ready to have a go at inducing psychic or intuitive skills, it tends to come relatively easily. And happily enough, it is not terrifying at all; it is actually rather easy and feels surprisingly natural.

Several years ago I attended a psychic night at the local Working Men's Club – classy I know! I was informed by a medium that 'they' were ready for me when I was ready for them and that I should not be scared. This frightened the life out of me, and resulted in my hiding further away from any small psychic ability I might have had. Eventually though, and following a variety of life experiences, I became less afraid and more open to adventuring in spiritual pursuits.

Through Spiritualism I have had access to a part of my soul I had buried before. As part of my enlightenment journey the 'psychic classroom' of Spiritualism has been invaluable. Though I would not consider myself to be a Spiritualist, I would certainly recommend a good spiritual development class to anyone who is interested. Spiritualism is very tolerant and easy to apply to the everyday world as such it is worth a sneaky peek.

Inspiration Spiritual Developments Classes

I had no idea what to expect from 'Spiritual Development' classes. Would it be heavy on religious teaching? Would I be witness to possessions, trances and exorcisms? Or would it be a forum full of egos trying to prove their innate spiritual abilities over others? Happily it was none of the above. What it actually consisted of was a group of utterly sane and friendly people sat round a living room learning from the very well informed and experienced Deborah Chamberlain.

Deborah has lived a lifetime of seeing and communicating with spirit. Following the death of her adored father she decided to make her advanced spirituality a constructive and meaningful part of her life. She credits the opening of the Inspiration School to her father's 'return home'. Following his death she was inconsolable, and her father came to her in spirit to let her know he was not truly gone. It was from this basis that Deborah realized she had a gift worth sharing. Through her father's sacrifice of his life, so many others could learn. Although the whole thing is tinged with sadness for Deborah, she at least, unlike so many others, can be completely certain of a happy reunion with her darling dad some time in the future.

The aim of the Inspiration School is to help induct newbies and intermediates onto a more spiritual and psychic path of life. There is no end result offered, you do not leave after six months with a certificate, but you are given the opportunity to expand your mind and open yourself to psychic and spiritual growth. This particular path to Spirit involved two hours a week that consisted of meditation, meeting angels and spirit guides, practicing psychic skills via various tools (pendulum, angel cards, colored ribbons, psychometry) and a variety of other interesting tasks.

The first week I was perplexed, by the second week I was becoming gently convinced, by the third week I was a believer. Debs must be the best psychic teacher in the west!

Without wanting to give the game away, or regurgitate any of Deb's lesson plans, I have set out some of my experiences and learning from the first few lessons. For more information I suggest you get yourself enrolled on a local course.

I can honestly say that development classes have been nothing but a benefit to my life and a huge ingredient in my spiritual growth and search for enlightenment. I have watched others in the class lose their cynicism and experience moments of peace or awakening. In one case the class bloke who played his cards very close to his chest and seemed determined to remain impartial, announced he was now a believer. Although his journey is no doubt hugely different to mine, I recognized the look of love and awe on his face as these words came tumbling out. Deb cheered, another part of her divine mission completed!

These classes have added structure to my spiritual path to enlightenment. They have given me plenty of proof to back up my heartfelt beliefs, as well as showing me my own innate psychic and mediumistic abilities. In the months since I began, my entire outlook on life has expanded and changed. I sometimes feel that I see the greater scheme of things, and certain things in life have become far easier to deal with. Spiritual development, although it can be studied alone, is in my opinion far better done within a group with a teacher who can structure and disseminate your learning.

In this section I aim to give you a taste of my experiences. I can honestly say that my Tuesday night group has become the backbone to my own development, and quite frankly I would not be without it! On that gushing note, here is a taste of some of the key themes and points for beginners.

Protection

The first week was really just an introduction. The second class covered the important matter of protection. This means protection from psychic energies and not necessarily the energies of deceased folk. I believe we all know somebody who can turn on the charm and brighten a room, but should they take umbrage at something and get upset, angry or distressed, then sure as hell everyone else is going down with them. Some people infect a space with their moods, insecurities and an almost visible darkness. Sometimes a person's bad mood can be passed on by their angry, disturbed actions; others can simply sit there allowing the stench of rage or misery to emanate to everyone nearby.

If you are sensitive to moods this can mean you are constantly on a merry go round of emotion, picking up psychic attacks from friends, or even strangers you pass in the street. I know I have certainly been a victim of this and it is horrible. You end up feeling exhausted, stressed, unhappy or angry for no apparent reason. If you trace your day back you can clearly see that your interactions with a certain someone are likely to be the prime cause of your unsettled self. The person often is not aware they are exuding such negative energy and it is not their intention to throw you into a depressive slump, however, they do so all the same.

Protection is therefore an essential part of Spiritualism. It aids your progress, as you are no longer being affected by other people's emotional problems. It gives you the ability to have tea and sympathy with a friend without taking home their baggage when you leave.

By using psychic protection you are not subjected to unwanted pestering from somebody's deceased Grandma in the queue at the local shop. According to Deborah, this can be fairly common and annoying once you become more psychic. By not putting up protection, spirits will be around you like a moth to a flame. They do not mean you any harm, but they will recognize your psychic abilities and attempt to use you as a conduit for a message for whomever it is they wish to contact. So to avoid scaring the life out of people on the street with unexpected messages from their loved and lost ones, protection seems wholly sensible.

Since starting to use psychic protection every day, I am so much happier. It actually makes a huge difference to my life; things tend to slide off me now, rather than sticking in my guts and dragging me down. In the past I have spent much of my energies struggling to cheer someone up who has made a conscious decision to be miserable. I am sure this is a familiar scenario to many of you reading this. As women we do tend to get lumbered with the hard work of sorting out other people's emotions. Occasionally this is fine but it is easy to get bogged down in an abyss of somebody else's misery. I have lived with people I would consider borderline manic depressive and no matter how happy you make them one evening, by the time the next morning rolls around, they are sad, crying, anxious or sullen all over again.

Being such selfless creatures we will continue to wrap our emotional bandages over what is likely to be an emotional problem the width of the Grand Canyon, not realizing how useless that is or how badly it is affecting us. My opinion now is that if that person has purposefully decided to be melancholy, grumpy or angry, and they desire to wallow in it, then more power to them! But if they think that I will be joining them in the wallowing then they are having a very large laugh. That is not to say that I am now insensitive and callous, but that when I have finished counseling or consoling them, I will walk away clear headed and able to get on with my own life. Some people you are stuck with forever and a little protection from their wayward emotions is vital.

Since I committed to protect myself, I am fully persuaded of its effectiveness. I am more able to cope with a fraught working environment and I appear to have less tolerance for bitchiness. I pander less to fake emotions, and I don't get in an emotional fluster over relatively unimportant things (well not often!). I cannot be sure whether asking for psychic protection is merely a mental placebo, or whether the angels actually drape an invisible coat of arms around my heart and mind. Either way it works and is a fabulous way to make the day brighter and the mind sharper.

The work place is an arena where protection is vital. Recently when I have neglected to protect myself I have become emotionally bedraggled by the end of the day. I might even feel claustrophobic when around large groups and vulnerable in a way I cannot really describe.

People's attitude and negativity is so much more apparent. I have become incredibly averse to bitchiness and I dislike listening to it especially when it is meted out for no good reason. In the past I would join in the catty gossip without giving it a second thought, it made the day fly by quicker! Now I just feel so uncomfortable I have to shut up, or leave the room. Yes we all have a moan some days at other people's expense, but full on attacks on a person's character because they have done something that niggles us is just plain wrong, it sends out nasty vibes and it does not help make the world a better place. I have come to realize that there is a huge dose of bullying and discrimination that flies around in the guise of comedy and allegedly witty banter. I have to tell myself constantly that such actions stem more from a person's insecurities than from a wish to harm others. That said it's still painful to hear or be a witness to. Protection from such antics is therefore essential, in my opinion it is definitely worth doing if you work with any manner of people!

When I have requested protection for specific events I have not been disappointed. Most interesting was when I requested protection before a meeting with a very senior, extremely pompous and powerful older male. This particular gent had a reputation for rampant, patronizing sexism and general obstinacy. What did not help was that the meeting was set up for me and my young, attractive female boss to turn up and tell him what he had done wrong – and this was predicted to go down badly.

In my request for protection I was very specific in stating whom I required the protection from, and also suggesting that this gentleman could probably do with a dose of psychic, happy, chill out juice. During the meeting, our senior colleague appeared to have had a personality transplant. When we leveled our criticism at him, he actually agreed with us. He then proceeded to spend the entire meeting grinning inanely at me. This was noticed and commented on by my colleague. The poor bloke did every-thing but roll over and purr like a pretty little pussycat. Have I made my point? Protection worked and everybody was happy!

Prayer

Praying in Spiritualism is fairly indistinct from any other form of prayer, although it is generally less formal. You are given free rein to be creative, relaxed and spontaneous. Should you require a serious spot of praying then that can be done too. Deborah instilled in the class that praying is a show of appreciation to 'head office'. It is a way of affirming your belief and thanking those above for protecting you. Prayer can be used in a variety of ways, you can send up some positive thoughts of gratefulness, you can request healing for yourself and others, or you can treat it in its classic format of asking for help. If nothing else, you can use prayer just to check in, whether you need anything or not.

Sometimes it's nice just to acknowledge your beliefs. There are no set format or specific greetings, your salutation can be as specific or vague as you require. This might be Dear God, Dear Spirit, Dear Angels, or Hey Almighty Dudes! Whatever takes your fancy really!

Since practicing prayer I have tended to keep it upbeat, as though I were talking to a close friend. My prayer practice is particularly random, it is not exactly the traditional kneeling beside the bed, closing my eyes and folding my hands together like a good girl! I have not done that since I was about four and Daddy was still a vicar! I have taken to praying incredibly indiscriminately and in all kinds of places. When I am driving my car to work I may send a thought upward to request a good day, or on my way home I might say a quick thank you for getting me through another day unscathed. If great things happen I will immediately say a quick, 'Thanks', eyes upward, with no real greeting or closing. If a stressful circumstance arrives unexpectedly then I may send a mental request for support and strength. I do not consider the formalities to be important, Spirit/Guides/Angel/ God and Goddesses will know I am grateful or in need without the requirement for pomp and circumstance. You should try it, whether you are on a beach, a train, a plane or sat at your work desk there is always something to be grateful for, and it is nice to remember that you are not alone.

My use of prayer is fairly new, I am not sure what to expect if anything at all. It is a helpful affirmation of my spiritual path, and if nothing else it will not do any harm. I also find it helpful as a form of mental preparation, rather than agitating about a meeting, or a falling out with a friend, prayer can help focus your mind on how to make the most of a situation.

You never know, an idea to improve things might drop your way. I am a huge believer in things being dripped into your mind, and I sincerely believe that the idea for this book happened as a result of such a spiritual drop! One minute I was contemplating breakfast, the next I was planning this book. Maybe I had it in me, or maybe I was prompted. Spiritualists believe that Spirit can affect their lives tremendously, so whether you require a higher wage, want to be happier, or need to send your love to a departed loved one, prayer is an excellent place to start.

Meditation

Meditation is a core part of spiritual development, it helps calm your mind and make the brain more accessible to Spirit. Spiritualism has a core goal of creating greater intuition and inducing psychic ability. Meditation is a fantastic tool for all this, as well as for assisting in calming the mind and body after a hard day's work. I have always longed to meditate but generally delayed, cancelled or postponed any session I had planned with myself. I always figured that I am far too busy and impatient. Being forced to do it in the class is a welcome benefit. Now I only have to work on being able to find the time and patience in my own time to follow through with this. I whole-heartedly recommend it, either as a pathway to a more spiritual life, or as an opportunity for a little you time.

Basic breath work meditation abolishes stress and promotes a truly positive state of mind, regardless of what faith or religion you might be considering, if any. Meditation transcends them all and is something we should all indulge in whether we are an atheist or the Archbishop of Canterbury. Until you join your own group, why not try walking meditations. These can be done by taking a walk in the countryside and allowing nothing to enter your mind except the wondrous beauty of nature. For those who liked Shamanism, this also happens to be a rather shamanistic thing to do – albeit Shamans would tend to walk for days as opposed to your quick lunch break stroll through the park!

If you cannot get into nature simply try sitting and focusing intently on your breathing, you should find this relaxes you, bringing superb physical and mental benefits. It will also help prepare you for any deeper meditations you may do when you join your own development class. Any decent yoga class should start and end with a basic relaxation meditation, so grab the chance to tone up and relax all in one fell swoop.

As you develop your meditation you may begin to see images or colors in your mind's eye. These pop us as pictures in your imagination. You may feel you are 'imagining' them, and yet they come from nowhere and often seem to materialize unexpectedly and sometimes quite vividly. This is nothing to be afraid of and is simply either your subconscious higher self, or perhaps a guide trying to pass you a helpful message.

I really struggled with this in the beginning. I wanted to believe I was seeing 'visions' or that I was communing with a force larger than my own mind, and yet part of me just did not believe it. Over time, however, it did become quite apparent that certain thoughts were mine, whilst other thoughts and images were dropped into my brain from a third party. Over time I put more and more of my faith into what I was seeing and now I can distinguish between what is my own imagination, and what is a psychic vision or message.

During meditation you may also experience a variety of physical feelings and sensations. These could range from a feeling that someone is standing near you, or you may suddenly feel very hot or cold, or perhaps get a tickly sensation on your head. This is entirely normal and again it is likely that an angel or guide is coming forward to be with you. These experiences, both visual and physical can be very gentle, or occasionally quite intense, which is why I recommend you seek the safety and reassurance of a development group within which to familiarize yourself with such intriguing phenomena.

Using meditation within the class actually brought about one of my most profound early spiritual experiences. During meditation I have seen wonderful mental images or had interesting thoughts, but on this occasion I was given utter proof of natural psychic ability.

What occurred was unexpected, unplanned and fabulously crazy! During a group meditation my thoughts turned to one of the women in the room. She was a woman who I had barely spoken to, nor did I know anything about her. Let's call her Amelia. I had persistent and insistent thoughts about a young female. I felt this girl treated Amelia very badly, almost with venom and disgust. The overwhelming message was that the girl did not mean to be this way, but that she loved Amelia so much, she could not bear to see her suffer, and would lash out as a result. I had an innate feeling the girl was Amelia's daughter, though previously I had not considered her old enough to have a teenage daughter. This thought started out gently, but as I tried to ignore it, the thought became more forceful and would not leave my mind. In the end I decided to accept that it might be a psychic message and I mentally stated that I would pass the message on, as long as the message calmed down and allowed me to enjoy the meditation. After asking for this the thoughts subsided.

When the meditation had finished I expressed to Deborah that I had had some thoughts regarding Amelia. Deborah asked me if I wanted to share. Although I was reluctant and concerned I was going to look silly, I knew I had to do it. I relayed the message and discovered that this was precisely the situation Amelia was in. Apparently, since her divorce her daughter had been behaving badly towards her, to the point that the daughter had moved out and they could no longer live together. She told me that that week had been particularly bad.

My mind was reeling from all this. Was I psychic, clairvoyant or what? The fact is that it happened, and there was no way I could deny, justify or explain it. Was the message planted in my mind by spirit or was it simply me being ultra attuned to Amelia and making an inspired guess, or was I somehow reading her mind? Instinctively I feel that Spirit put the thought there. The fact is that the thought was so insistent that I had to bargain to get it to back off.

I do have a touch of cynic about me believe it or not! However, I think that after this experience the cynic in me rapidly dissipated. As I have gone on to do many more months of spiritual development, such instances are becoming more frequent and easier to deal with. It is through such occurrences that I am reminded of our innate ability to be spiritual. I do not think I am particularly special or gifted, and I am sure that you could develop some psychic ability if you wanted to.

Please excuse this diversion, but upon finishing writing the above paragraphs regarding my spiritual experience, I noticed that my word count for this chapter stood at exactly 3333. Thinking this was interesting I looked up the meaning of the number 3. Significantly enough I learned the following. The number 3 generally represents the union of the divine and the human. Now that to me reflects exactly the circumstances I have just described: my human mind, being influenced by the divine. These two elements came together to pass on a valuable message to Amelia. Maybe my precise word count was a little bit of validation to help further the rapid dissipation of my cynicism! Please note – the word count is subject to change, therefore by the time you read this it will likely have altered – so please don't bother counting!

Angels and Guides

Angels and guides are at the heart of most spiritual teachings. For it is through working with our angels and guides that we develop our abilities. I have been lucky enough to meet and commune with a personal guide. His name is Celebrielle and he is a lovely winged horse. He came to me via a guided angel meditation and his presence has been a truly amazing gift. He affirms himself to me regularly and barely a day goes by where I do not stumble across an image of a Pegasus style winged horse. More often than not these sightings coincide with spiritual tasks I undertake, and are now so frequent that my boyfriend and friends have started to point them out to me.

I will go on to mention the lovely Celebrielle several more times in this book, so I will not rant and rave about him here for too long. However, what I will say is that prior to meeting him, I am not sure I really believed that angels existed in anything other than fairytales and bible school stories. Following this I am a believer. The cynical, grown up part of me that scoffed at winged creatures sent for our protection has been silenced. It may sound airy-fairy and quite contrary; but I now believe angels, in all shapes and forms, exist, they are kind, they are cool and they are clever. Angels rock!

Other than my personal angel, Deborah also introduced us to some of the top dogs in the angelic world, the Archangels. Deborah certainly has contacts in ridiculously high places! These lovely beings certainly get around and are worshipped as powerful entities in a number of major world religions including Christianity, Judaism and Catholicism. Kabbalah is also keen to acknowledge these bigwigs in their tree of life. Each of these profoundly talented winged beings has a particular area to take care of, for example, protection, health or animals. Think of these Archangels as directors of specific earthly needs.

One such example of an Angelic Deity is Archangel Michael and he certainly is a handsome one! Think of an Adonis with wings, a sword and body armor. Ooh ladies, calm down now. In my mind he is a bit like Hercules but with more brain. It is not entirely appropriate to have a crush on a servant of God, but as long as you do not compromise his angelic mission I am sure a long distance admiration will not do any harm!

Michael is an angelic knight in shining armor. And we all know how lacking those are these days on earth! When things are going awry and you need protection, strength or a helping hand, Michael is the man. All you need to do to invoke this Archangel is speak to him in your head, tell him what you need and do not forget to say please and thank you. He is perfect for taking on a long road trip, or an exotic holiday. He will protect you while you travel and help you land safely in your destination without a hitch. If you ever feel unsafe or frightened in a bad or scary situation, call on Michael, although if need be call the police first! I certainly have requested his help in the past and things have worked out well. On a recent flight I got a bit fraught over some turbulence. I will not be so dramatic as to say Michael stopped the plane from crashing, but calling on him made me feel better. The plane was soon flying smoothly and my fear quickly disappeared.

If you wish to work with the angels more closely and sending them requests for help is not enough for you, then there are several ways you can bring the guidance of these celestial beauties into your life. Angel cards are one such way. These fabulous decks of cards are decorated with images, words and guidance. You can use these cards to ask complex questions, or to get daily guidance on life situations. I have included a bit more about these in the Divination section later on. As well as cards, you can also listen to Angelic meditations, these can be purchased on CD and they aim to introduce you to the angels whilst brining their qualities and benefits into your life.

Doreen Virtue is an angel expert and she does an array of books, CD's and cards and is one of the leading people in the field of Angels. I did find her stuff a bit girly at first, but upon further usage I think it's rather marvelous.

Alongside your personal angels and all the other hosts of Angelic beings, you also have a personal guide and possibly power animals. A guide is like a teacher/mentor spirit who is always with you, always helping you and is likely to be one of the little voices in your head – usually the sensible one. By going through spiritual development you will eventually meet with your guides, though this is not a process I am able to impart to you here. It is important that you are closely guided and monitored and that your first meeting with your guide is done gently and at the right moment for you. Your guide has been holding your hand since your birth, so they know you intimately. However meeting your guide can be an unsettling and emotional experience.

For some reason I feel utmost reverence for my guide. With my Angel I am very relaxed and feel like he is a good old buddy watching out for me and keeping me safe. With my guide I feel a very different relationship, one that is deeper and heavier. He is here to make sure I make the right choices and to help me achieve my potential. In that respect a guide is like an educator or a mentor. Whilst I can fool around with my angel and ask him to find me parking spaces, I would never deign to ask my guide for such a thing! My guide is my spiritual teacher, he loves me in a different way and I look up to him. It is a weird thing really and it cannot be explained properly or sufficiently.

Whether or not you ever come into contact with your guide, they are still there for you, they always have been and they always will be. Feel free to talk to them in your mind, or even out aloud if you fancy it! Watch out for useful thoughts, dreams or inspirations coming your way, it is likely that your guide has dropped these into your mind for your benefit. Pay attention to your instinct, as that may be your guide's way of trying to direct you. Listen to your own needs and ask your guide for their guidance with anything you require as that is, after all, what they are there for and what they love to do.

Psychic Readings

I have kept this intriguing section relatively short. Later on in the divination section I delve into 'psychic readings a little deeper'. For now I will look at the readings I have had that are closely linked to my development classes! Within a week I have had three superb readings. All for the purpose of this book of course and not because I am a psychic junkie! I feel all 'reading-ed out'. I could not cope with another valuable insight or prediction and I reckon I have enough to keep me going for a good few months!

Most impressive was my psychic reading with Kate, one of Deb's star students. Although I have had plenty of proof of spiritual existence through my own spiritual practices, I did not know what to expect. It was hard for me to imagine a psychic getting anything meaningful about me, my life or my character. Kate hit all of these spots, one after another, after another. At one point she looked me dead in the eye and asked me if I knew someone called Reina. I just burst out laughing as Reina is one of my best friends and her name is so very unusual. Plus, I had never mentioned my friend's names to Deb or anybody in the psychic development group. Kate got information about this book, about my love life, past and present, about my future children and she even described a past life link with a little girl I know who I have always felt an incredible bond with.

This was the icing on the cake for me. As time has passed more of Kate's predictions and comments have come to fruition. This includes a rather murky prediction about a legal situation, and I believe I have realized who one of the spirits was who came to me with positive, life-affirming messages is.

Kate described a Native American Indian looking woman named Annie. Having given this plenty of thought I remembered that my Mum had recently shown me a family tree harping back many generations. Within this I learned that my great grandmother, many times removed was a Cherokee Indian lady. Her name was Fanny. Now Fanny was a fairly typical name way back when, and certainly does not have the same American and British connotations it does now. Next time I see Kate I shall have to ask if she was actually hearing 'Fanny' but changed the name. Perhaps she had allowed her Great British sentiment to over rule her natural instinct, in effect censoring the name to the tamer version of, Annie!

I am still attending Inspiration School and can only hope that I am well on my way to developing a skill such as Kate's, or indeed

Deborah's. If you have any doubts please bear this in mind, prior to her psychic development Kate was a hard-nosed scientist. Ruled by her scientific intelligence she believed what could be proven and by no means dabbled in Spiritualism, and then, well then she met Deb! There is hope for us all!

Spiritualism Conclusion

My development through the attendance of spiritual development classes has been awesome. Not only have I learned a great deal theoretically, I have put it into practice and watched in awe as my own abilities have taken shape. On beginning my classes I was not sure I believed that I could be psychic or that my spirituality would ever make itself known to me so clearly. However, almost immediately both of these things took shape and my eyes were opened to a world I had hoped was there but that I did not dare explore alone. As I write I continue to visit my class every Tuesday and I will continue to do so for the foreseeable future, indeed I have been honored to be invited to be Deb's next trainee protégé! This was a perfect conclusion to the spiritual path that began with me meeting Deb's current protégé Lynda a whole year ago when I was a very different person.

I hope I have displayed a good taster of the amazing and thrilling events that could be yours should you choose to experiment with such a development class. These classes have blown me away! As yet I have no intention of carving a career as a famous psychic or setting a stall up at the local market offering fortune telling. However, from what I have seen, psychic abilities and intuition are a natural gift that most of us simply do not access in our daily life. Now that I do access mine, I am beginning to see where my future is headed. Having spent my whole life wondering about my direction, I am now certain.

Many people think of psychic skills as nonsense or imagination, when in fact I am now sure that they are quite natural. It is my thought that put to the test on a daily basis spiritual skills are frequently helpful and generally an accessory to a well lived life.

Furthermore, by thinking in a spiritual manner we are kinder to those around us, we respect ourselves more, and through being grateful and utilizing positive thinking, we can usher in a whole new successful life for ourselves. Spiritual development classes with a good teacher are much like a crash course in, "Learning how to live a Fabulous and Abundant Life 101". It can be put to practice on a daily basis between applying makeup, dropping the kids off or preparing a four course masterpiece dinner for your in-laws. If the thought still lingers in your mind that Spiritualism is full of kooks and crazies, then think again, it is my belief that you would be crazier not to...

Spiritualism as a formal set up is perhaps not my idea of fun. The churches I have visited have been too restrictive, old fashioned or just plain creaky. Although as a basis for a set of personal beliefs, I think Spiritualism is remarkable. I am not necessarily an occult lover, nor am I hugely motivated by a need to speak to the deceased. However, as far as attuning my intuition and psychic abilities for my own benefit, and for that of friends and family, well, I think that is a great idea. I have no problems whatsoever having a chat with the Archangel Michael and asking him to protect me from a negative vibe or scary backstreet. But having a word with Aunt Doris or Great Uncle Arthur is not necessarily right for me (not yet anyway, I may still be convinced). Thus far the spirits have treated me well and as long as they steer clear of midnight visits in strange hotel rooms, we will get along just fine.

Spiritualism, or at least my version of it, is great because I see it as an amalgamation of other stuff. There is a bit in there about Angels, so it is clearly influenced by traditional Jewish/Christian/Catholic belief.

Meditation is nicked from Eastern Mysticism, whilst prayer is universal. The one defining concept of Spiritualism is that of communing with the dead. Although this might be seen as coming directly from a background of occult practices, Ouija boards, Victorian era séances or even voodoo, others might think it derives from the Norse and Celtic shamanic tradition of contacting our dead and ancient ancestors. I would certainly reject any belief that it comes from anywhere dark or demonic. Spirituality is all fluffy white clouds, positive energy and harp playing celestial hosts. It is a 'living room' based religion that can be shaped nicely to fit into your needs, and there are a thousand mind, body, spirit websites and books to help you to do just that.

As for paranormal activity, I guess if you ask for the help of the unknown, sometimes you will receive it. Just this week I have been 'haunted' – although do not let this little ghost story put you off.

At the time of this bizarre event I had been getting into my spiritual development and actively going about being more and more spiritual. Using prayer, protection methods and a spot of 'cosmic ordering' I had asked that I was guided in the right direction, and that my boyfriend was too. James had had some health problems that were aggravated by drinking alcohol. Yet like any talented guitarist worth his salt he had little intention of cutting back (God Bless Rock 'n' Roll). I introduced this into a cosmic ordering style request, and asked that he might be helped to amend his ways until he was fully healthy again.

Following my request came a bank holiday weekend. At the end of a long and alcohol soaked weekend I toddled off to bed leaving James alone downstairs. He was watching the television with a can of beer that he had not yet opened. He felt himself drifting off to sleep and struggled with his mind to stay awake. At that point he became acutely aware of freezing cold liquid being poured down his back. He jumped up to find himself totally drenched in beer. Confused and slightly groggy he reached to make sense of events, immediately looking for the can of beer he had previously brought from the kitchen. That can of beer was exactly where he left it, on the floor, unopened. He looked all over the sofa, behind cushions and all around the living room for the offending beer can/bottle/glass. None was to be found. Needless to say he came to bed totally freaked out and shared the story with me, starting with "Babe something really weird just happened..." And as he promptly fell asleep snoring, I was left wide awake, super alert and praying to the good Archangel Michael for his love and protection.

The next day I tentatively made my way downstairs to investigate the scene for myself. I found a beer soaked T-shirt and a telltale trail of beer splattered on the floor leading to the sofa. The pattern of beer on the T-shirt led me to believe that liquid had started at the neck and traveled in a downward direction – as though it were being poured. His story checked out. Strangely enough I could not find a single drop of it or wet patch on the sofa, nor could I locate any can or bottle that might have been used to commit the beer pouring act.

I was exhausted, a little perturbed, but pretty sure that somebody had just got a bit of a telling off. Later in the day I spoke with Deborah for her opinion, and between us we came to the conclusion that James had been visited by an aggrieved relative in spirit, or guardian angel that was concerned for his well being. To me there is simply no other viable explanation, and as for James he cannot explain it, so he will not talk about it (typical man!)

Happily enough, I am not scared. As I write this, I am sat in that exact room right now, I can see the sofa and I feel fine. I am sure there is no crazed poltergeist and I am happy in the thought that my recent spiritual development may have helped bring about this somewhat bizarre turn of events. Furthermore, I do believe that James's drenching does appear to have reversed his fortunes; a baptism of beer has helped cleanse his soul! This was sufficient to help him cut down and get back on the healthy track! Now I do hope this does not occur again for a long while, it was an intense and scary experience. But in retrospect it is kind of funny, very apt and has had a very positive impact on us both.

My forays into spiritual development have been fun, exciting and eye opening. In light of the above I guess spirituality may not be for the timid, though I am certain that nobody would pour beer, or any other alcoholic substance down your neck unless they thought that you could cope with it! I believe that the Spirits go easy on newbie's, and they know when is the right time to make themselves known.

My experiences range from very subtle to undeniable. I am sure that your experiences would be relevant to how ready and prepared you are. The learning captured by spiritual development has been of great use in my every day life, whether I am judging a person's mood by the color of their peep toe kitten heels, or protecting my sensitive side from negative outpourings at work. It is all good and extremely helpful as tactics to help make life more pleasant.

Spiritualism has allowed me to accessorize my spirituality in a hands-on manner whereby I can almost chart my progression. It can also be very girly and creative, it's a one size fits all kind of faith and it is good fun too. Practicing the various development techniques is like playtime. If you respond well to learning through play, or if you did when you were four, then this is a great way to go about it. It takes the edge out of dogmatic religion and makes you responsible for your own development. By embracing Spiritualism, spirituality can become relevant to you as a growing person, to your day-to-day life and helps you to forge clear, usable links between normality and your inner soul. Join a spiritual development class of your own, I promise you, you will not regret it!

The High Heeled Witch

When Daddy announces that he is a witch, what is a girl to do? Is this a question for Jerry Springer perhaps? Having lived through that very experience and without wanting to sound like a halfwit in a salacious women's 'real life' magazine, I can proudly say that my Dad was a witch, and prior to that he was a vicar. Let me assure you it is not half as exciting as it sounds. My initial thoughts upon learning of my father's newfound beliefs were something on the hysterical lines of 'Does that mean you worship Satan?' This was followed by a fleeting thought about my potential imminent demise as a human sacrifice to that demonic overlord. Once I had been well assured that the devil had nothing to do with it, and that no young virgins (or anyone else) would be harmed, I settled into a state of sheer bemusement. After all, aren't witches generally ladies; crusty, cackling, green tinged old ladies? As a huge fan of the Wizard of Oz, to say I was disconcerted is an understatement.

Little did I know it, but Dad's shock confession led to my own (closely guided) experimentation with witchcraft, or Wicca, which is the official religious title.

I grew a healthy respect for the occult and unlike many of my peers I did not experiment drunkenly with the Ouija board, nor did I dabble in black magic hoping that the prettiest girl in school developed acne. Mine was a studious venture, gently taking in an understanding of Wicca, healing, spiritual energies, tarot and meditation. Nor was it anything I advertised, it had originally been beyond my comprehension, so how could I expect my schoolmates to understand?

In time a few friends were informed and were curious, often surprisingly so. At this stage I began to realize that this part of my life was not only of interest, but was also of some comfort to others.

My first proper boyfriend was particularly intrigued. I took him to meet my Dad and stepmum one weekend, in a cleverly designed ploy to actually stay overnight together in the same bed! However, the boyfriend was so smitten by the whole concept he proceeded to have deep and intellectuals with my Dad all evening. I looked on rather sadly, getting increasingly drunk on some rubbishy alcopop. In between trips to the toilet to vomit and attempting to make the room stop spinning, I gave up the ghost and probably turned all teenage and grumpy. Having failed to get my love machine to myself I promptly passed out for the night, how embarrassing. Without too much detail I never did get an overnight stay and we split up not long after. I was sure he only used me for my interesting esoteric contacts!

Like many religions, witchcraft is inherently about doing good and living for the betterment of humanity. Historically, Wiccan practices are steeped in folklore and stereotypes, although without doubt, Wiccan practices are not so different from well-established beliefs. Wiccans wear robes to their ceremonies, as do monks and bishops. Wiccans carry wands and use cauldrons; while our churches house pulpits, altars, and a symbol of the cross that can be used to rebuke evil spirits and vampires! Some Wiccans dance naked in the woods as a celebration of nature, but every Sunday respectable folk queue up to munch on a representation of the blood and body of Christ. When a witch casts a spell, a request is sent out to the universe; is this not just another version of a prayer or its modern day equivalent – cosmic ordering? And where the established church has its strict commandments of behavior to keep its followers in line, the Wiccan Rede has just one, "if it harms none, do what you will". Once you cut through the centuries of archaic nonsense, then broomsticks and bibles are not so hugely different.

Witchcraft and paganism were Britain's first known belief system, stemming from times before Christianity, before the businesslike structure of churches, cathedrals and temples that we are now familiar with. With the beginnings of Christianity, the term Pagan became a dirty word, summoning an image of the muddy, uneducated heathen, too ignorant to put their faith in the newly imported Christianity. Pagans were forced underground to worship in secrecy. Anyone found worshipping earth-based religions such as Celts, Druids, Witches and Wizards were seriously frowned upon or even worse they were hounded, tortured and burnt at the stake!

My reaction to Dad's decision to turn witch is evidence that these attitudes persist, and that ideas implemented centuries ago still haunt our thinking. Sadly the personification of a witch in many peoples' minds is still that of an old hag turning good men into toads and setting a vile curse to her neighbor's petunias!

Witchcraft's essence is as pure as what lies at the heart of any religious teachings. Wicca is basically the worship of nature and of Mother Earth. In that respect it is not dissimilar from shamanic beliefs, and Wicca is perhaps the Shamanism of the British Isles.

Wiccans enact reverence for the miracle of the universe, and in their rituals they often call on one of the many goddesses or gods. By worshipping a deity (god or goddess) a witch is truly worshipping what that deity represents. For example; Diana is goddess of hunting and the moon, Hecate is goddess of the underworld and of witches, Pan is god of the wild wood, whilst Aphrodite, Venus, Eros and Cupid are, of course, the deities of love.

A word of warning here; naming pets or children after all-powerful beings is not a good idea. We had a really cute grey and black tabby kitten that the folks decided to call 'Kali-Ma'. It is a pretty name and sat very well on the sweet little trinket of love they had opened their home to. If you do not know already Kali-Ma is a 'goddess of darkness' who is reputed to have worn a necklace made from human skulls. She was not very nice. As we invoked this name everyday, our little Kali cat soon turned into Cat of Darkness, scratching and maiming the hand that fed her, acting like a lunatic and wreaking evil vengeance on her pussy cat companions. If you are not convinced then hear this, we also had a cat called Kennedy, named after JFK. Kennedy cat died at a young age in the prime of his life, possibly assassinated by a Russian crow who pushed him from the roof of the house to his death. If that is not proof about the dangers of pet naming then I do not know what is. Moving on...

Hundreds of years of bad press are a powerful indictment. In spite of this I have had the pleasurable company of many a witch. Some of them are stereotypical looking, punk/gothic types, however that is not so unusual these days with metrosexuals like David Beckham sporting a mohican, whilst his wife does a wonderful Morticia impression.

I have passed many a fine hour in the company of a variety of male and female witches. Dad used to let me join them in meditation or healing practice, they always made me welcome and treated me like a little adult. I never once got the impression they were grooming me for any kind of ritualistic sacrificing. Nor did they ever pluck my virginal hair for use in their spells. They were cool, sometimes I had a glass of wine and we would all sit round and talk about pagan beliefs or healing or the television. I have been to pagan picnics with whole crowds of witches, warlocks, Shamans, magicians and their children! Just like any other picnic, we all ate food, games were played, and I remember that Rounders seemed to be a favorite. Once we went to Sherwood Forest, I got food poisoning and vomited all the way home, but the witches really looked after me.

Most recently I went to 'Witchfest' 2007, a mini festival for the witchy community. They were having a right good time; there were many stalls and a big barbeque. Some of them were getting started on the drinking early and enjoying the amazing sunshine. A few people were wearing all black, and on the hottest day of the year I do not know how they managed it. That said, Muslim women manage to wear black burkhas with the Middle Eastern sun blazing down on them day in, day out.

Witchfest was actually a great day out, kids were running around happily, the stalls were interesting and everybody was just as friendly as they could be. One thing is for certain; none of the witches I have met bears even a passing resemblance to the Wizard of Oz's wicked witch of west. Witches are ordinary people brought up in our society, doing our jobs, teaching our children, and probably sitting next to us on the train. They enjoy all of our 21st Century luxuries and have even harnessed the power of the web to help promote their causes, simply type 'Wicca' into Google and you will find hundreds of sites offering helpful support and information.

In these modern days the mysteries of witchcraft are becoming normalized. With the rise of alternative therapies, self-improvement and environmentalism, we can see the beliefs that sit at the heart of witchcraft are very much in vogue. The move toward cleansing our planet is a reflection of what witches have always done. For these reasons the practice of witchcraft is becoming a viable, if not sensible option for many people. With the recent move toward ecological lifestyles becoming excessively chic, I predict that Wicca could be the next big thing!

Wiccan Worship and Rituals

Wicca can be practiced alone or in a group known as a 'coven'. If you do go down the coven route be sure to carefully vet your membership. Sadly a lot of people see witchcraft as something very different to what it is, influenced by Hollywood films like 'The Craft' (cracking film) rather than a love of nature and the Goddess, you may find some peculiar types come your way. I know that my Dad had this problem with his coven, it occasionally attracted either needy, or slightly strange people who wanted more than the group could offer them – and that is putting it diplomatically! I am not personally a witch but if I were I would choose to practice alone, or with closely trusted friends. It may be that a group worships locally to you, and reputable organizations exist to help any aspiring Witch find her way.

Wiccans truly embrace creativity and diversity and there is no strict format on how worship should be performed. They customarily celebrate the eight seasons of the ancient Celtic year; these form the major crux around which worship is based. With eight excuses for parties a year, I cannot think of a better religion for having a regular shindig! Rituals and spells can be performed alone, although when it comes to those eight parties a year I guess you may prefer to hook up with some likeminded individuals for dancing, drinking and good times! Some of the festivities coincide with mainstream religions; Midwinter Solstice overlaps Christmas, whereas Samhain or Halloween is a bigger holiday to witches than it is for the pumpkin smashing, costume loving Americans!

All of the eight seasons are celebrated equally by Wiccans, as each season is just as important as the next. Each of the eight dates represents part of the ongoing cycle of renewal, the rhythm of nature and the four seasons of spring, summer, autumn and winter. Unlike the traditional calendar you have on your desk at work featuring kittens or 'hottie of the month', there is no defined beginning or end. No singular season or celebration is seen as the definitive start to the Wiccan year. There is no figurehead akin to Jesus, Mohammed or Buddha whose birthday must be celebrated; every day is a miracle, every moon position or budding leaf is worthy of worship. The hero and heroines in the tale of Wicca are the elements themselves, the cycle of birth and death, caterpillars, baby chicks, sunny days and the frost on your car windscreen that makes you late for work.

A word to the wise, before you set the date for partying and send the invites out, be aware that some of the following dates are approximate. They change year to year and so before holding an Equinox party a day too late consult a Wiccan calendar or somebody in the know!

Halloween / Samhain – Oct 31st

Halloween (Samhain) is of course a familiar date to anybody living in the western world and you would assume it is the biggest date of the Wiccan calendar. This is not the case.

It is believed that on Samhain the veil between the living and the dead is at its thinnest; therefore an offering is left for the delectation of passing souls. Funnily enough, Samhain was never traditionally about children parading the streets dressed as ghouls and ghosties, or knocking on the door demanding treats! Nor in traditional Wicca was there ever a place for flour and egging the homes of those who were too poor, unorganized or too miserly to provide a treat for unruly youngsters!

However, given the original meaning of Samhain, I can understand where this modern phenomenon stemmed from. Witches often leave 'treats' out for the wandering deceased and this is obviously reflected by the modern day ritual of kids, high on sugar, dressed as vampires, knocking on doors and giving cheek! It is a direct correlation to those Wiccan traditions of leaving food out for the souls of loved ones departed, although my guess is that those reasons are long forgotten to the youth of today and their parents!

For the modern day witch Samhain is a date of reflection to remember those loved and lost. It may be a date when they feel particularly close to deceased friends and family. Rituals are performed in honor of loved ones and ancestors, food particular to those people may be left out. If Granny loved Murray mints, a bowl of those sweets may be provided, alongside some more generic candy for other passing spirits. Any magic entered into on Samhain would be focused on divination and fortune telling. 'Scrying' is a form of 'do it yourself' fortune telling that involves staring into a blackened mirror or crystal ball. Scrying is frequently undertaken by Wiccans at Halloween. The purpose of this is for believers to stare into the glass until they see images or snapshots of the future. My Dad informs me he was pretty useless at this and I am reluctant to try it, I think the Candyman films have scared me off the whole mirror, spirit, occult thing!

It seems that much of the traditional 'witchy' stereotypes have been built up in society solely based on the practices of Wicca on Halloween. Samhain will see witches placing apples and twigs on altars or alongside their cauldrons. Bobbing for apples comes to mind, and again we see the modern day practices of Halloween reflected in the serious worship practices of Samhain!

It is worthy to note that as I was writing this section on Samhain, two young boys knocked on my door asking for money for an alleged charity. Bizarrely this occurred concurrently with me writing about the youngsters turning up and asking for treats at Halloween. Despite the fact that these two were clearly trying their luck, and the 'charity' was no doubt funding their next trip to the corner shop, I must say they were ever so polite. One of them even said that my house smelt nice. When I declined to give them money they thanked me and moved on. In spite of being little scam artists, they were lovely. More importantly what an excellent coincidence, perhaps a jab in ribs to me for calling kids cheeky!

Yule / The Winter Solstice – December 21st and 22nd

Yule pretty much coincides with Christmas, and Wiccans may send 'Christmas cards' saying Happy Yule or Winters Greetings to one another in keeping with the spirit of the season. In the Wiccan calendar Yule represented the dead of winter, a time of desolation, barren fields and the likelihood of disease, suffering, cold, poverty, and death. Prior to central heating and when the majority of us worked on the land for a meager living, Britain was understandably not such a great place to live. Yule, in pagan traditions was a call to the deities to help see the people safely through this cold and frightening time of year. It was a transitory celebration, to recognize that the nights would start to get longer and that spring was on its way. The fertile and bright colors of evergreen, red and gold were often used in celebrations, and have clearly followed through into Christian times as festive colors associated with Christmas.

I would think that witches of ancient times would heartily approve of our current Christmas festivities. The idea of eating till your belly burst would have been a mere fantasy back in the day. I imagine their utter approval at indulging to your heart's delight in an attempt to stave away the chills of a winter's night! Although Christmas has become a secular festival of gorging, giving and receiving, the manner in which we all celebrate Christmas is typically pagan. So for any potential witch a transition to Wicca need not see you neglecting the yuletide festivities, indeed you would have more reason than most to tuck away heartily and drink till you fall over! The goddess implores you, go to the office Christmas party, gather family and friends round, eat drink and be merry!

Imbolc / Nature's New Year – February 1st and 2nd

Imbolc is a representation of new beginnings; spring is starting to show itself and everyone is feeling optimistic. Snowdrops and candles are placed on altars to represent all things new, pure and hopeful.

Magic undertaken at Imbolc is to purify and renew with the purpose of ushering in a prosperous harvest that year. For a half-hearted witch it is a fabulous time of year for a spring clean, starting a new fitness program, clearing clutter and setting the year's goals. If you failed to keep your new year's resolutions from a month earlier, then Imbolc is your second chance – you know the gym is still there and waiting for you and spring is just around the corner!

Imbolc is literally seen as the new year making itself known in nature, although the connotations are different from those celebrated at New Year's Eve in the every day calendar. Some things remain the same between the two. Witches, just like New

Year revelers, are all putting their faith in a turn of good fortune and fresh starts. Wiccans are overjoyed at the thought of new life bursting out of the barren ground and the promise of fertility, babies and the return of life to the world around us following its wintry hibernation.

Imbolc is the calm before the storm. It is a time for making plans and getting prepared to set them in motion. Yawn, stretch, and open your eyes. The world is waking up after winter so buy some new shoes, get a spring in your step and anticipate the barbeques, sunny days and laughter that lies ahead.

Spring Equinox – March 20th / 21st

A time for making sweet love perhaps? Why the heavens not! Spring is when all the animals are at it, romping around the fields like little loved up critters and eventually popping out the next generation. Quite frankly the 'rising sap' in spring does make us all feel a tad bit frisky. As we emerge from the oversize jumpers and indoors incarceration that winter enforces upon us, it seems entirely natural that we get a slight bit excitable! Now that may come in the form of turning into a sensual seductress overnight, or you may just indulge in the urge to go out, be seen, have fun, get some new make-up and let your hair down.

Spring Equinox is all about living and loving life. It is about reproduction and recreation and breathing a massive sigh of relief that finally the sun is in the sky. Because Wicca follows the natural ebb and flow of the seasons it coincides very nicely with the feeling of the general population at various times of years, and spring of course is a welcome relief to us all. So whilst Christians are celebrating little eggs, chickens and lambs, so are Wiccans. It makes me wonder how much Christianity borrowed from Wicca when it arrived in Britain. That said we are all loved up, happy and basking in a warmer glow from the heavens above! Get your T-shirts out and enjoy it!

Unsurprisingly the color most used by Wiccans at the Spring

Equinox is green – grass green. Any magic they perform involves new beginnings. Spells might be cast that represent new starts, so this is yet another chance to attempt to live by your new year's resolutions. Third time lucky!

For those not in the know, an equinox is a time of year when the sun spends an equal amount of time both above and below the horizon, and is seen to do so from every place in the world. After the long hours of darkness every day during winter, and the long hours of daylight all summer, at the spring or Autumn Equinox it will be light outside for nearly the exact amount of time that it is dark, wherever you are on the planet.

Beltane / May Day 30th April / 1st May

So you thought Spring Equinox was a little bit saucy, well stop frolicking like frisky lambs and check this out. Beltane is about burning passions, love, lust and sheer sexual energy. Wiccans love it, but don't we all! Reproduction and all that leads to reproduction is unashamedly worshipped and celebrated. Beltane is all about the Goddess, and it is a big party time. Get your glad-rags on, flirt, dance and celebrate your Goddess like wonderfulness.

Beltane lands on May Day and can be associated with all things positive in nature and a celebration of the glorious weather. It marks the beginning of six months of summer and lighter evenings, and that is one thing I am always grateful for.

Summer Solstice / Litha – June 21st

Summer Solstice coincides with Midsummer, the time of year when the Sun is beating down longest and hottest onto the earth. If Beltane is for the Goddess then Litha is the big solar celebration for the God. Male energy is worshipped, completing the adoration of the two genders and setting an equal footing for the year ahead. The Sun King sits at the core of the Summer Solstice celebrations and you can party all night as he sends his strongest rays down to earth. This is the event that tends to draw the hippies to

Stonehenge. Summer Solstice is the last big blow out before it gets darker and the world turns her mind toward winter and a very sensible hibernation.

At the Summer Solstice Wiccans practice magic to create material good fortune, so get your cosmic orders ready. Spells might be to request success at a job interview, a pay rise to provide for your newborn offspring, or simply that the year ahead brings material warmth and security. Think of Litha as a Fraternity party or Stag Do (only without the strippers, lap dancing clubs and/or being tied to a lamppost naked).

Lammas August 1st and 2nd

This is the bringing in of the harvest; make hay while the sun shines. Despite the obvious celebration, at Lammas life starts to get a bit serious as people think ahead. With the cold and frost looming this was a time when people would accumulate stocks for the winter and have to accept that life was about to change. It is a time to consider the passing of great joy. Lammas itself means to 'bake bread'. Of course, these days those of us not on the Atkins Diet need only pop to the shop for a loaf, but the theory still applies. At the harvest feast we break bread with friends, although sharing a pizza may be more satisfying! Though 21st Century folk might not be saying goodbye to bread, we are entering a darker period of year, and we all feel a small loss at the end of summer and friends start to suffer the dreaded SAD (seasonal affective disorder).

At Lammas it is time to take stock of your life and put your sensible head back on. Probably as an ancient means of survival Wiccan thoughts turn to partnerships. If you have been playing the field all summer, then now might be a good time to find a soul mate to snuggle up with till spring. As the sun is becoming more reclusive, our thoughts should turn to spiritual acts and worship.

Now that the fire laden passionate physical months are done and dusted, you may want to pay more attention to your spiritual growth and needs. This book would make perfect reading at Lammas, or if you happen to be reading this in spring then when Lammas comes around why don't you check out my reference list at the back and expand your mind baby!

Autumn Equinox – 22nd September

At the Autumn Equinox thoughts continue to turn inward to self-improvement and spirituality. It is time to harvest the fruits of your efforts. Spiritual projects or paths begun at Lammas should really show progression at this time of year. I must admit that my spiritual path probably really kicked off around Lammas and it was around the Autumn Equinox that the idea for this book popped into my sleepy head one morning. This is some sort of (very casual) evidence that the body, mind and spiritual self closely follow the patterns of the year and the natural evolution of the seasons.

As the nights start to draw in, it is time to check the boiler is well serviced, and buy a tog duvet to snuggle up in over the winter months.

It is believed that at Autumn Equinox the Goddess takes refuge in the underworld – I guess it must be warmer down there! Wiccans might float candles down the river as a symbolic goodbye to the Goddess and the Sun. Now is a time to practice magic and develop your witchcraft spells.

The Moon

The moon and its various phases is of great importance to the Wiccan tradition. Just as the cycle of the year is vitally important so is the cycle of the lunar month. It is often used to plan spells, magic and those infamous Full Moon partying sessions.

There is actually a great deal of scientific evidence to suggest that the moon plays a big part in human moods, emotions and even mental well-being. Having worked in a customer service office dealing with complaints, it was common that the phone lines tended to go a little crazy on the day of a Full Moon. Following the night of a Full Moon, it was not unusual to come into the office to have some irate person ranting and raving into the answer phone until they get timed out.

I can attest to the fact that a Full Moon affects even the sanest of us. I have been keeping track of the last few Full Moons and I can fairly say that I too go a little off the wall around that time of the month, as do my friends (no offence intended). The symptoms of a Full Moon are very similar to the symptoms of Pre Menstrual Stress symptoms. A Full Moon seems to accompany mood swings, feelings of unrest and inexplicable sadness. Some people seem more volatile and emotions are highly strung. And yet, the Full Moon is supposed to be one of the best times to have a wild party. I suppose the vibrancy of a party might shake you out of your negative mindset and help you indulge in letting your hair down and forgetting your woes. The best parties are the ones that help us forget and remind us that the niggly little things in life are really unimportant when you are surrounded by friends, wine, dancing and music. My advice at the Full Moon is to let it rip. Dig out your party heels and dance like a werewolf woman!

Under the advice of Wicca, you may wish to simply stand beneath a Full Moon and absorb her power. Indeed my mother reliably informs me she was once given this exact advice by a specialist consultant at her local hospital. He advised spending ten minutes outside in the rays of the Full Moon to help sort out her crazy hormonal situation! Perhaps my problem is that I have not been doing this, so instead I get grumpy and fickle. Even better is the idea of mixing both the doctor's and Wicca's idea together and have an outdoor Full Moon party. The best of both worlds! Full Moon parties are quite common for revelers as well as witches. Places such as Thailand are world renowned for their Full Moon parties on the beach. Who needs pyrotechnics and flashing lights when you have the glowing luminescence of a Full Moon beating down on the sea and sand. Heaven!

The time of the New Moon is a much more positive phase. It is a great time for self-improvement and starting new projects. I do find that I am far more productive around this time and much more likely to sit down and get stuff done. As I write, it happens to be a New Moon, which is peculiar seeing as it is the middle of the day, however as I went out into the garden to water the plants, there it was a misty wisp in the bright blue sky.

For a Wiccan a New Moon is the perfect time to perform rituals or spells that plant the seeds of new beginnings. The idea being that as the lunar cycle progresses from New Moon to Full Moon you will see the benefits of any magic you have performed. The voyage of the moon from new to full is officially termed 'waxing'. So if you hear or read about the 'waxing' moon this is not a reference to a time of month that the moon dictates you should visit the beauty salon. Waxing simply refers to the moon getting fatter.

The moon is a bit of a yo-yo dieter and once it has expanded to its full size, it will then dramatically reduce its body mass by half in a very quick 14-day period. If only we could all tap into that power! The period of the moon getting smaller is officially called 'waning'. If you or I were to drop half our body size in two weeks, we would be called anorexic, but the moon is simply waning.

This is a great time to do rituals or magic that aims to purge something from your life. So whether you wish to actually lose weight, get rid of a harmful relationship or leave your job, then the time is now. The waning moon is about getting rid, whilst the waxing is about attraction.

So do your cosmic ordering in the waxing moon and clear space for your new life in the waning. It may be a bit tricky to figure out whether the New Moon you see in the sky is waxing or waning, but you might be surprised how easy it is to find out. My personal diary actually has little symbols and a key for the year. It is really just a normal diary with no Wiccan connections whatsoever; however, the state of the moon is clearly of more importance to many more people than I gave it credit for!

When the moon has waned it will then vanish. Oh how I wish I could wane away my stubborn belly fat! This is the period when there is no moon in the sky and it lasts for three days. This is a time for little action, but it may be a good time to think deeply and consider your future plans. I believe that it is definitely worth keeping a check on the moon, and perhaps experimenting with tracking your daily deeds by it. If nothing else you will be very organized, and at most you could really click into your optimum performance levels. It is worth a go! Perhaps next time the moon is nowhere to be seen you can sit down and make some plans for your lunar month, including that fabulous Full Moon party half way through!

Temples and Rituals

Most Wiccans create their own temples for their worship. At my Dad's house my old bedroom was converted into the temple, much to my dismay. However, by that point in time I was far more concerned with flirting and clubbing to really notice. My room was probably the best room for it. I had experienced some very bizarre phenomena in there myself and I am sure it certainly had potential to be a great housing place for the supernatural energies of any Gods and Goddesses called upon to join my Dad and his coven in worship.

The Temple was basically a table, covered by a cloth and then covered again with all kinds of symbolic and meaningful items. There was loads of stuff on there, and in fact a lot of it bore a cow motif, due to the Coven's mascot animal being a cow. Other things included incense, knives, broomsticks, and statues of deities, all kinds of random stuff. It was a bit of a crazy, mystical mess actually, although, I guess the neatness or rambling madness of your temple depends entirely upon an individual Witches tastes. An altar need not be any specific size, and if you wish to use a shoebox, then that is your prerogative. As long as your altar houses things that are meaningful to you and your practice then anything goes.

Many Wiccans choose one or two gods or goddesses to be their main focal point of worship. You may wish to place a statue, painting or other representation of them on the altar. If you feel like putting a picture of Buddha or Jesus up, then go for it. As long as your intention is right then your altar is yours to play with, fill it with whatever inspires you, makes you happy or that appeals to your eye.

You might be quite concerned about the use of knives in my Dad's temple. Knives are a fairly common addition to any temple, and as the police never came a knocking. I am reliably informed that they were there just for effect and to act as pointing devices during ritual. Indeed Knives and Swords are an intrinsic part of most rituals and are used to 'draw the circle'. I will explain in more detail shortly...

Once you have a temple you can prepare for your rituals. The word 'ritual' sounds a little archaic and scary, but really it is nothing more than worship, praise and/ or connecting and thanking your favorite deities. You might use ritual simply to express your allegiance to Wicca and to help reinforce your own beliefs. At other times you will be celebrating the various festivities. Ritual can also be used for casting spells, healing and making requests.

You can be creative and do whatever takes your fancy, whether that means lighting a candle and meditating, or inviting your coven round and having a full on and formal invoking of the Goddess.

If you are going to 'invoke' anything formally then there are some things you may wish to consider taking into consideration. Firstly, what are you going to wear? I know this is a very important question for most females who have ever existed. Some Wiccans actually have found a very easy answer to that lifelong question and they wear nothing! Yep, that is correct, they perform their rituals in the nude, the buff, naked, as they were born, without clothes on. Completely and utterly starkers! This is officially known as being 'sky clad', which is a very delightful way to put it. If you decide you do not wish to be separated from your Levis then you might prefer to do your rituals robed. If you are a serious Wiccan you might even think about having some special robes made up. Otherwise robed, could simply refer to being 'clothed'. Perhaps if there is a group of you, you could make the effort to color co-ordinate, which would be fun.

Rituals and Circles involve huge amounts of energy and items such as watches should be removed so as the energy surge does not damage them. We were never allowed to take electric goods such as watches or clocks into the temple, even when no ritual was being performed. I never tested the theory myself, but apparently it was common for them to break or stop.

Dancing, chanting and scripted invocations are all involved. An invocation means asking the gods and goddesses to join you in the circle, the effect of which, according to my Dad can be tremendous.

Following once such invocation, Dad did not clear the space properly afterwards. He was out and my poor stepmother was alone in the house. She was woken by what she thought were burglars having a party in the Temple room. She lay there terrified until my Dad returned. On his return she sent him into the Temple to check out what was going on. He bravely took up the gauntlet, only to discover the Temple was completely empty. Realizing that it must have been the invoked spirits wreaking havoc, or at least enjoying their newfound Temple, he told the invisible revelers in the empty room to 'please keep it down'. This apparently worked wonders and if they did continue partying they did so with a little more reserve.

I think it is very important to mention that according to my Dad's own book, after a ritual is complete it is necessary to indulge in Wine and Cake. Hearing this I felt like turning my

Yucca plant upside down, calling it a broomstick and inviting mates over for a glass of red and a slice of gateaux, but I am on a diet, so I didn't. If nothing else, a ritual sounds like a great reason for a get together with like-minded friends. It can help channel your focus on matters of importance, whilst invoking powerful magic and wondrous entities for the highest purposes of the participants. I imagine that as a path toward heightened spirituality, psychic ability and communing with nature and the elements, performing rituals will put you on a fast track.

Spells and Healing

In this modern day Wiccans still cast spells, although unlike in the fairytales, these are strictly for the benefit of others, and never to the detriment of any being. Contrary to popular belief, it is unlikely that any witch can conjure a pumpkin into a horse and cart, or magic the washing up clean. My personal favorite was when Dad cast a spell for peace in the Middle East, a grand task indeed. A handmade boat represented the spell. When I was told what the boat represented it promptly fell to bits in front of our eyes. I took this as the universe's way of saying this spell was perhaps a little too ambitious!

When casting spells the Wiccan Rede's rule of harming none comes into force strongly. Witches believe that any act they commit will revisit them threefold; therefore any spell undertaken with negative intentions will comeback to them in the future. Black magic is strictly forbidden.

Spells, like much of Wicca, are open to creative interpretation. Just be careful what you wish for, because some things are not meant to be ours. For example, casting a spell to make another person's partner fall in love with you is foul play. No matter how attracted you are, or how attracted that person is to you, it is very bad and naughty of you to try to steal them away via magic. Having said that, it is unlikely that such a spell would work anyway, not unless you were indulging in some form of black magic or voodoo.

What would be far more appropriate than dastardly intent would be to request via a spell that the universe sent to you a soul mate. You could search the library or Amazon for spell books, or you could make it up as you go along.

I believe that with magic, as long as your intention is there and you perform it with full concentration then the Goddesses will hear, wave their magic wands and hopefully somebody perfect will head your way. Feel free to light as many candles as you like, burn incense and wrap up rose petals on a Full Moon, whatever you feel suits you best is worth doing. As long as you cast the spell with your heart and mind in the right place, and with good, clear intention, then it may very well work!

For your benefit, I have stolen a couple of spells from my Dad's book of witchcraft. He and my stepmother Aileen were the first authors in my family, and I am keen to plagiarize their ideas. I am certain that they will be more than happy to allow me to do this. For more information on witchcraft you can also see their very easy picture filled guide, 'The Illustrated Guide to Witchcraft', but for now here is a useful little number that I have lifted.

Love Magic

Oooh err missus. My Dad and Ailz have been married near on 20 years, so this must be potent stuff! Here goes, my dear old Dad says...

Love Magic is about making you or your friend, feel lovable. For this you need to be relaxed, unstressed – and to love yourself." Wow my Dad really is an old hippy!

He and Ailz go on to tell you...

"Before an evening out, light a yellow candle in the bathroom. Run a warm bath. Add some of these oils: gardenia, lavender, lemon verbana, rose, vanilla, lime, patchouli or ylang ylang. Lie back and soak."

Anyway I am sure you get the idea, it is all about preparing a little ritual for you that you feel works. It is about putting positive vibes out into the atmosphere and truly believing that they will come true. Creating a little spell or ritual around those vibes helps you to concentrate and focus on exactly what it is you desire. As long as you do not mean any harm, then it cannot do any harm. Have fun concocting your own spells and send them out to the world with happy affirmations! You may just have a dream come true!

Healing is much the same and witches take a sensible, creative and modern approach. Of course, healing is never a substitute for hospital treatment, counseling or medication, but it can be helpful alongside medical treatment, to help you relax, recuperate and recover your energy. The form of healing performed by witches calls on spiritual energy to be brought down from the universe and sent through the hands onto the person afflicted with illness or injury.

This might be done in conjunction with the chakras. The chakras are seven energy points placed at key points on the body. Although the system of chakras has effectively been borrowed from Indian religions, it transfers very well to Wicca. The chakras are energy centers that can be found at the crown of the head, the middle of the forehead (third eye), the throat, the heart, the solar plexus (between ribs), the base of the spine, and one just about where your private parts are! For a bit more info check out my section on Chakras later on... A Wiccan will meditate on these points, opening them and receiving universal energy into the body. This energy purifies the energy streams of the body, making it a better channel for healing energies.

Conducting spiritual healing is actually very easy and I did it often as a teenager. You simply imagine a stream of golden light coming down through the top of your head and accumulating in your stomach. I was taught that you then imagine the energy building and swirling around in your stomach, at which point you basically aim with your hands and fire. I appreciate that may not be the best or most accurate description but that is what I did. That very scruffy and basic technique is what brought my gerbil back to life when she was at death's door. She had not actually died of course, I am not claiming I performed a miracle, but she was very poorly indeed. Following the healing she stayed around another six months before popping her gerbil clogs.

Wiccan spiritual healing is not unlike Reiki or generic spiritual healing, and no doubt comes from the same unknown mystical healing source. With all things Wiccan you must ensure healing is done with a pure mind and good intention toward the person you wish to heal. If it is your plan to visit a plague upon somebody then you have come to the wrong place.

Wicca, Women and Sex – My Wiccan Conclusion

Sex is pretty high on the agenda in the Wiccan world, as you may have guessed from the frisky and saucy summer celebrations! I am not saying that Wicca is populated by playboys and swingers, but that the Wiccan faith worships sex, reproduction, birth, pregnancy and all the good old-fashioned, honest stuff that sex represents. Boy meets girl, they get feisty and horny, they play the naughty tango and then baby pops out. That kind of thing. Sex is recognized for what it is, the fun and passionate act that makes the world go round and ensures that all species, animal, human, flora and fauna continue to exist.

Sex is the source of everything and everyone's beginnings. As a result it is celebrated by the Wiccans as a happy, essential and spiritual act. That said it's important to stress that Wicca is not a heterosexual only religion. Yeah we all know how babies are made, but it goes beyond that, encompassing other important relationship aspects such as love, passion, companionship, nurture and care. Sex is seen as one expression of being alive and quite clearly you don't have to be straight to indulge in sex, parenting, nurture or love. It therefore follows that you don't have to be straight to indulge in Wicca. Just felt I needed to clear that up and avoid any confusion, now back to sex...

Sadly this train of thought, that sex is natural, goes against the grain of the society we live in. Even in the 21st Century with sex all around us we can still be prudish and judgmental. Indeed when we aren't being uptight and scared of sex then there is the other horrific extreme. Women are abused, raped and vilified at every turn and in every nation on this planet. Women are trafficked to work as sex slaves; women are abused and attacked by strangers on the street, or even by their husbands and lovers in the home. Our bodies are adorned in pretty swimsuits and touted as flesh for men to fantasize about. We all buy into this to an extent.

I know I do, and for my sins I have been one of those girls in the swimsuits. I wear revealing clothes, I show off my sexuality, which I believe I have every right to do. But sadly the overwhelming evidence shows that this is not always safe. There are still regular debates on whether girls wearing short skirts are 'asking for it'. I have been groped and grabbed in clubs and on dance floors, I have had men yell obscenities at me as I pass innocently on the street (wearing jeans an old T-shirt and trainers). I have cried about it. Women I know have been raped, assaulted, abused, and beaten.

It is not entirely safe to be a female, and that is because we live in a world where sex as a natural, loving act has been twisted and contorted out of all recognition. Women are flaunted as victims, as available, as easy. If we are not good girls, we are sluts, and we all deserve what is coming to us. Or so many people, including some women, seem to believe.

I know this is terrifying but in spite of this I also know that women are reluctant to label themselves feminists. I guess we are all straddling a fine line between keeping our adored femininity and requiring equality. Wicca, however, presents a different view of women. They are to be adored, cosseted, and worshipped even.

The very fact that it is our bodies that will produce future generations is enough to venerate us and raise our status. For this reason Wicca is extremely awesome. It is a welcome and refreshing change to view sexuality as something to be adulated without it being adulterated, violated or deformed. In spite of Wicca being an ancient tradition, it appears that the Wiccan attitude toward sex was far more forward thinking than the attitude of some of the Neanderthals that trawl our streets looking for their next easy lay.

In my opinion Wicca is a bit of feminist religion. Don't shirk or cringe. The only reason we see feminism as a dirty word is because that is probably how a male dominated society would have us react. I do not see feminism as a way to get one up on men, or as a cause that means we must surrender our innate womanliness. In my perfect little world feminism and the Wiccan attitude toward women would be one and the same. Through Wicca women can still be feminine, sexy and alluring, whilst also possessing mental traits of intelligence and wit. I guess what appeals about this is the 'equal but different' philosophy. 'Different' meaning our bodies have different functions and we are emotionally and hormonally different to men. 'Equal' meaning that despite our differences, women are just as precious, capable and intelligent as any man ever was.

Like many other religions Wicca worships the Goddess. Standard western religions tend to see only one religious figurehead, that of a male god. Furthermore according to the Bible the first woman in history (Eve) was a bit of a slut and a traitor, so no wonder we all have a bad rap.

To me it makes infinitely more sense to worship both a male and female deity. Like the Chinese yin and yang, you need both to make a whole and to make the world complete. It is only in loving the opposite that we can love ourselves, for without the opposite, no matter what opposite that is, none of us would be here today. Wicca's spiritual stance on the genders is perfectly natural and predates rampant sexism. Wicca is a good one for the girls so get yourself a broomstick, candles and a cat and maybe we can change the world!

The High Heeled Kabbalah

Ok who loves Madonna? The material girl has certainly done a lot for this otherwise little known Judaism based religion. Yet other than it involving a red string worn round the wrist and a possible association with macrobiotic food, what else do any of us really know? I know that my Dad used a form of Kabbalah, known as Qabballah, alongside his Wiccan religion. And I know that Kabbalah can be utilized alongside other religions – an optional extra so to speak! But beyond that I did draw a bit of a pathetic blank. So what is it about this mysterious faith that has Miss Vogue herself espousing its greatness? What is this amazing spiritual philosophy that has managed to bag one of the most iconic pop stars as a follower? And what is the key to a faith that has Hollywood's elite clamoring for red wrist strings and a way in to this glamorous faith?

The main big, shiny, focal hubs of Kabbalah are the Kabbalah Centers based in big cities such as London, New York and Los Angeles. There is much in the press about The Kabbalah Centre being a dodgy, brainwashing outfit, but my exploration of their beliefs makes me question this view somewhat.

Kabbalah essentially comes from the Jewish faith and is traditionally only open to married males over the age of 40 – or some such nonsense! I think that the popularity and accessibility of Kabbalah, thanks to the Kabbalah Centre has ruffled some big wigs' feathers, which may perhaps be what is behind some of the more negative press cuttings.

I was assured to see that the Kabbalah Centre offers scholarships to those who cannot afford to study; the scholarships provide costs for courses, books, DVDs, classes and any other relevant Kabbalistic learning materials that will help improve that person's life. Furthermore the Kabbalah Centre is an official not for profit charitable organization and I am aware that they are doing some exciting, albeit controversial projects in London schools. So rather than having stumbled upon something rather cult-like and murky, I realized they were not bad at all.

Kabbalah, however, does not start and finish at Madonna's chosen place of worship in fair old London town. Kabbalah, Qabballah or Cabbalah as it may be known, has been adopted and interpreted by all manner of people who are interested in the etheric wisdom it offers.

Some groups choose to study the 'Tree of Life' solely. The Tree of Life is at the mystical heart of Kabbalah. By utilizing tarot, astrology and a plethora of other symbols, the Tree helps to describe the entirety of existence. This is the existence of you, me, the universe and all the levels of being that right now we cannot even conceive of. Though I will touch on this later, there is only so much of 'existence' that I can fit into one chapter of one book!

As a result of the varieties of Kabbalistic thought, we can see how flexible (and intense) the wisdom offered is. Indeed, flexibility like this is only fitting to one other spiritual practice I can think of, that being yoga. No wonder Madonna is so darned toned, with a mix of yogic workouts and Kabbalistic thinking she is stretchy inside and out!

Kabbalah's routes are originally found in Jewish and Hebrew tradition. Though finding a place of worship or further information may at first seem daunting. Kabbalah is easily studied alone or alongside like-minded friends. Unfortunately, the internet is not exactly awash with wholly reliable Kabbalah groups. However, with a bit more detective work, and a membership card for the local library most information you require can be at your fingertips. If, like so many others, you choose to study Kabbalah alongside other beliefs or as part of your own DIY religion, then all you need to start with is a basic knowledge of the theory. And intriguing theory I think you will find it is.

Now the problem with Kabbalah, or at least my problem with Kabbalah is that people do not worship it, they study it! My attempt to explain it to you is fraught with headaches, minor anxiety and confusion.

Learning about Kabbalah is at first glance a little like mingling ancient religious 'fact' with super modern science fiction fantasy. At second glance you realize just how damned much of it there is to learn. This is probably the hardest chapter I have had to write. Between grasping the knowledge myself and then disseminating to you the relevant bits, I have probably aged five years! That said, let us carry on and see how I did....

(Some of) The Theory

Central to Kabbalah is the idea of Light. Think back to the beginning of the Bible when God piped up with, 'Let there be Light' and you will see what I am getting at. Kabbalists see the Bible as very relevant to their religion, though they believe the Bible is in fact an encoded version of their belief, and that to take it as read is the fatal flaw of modern day biblical based religions.

Light is at the very heart of Kabbalah and at the heart of you, me and everything else that exists in the world and in all other worlds. What is that, I hear you cry, 'other worlds?' Yep, you read me right. Kabbalah believes that existence goes on beyond our little version of it and that other worlds or dimensions surround us.

In his easy to read book 'The Power of the Kabbalah', Yehuda Berg points out that we currently exist in only 1% of all existence. The other 99% consists of three other worlds. These other worlds are said to be 'beyond the veil', in other words they are slightly beyond our reach, and we cannot directly access them from where we currently are on earth.

Through Kabbalistic practice, we may have glimpses, or become able to access the benefits of these other worlds. The worlds are not other planets that we could fly off to in a space ship. They are worlds that exist in other dimensions and on other vibrations, but that are also all around and within us.

As humans our vibration is a slow vibration. When we increase our access to the light through Kabbalah, then our vibration increases. As it increases then we have a little more access to the other worlds. This access may come as messages from spirit or guidance from angels.

When we die our vibration again increases as we leave our human body and return back to our original form as a divine being, a soul. This focus on light and vibration and other worlds is like an explanation of spirituality as a whole. Whilst various spiritual thoughts describe that we can contact the angels or the Great Spirit or God or our Guides, Kabbalah gives us a step-by-step manual on how to do this and why it happens.

The other worlds are not unrelated to us, and really in my mind they are simply a very specific and complex description of heaven, 'life between lives' or Nirvana. And yes, this includes all of those traditional things that a storybook heaven might have, such as angels, ascended beings and wise spirits, but it also has a whole lot more, a whole 99% more. When you consider how much stuff is known on this planet today, and put together the combined knowledge of every single human being, animal and plant, that has ever lived, this still only ever represents 1% of everything, you begin to realize how massive existence is, and how very, very little we have access to.

One of the downfalls with our ability to comprehend our world is due to our heavy reliance on our five senses. We only comprehend life through the five senses that we deal with on a daily basis: sight, hearing, touch, taste and smell.

Because everything we know and understand is beholden to these, it makes us very desirous creatures indeed. We are in fact creatures who generally cannot see past our own needs and our own desires. Everything we do, need, want or crave stems from our body's needs and we tend to spend our lives wanting stuff. This is not necessarily selfish stuff, but it is still as a result of our needs. You may want to see a film at the cinema, or you may need a glass of water, a long bath or some delicious food. All of these things are ultimately things you want to make yourself feel better and/or happier.

As a result, the whole of society is set up around performing tasks that appease all of our needs. From big to small business every need that stems from one of our senses is catered to and provided for. According to Yehuda Berg, we are desire in action, or as he puts it 'desires on foot'. Basically, nothing at all occurs within our world that is not the result and whim of somebody's desire. We are slaves to our desires, wants and needs, in the process of constantly ensuring they are satisfied we have little time to think of anything else. Life has become a thousand quick fixes a day, whim after whim fulfilled until its finally time for bed.

This brings me back to my earlier comments about light. Light is the Kabbalists' code word for happiness, pleasure, contentment and never ending peace. Light is at the beginning of our universe and apparently exists in great bounty everywhere. So although we are surrounded by light, and we desperately desire this light, we cannot necessarily access it. We are too busy fulfilling our basic needs and petty wants to even begin to think that light, and happiness might be found through another route. Light can be found in abundance in the 99% that we cannot yet comprehend. Although we cannot comprehend it, we do access it for temporary moments all the time. Whenever you feel joy, happiness, safety or stillness, you are receiving the light through the veil. Whenever a need is catered to, a nice glass of wine, or a delicious meal with friends then a small piece of light creeps in though as we all know, such happiness tends to be fleeting.

Kabbalah aims to help us view life differently so that we will have better access to the worlds beyond the veil and get a better deal on the amount of light we have access to. Kabbalah wants us to see beyond our quick fixes and set our eyes toward a more permanent prize. We all know that a full, satiated belly, quickly leads to an empty, hungry one. Kabbalah helps us to control how we find happiness so that our good times are longer lasting and our happiness comes from within our selves.

Currently, whenever you feel great happiness it is because the part of you, your divine part, that exists in other worlds, has allowed you to feel it. You have in essence made contact with your spiritual self. Kabbalah believes that although we are physically living on this planet, we also exist through the veil in our spiritual capacity. As humans our physical bodies and needs limit us, but we do still retain some contact with part of our soul. If we can strengthen our link to our soul then we can increase our access to the light, Kabbalah teaches you how to better forge that link.

This reminds me very much of the work done by the likes of Michael Newton (see past life regression section). Newton uses hypnosis to go to a place he calls 'life between lives'. Some of Newton's work suggests strongly that whilst we are on earth, we leave behind part of our soul in this other existence. This soul can interact with us, and others on earth, perhaps through sending thoughts down that we perceive as moments of inspiration, or even moments of divine madness. I like to think that in writing this book I am perhaps accessing my 'higher self' and channeling the words I type.

Currently most of us access our higher selves by happy accident. What Kabbalah teaches is that we can access these other worlds, and our spiritual selves, quite easily and whenever we want to. The result is that our desires become fulfilled differently, that we have greater happiness and a better understanding of existence fills any voids.

So out with pizza and white wine spritzers and in with divinity, love, spiritual understanding and bags of light!

Who are you?

Kabbalah believes that we are all individual manifestations of God. We are part of God and s/he is part of us. We co-exist in a dependent relationship whereby neither can exist without the other. As far as relationships go this sounds pretty unhealthy, however as we are speaking of a celestial, all-powerful spirit, I will let this one slide! You may like to think of God as the source of the light, I certainly do. I do not consider God to be a male entity somewhere in the sky. So when I refer to God throughout this chapter I mean the source, the light, the heart of spirituality, I do not mean a jolly old dude in a white dress.

As a result of our close affinity and connection with God or light, the Kabbalah believes that we are all precious divine beings. One of our first lessons is that we must begin to view ourselves as divine beings. This level of respect must then be leveled at all human beings, even the ones who make us want to scream and throw furniture. The catch is, that when we view ourselves as divine we are looking deeper than our likes, dislikes or even our charity work. Our divinity comes from our very being, our inner self, and the self that is at our core. This is the self that exists on other worlds and that has a higher vibration than the self we live with on a daily basis.

Rabbi Esther Ben Toviya suggests a simple exercise to help understand what precisely our divinity is. In her book *Created in the Image of God* she asks the reader to draw a circle and label it 'Being'. From here you draw lines coming off the circle that describe your hobbies, favorite colors, restaurants and friends. She then asks you to disregard all these things, all of these elements of your life are things that you do, or things you enjoy, and none of them are part of your divine essence. All these things are merely human accessorizing and therefore they are not divine. Your shoes, your car, your beautiful new dress, your wedding ring, your love of sushi, none of these are divine. These may mean a lot to you, but only in so far as fulfilling your desires and making your life on earth more tolerable.

By doing this exercise it may feel that you are stripping your soul back to nothing. But actually the exercise shows that you cannot be judged or prejudiced against based on these things as they are not truly who you are. For example, you love carbohy-drates more than the next person, so what, that is not reflective of your soul. You have a new flash sports car, big deal that is only an appendage, a symbol of success that you have purchased. You enjoy doing yoga twice a week, who cares, you do that for yourself, such acts do not really speak volumes about your innate divine or spiritual character – even if you think that they do.

We are conditioned to define ourselves as a measure of what we buy, or by our work or hobbies. Kabbalah teaches us that these things are not part of our true divine being. Do you see what I am getting at? Strange as it might seem your love of olive oil and dark chocolate or your desire to climb Mount Fuji do not amount to part of your divine being. Yes, they are reflections of it, and yes these desires might stem from your inner self, but essentially they are human add-ons. They are things you enjoy doing with your physical human body in this lifetime's incarnation.

Culture, society, parents, lovers and friends all judge you to some extent by this external clutter, just as you judge them. No wonder we all desire so very much, if we did not desire things, we may not fit in with the rest of society and the people around us. If we do not fit in here, where will we fit in? Maybe by opening your heart to Kabbalah, you will see that you do already fit in, and that the 1% is so full of irrelevancies that even though you do fit into the clutter, your heart and soul is bored and lonely. The clutter is nothing but a huge diversion from the divine inner you. Our obsession with earthly objects and clutter and desire does nothing but block us from contact with our divine selves. To access the divine we must tear our eyes away from the online shopping site and learn to see and appreciate our innate and pure godliness.

Kabbalah is dissimilar to beliefs such as Buddhism in that they do not actually see a problem with you accumulating junk, or indeed wearing this season's new expensive Manolo Blahniks. But Kabbalah does see that you must desire more than this if you are going to achieve ultimate happiness. Although your Manolo's may bring you great, deep, previously unknown joy, as soon as they are scuffed and worn you will feel disappointed and will eventually crave more of the same, more approval, more identity. So whilst you can collect clutter if you wish, Kabbalah simply wants you to seize your divine identity and think of shoes a little later…

We live in a world where success and character can be bought and measured. Take away our purchases, disguises, Curriculum Vitaes and the content of our kitchen cupboards and what we have left, our inner being, is what is divine about us all. Our divinity is what will continue to exist after we are dead and into our next life. Our divinity is our inner soul and wisdom; it is the part of us that links us directly to light, the angels and everlasting life. Our divinity exists here and in the other Kabbalistic dimensions, and it is this that we must access to ensure a better time here on earth.

Kabbalists believe we are all precious, no matter what our social status or bank balance, they see that we are all little pieces of God. And it is that aspect of a person that you must recognize in others. Kabbalah asks you to see beyond any pretence, diamante bling, Jamaican sun tan or penchant for cocktails and view the divine eternal being that lies in us all.

The Opponent

The Opponent is what makes all our good works and good intentions so difficult. He is a an important part of The Kabbalah Center's teaching on Kabbalah, but not so much a part of the more mystical approach. Whether you choose to embrace a belief in the Opponent is entirely down to you. If this makes uncomfortable reading for you then I suggest you take it as simple good advice to keep you on your best behavior. The Opponent is basically Satan. He is the darkness that wants to destroy the Light; he is the nasty little thought at the back of your head that makes you want to do bad things. He is the self-critical voice that says you are too fat, too ugly, too short. He is the voice that is cruel about your friends and family, and the one who lets the gossip slide from your tongue. He is the voice that comes to you late at night and scolds you because you failed, or you did not have the will power to stand up to him.

According to Yehuda Berg he is so clever that he has tricked you into thinking he does not exist!

I am sure that the idea of the Devil is somewhat archaic and ridiculous to you. In spite of this, some Kabbalists seriously believe in his power and influence over us all. You may choose to see the Devil as a red horned beastie, or a malignant power, as a force that tests humanity or simply as darkness. Whatever format you give him, he is the 'force' that you can blame for everything you have ever done wrong. Although of course it is not that easy. Yes, you might blame him for the time you passionately kissed Mr inappropriate, or the spurt of shoplifting you indulged in when you were 15, you may even blame him for that deliciously tempting pecan pie you sank last night, but really is it him? It is not as though he is standing in front of you cracking a whip and threatening an eternity in a fiery hell should you refuse the pie. He is nothing more or less than a voice in your head, as powerful as this may be, you have to accept that you are the one to blame, because you are the one who did what he said!

The Opponent is determined to make you feel bad. And he very often succeeds. He offers moments of pleasure that give way to all that murky sadness and darkness you feel afterward. He does not like the light so he makes you an addict to your desires, and he makes your desires very cerebral, physical and immediate. He makes you obsessed with what is in front of you, so that you exclude the bigger picture. He makes the extra sambuca shot more appealing and shuts out the repercussions of drunkenness, hangovers and humiliating yourself on the dance floor. He makes you think you look cool when you start an argument with another reveler on the street and he throws your inhibitions out the window and allows you to dance drunk and naked on a beach with total strangers. (Not always a bad thing of course, but you can see where I am going with this!) He makes you want stuff badly and he makes you want it now, and he makes you go to all kinds of lengths to get what you want. In wanting stuff and getting stuff you lose track of yourself, you become a big nervous bundle of wanting, you become a desire addict. The opponent is the bad guy, but you are the one bending to his whip and allowing him to crack that whip harder day after day after week after year.

To overcome the Opponent, first you must recognize him. Pump up the volume in your head so that you can examine your thoughts better. Don't allow the greedy beastie to always get his way, and when he does get his way recognize that and acknowledge how it makes you feel. Yeah, it was great when you succumbed to that crazy shopping spree, but how do you feel later when you have no money left to pay the electricity bill, the car needs petrol and the cats are whining for food. Yeah, you can probably provide all of that stuff, but you have to go into your overdraft and ruin all the good work you did paying off your debts. The Opponent tricks you into believing that the fulfillment of your measly five senses is ultimately important. When really it is less than important and does nothing more than make you feel shitty in the long run.

I am not personally convinced that the Devil exists as a real life entity determined to see my downfall. That is all a little bit too old school biblical for me. Most of the alternative strains of Qabballah do not feature this particular quirk. The Kabbalah Centre, however do promote the Opponent as being our true enemy. I think that the Opponent as a metaphor is a pretty good way of getting across a message. If we blame the Devil for our behavior, then we may become more able to recognize when we are being out of line with what is good for us or in our best interests.

The thing that worries me a little is the control aspect of

blaming someone else for your behavior. And the fact that Satan, and Hell are both concepts that have caused a great deal of repression within many societies over the years. I feel the need to disassociate from that concept. Yes, I can see how it works within Kabbalah, as an illustration, and as a way to bring peoples' attention to their temptations it is likely to be very effective. But as far as taking responsibility for one's actions I am afraid that it just seems it could be used by the vulnerable as a bit of a cop out. If you commit a crime and say that the Opponent prompted you, do you feel less shame? Though perhaps it may even provoke you to seek help and refuge from the behavior.

I am of the mind that all things spiritual are inherently good. Any badness or murkiness around the edges comes purely from messed up human minds. Yes, I believe in the light, I am certain of it, though in my personal philosophy I would probably call it something else. But the Devil? I just cannot take that seriously, and if you have ever seen South Park the movie then I am fairly sure you will not be able to either.

Divinity

In loving and appreciating everybody as a divine representation of God, we must look closely at how these divine/human beings have affected our lives. Kabbalah asks you to realize that everybody you have known has helped make you who you are. You may be reluctant to see or admit this if you have been badly treated or if you dislike a person. However, no matter what your personal feelings are towards people you have known, it is likely that each person has had some lasting effect on your character.

This is an intriguing way of thinking about the world, and the more I thought back, the more I realized that people's presence in my life had deeply affected my own character. Now this may have been in some parts purposeful, as in when a parent prompts a child to be brave or to improve their spelling. In others it may be a more subtle influence or the result of somebody's character rubbing off on your own. When I was at university I befriended two very popular and outgoing girls, as a result I became more outgoing, I learned self-confidence and much about the closeness of friendship from them. They did not set out to help me in this way, they simply influenced me, their very presence and the gift of their friendship was enough to mean that I made changes in myself. Indeed the changes I made were barely perceptible at the time. But I did change, partly purposefully and partly on a subconscious level.

In other instances it may be the pain a person has brought us that makes us stronger, be that person a playground bully, an ex-partner or an abusive parent. Though a person's intention may have been to hurt us or to spurn us, in the end it is likely we become stronger. This is often a more painful, drawn out process, but we will eventually see what we have learned and how that person has helped us to grow whether they meant to or not. Through our connections with people we understand ourselves more, and each person can have a massive impact on the person you are today.

If you try to claim that people have had no such impact on you, then I reckon you are in denial. We are all guilty of hurting others and as a result changing their characters, although hopefully this will be for the better in the long run. We have all offered friendship or love to somebody and perhaps given that person a great deal to think about and eventually grow from. Our effect on others is tremendous, and yet we go about our lives as though we have little effect on them. How often have you acknowledged any of this to yourself? I can admit that I have barely thought about it. If a friend does me a favor, of course I thank them, but if their presence in my life makes me braver, more compassionate, more thoughtful or a better listener, do I thank them? Do I even acknowledge it? Do I even realize the impact they have on me?

Kabbalah helps us to recognize that all these people and the events they cause, or contribute to, are sent to us on purpose to help us develop into the best example of our true being that we can be. In some respects this can be seen as a reason, or answer to the conundrum of 'what is coincidence'. The answer being that every coincidence is in fact an example of our divine purpose being made evident to us and being handed to us on a plate.

I know I have always been surrounded by a succession of impressive and confident females. Each one has taught me more about my own femininity, my strengths, my weaknesses and myself. In turn I hope I have influenced them, maybe I have given them something to think about or at the least added some small value to their day.

As divine beings this is how we will progress and how we evolve. Our lives are characterized by seemingly random events that when viewed from a distance become vital to our existence, and an essential part of the road map of our lives. Because every person is a small piece of God made real, then all actions toward, against or for us are actions done by God. Whether they are sent to test us or to offer us help is immaterial.

By recognizing this we must learn to accept and appreciate it. No matter what sadness a person injects into our lives we must not blame them. Everyone we meet is a gift from God, even if the Opponent influences his or her behavior. It is still true that they are a divine being. Blame is unacceptable. Because Kabbalah asks us not to blame others, we must adjust our own instincts and I will go into this a little bit more in the next section on reactivity and obstacles.

It is essential to remember, on a daily basis that as a result of our precious inner divinity we are all interlaced and fully connected to one another at any one time. If we pray to 'God', we may actually send a prayer to the mass of divine beings, one of whom may answer that prayer by sending their human incarnation to assist you. Still confused? Let's try this approach: Have you ever been distressed or upset and a friend has called out of the blue and seemingly comes to your rescue. Kabbalists would say that this happened because your thoughts had been sent to your 'divine part' that exists with God and everybody else's divine parts; your divine part has then had a word with your best friend's divine part. Your best friend then has an unexplained urge to call you, prompted by her divine part.

I told you it was complicated. And this is just the bare essentials!

Reactivity and Obstacles

Kabbalah is really hot on the idea of reactivity and the conscious control of our reactions to defeat the Opponent and to improve our lives here on earth. Kabbalah is a religion that advocates pain, struggle, stress and torment as normal aspects of life, and therefore to be expected. It does not want you to go out and commit horrible acts on others, rather it wants you to embrace the harder bits of life and turn them around in your favor.

Kabbalah is not a religion that sees chanting, praying, meditation and communing with nature as a particularly effective way to attain enlightenment. Kabbalah believes that we are here for a purpose, and that purpose is to experience and understand the human experience. What comes with the human experience is the volatility of emotion, in other people and ourselves. For a light seeker there is no point hiding in the garden practicing your mantras and singing to the butterflies, oh no, for that would be defeating the object of being here.

We are here to learn and to do so we must immerse ourselves in all that human life can bring. In doing this we will only better ourselves by bettering the way we react to events that come our way. This can be something as trifling as refusing an extra slice of toast so as not to ruin your diet. Or it may be that you handle arguments differently or consider how you deal differently with tricky situations. Yehuda Berg tells us in simple detail that to understand our spirituality and to bring light toward us we must not react to situations. Reaction is based on gut instinct and primal emotions. By reacting we are not allowing our higher self to kick in and assist us. By reacting to temptation or trouble we are our own downfall. By reacting to the extra pizza by eating it, we may have some small parcel of light come our way, but this soon is replaced by darkness and self doubt and self anger and an extra inch of shame around our waists. By reacting to another person's anger we may feel justified and powerful, but this will give way to darker emotions and the Opponent will achieve his goal.

Berg tells us that we must stop the instinct to react in its tracks. We must be open to possibilities and let in positive thoughts. When things do not go our way, we must not give way to the natural reaction of negativity. Instead we must sit back and contemplate how we would like things to end up. We must embrace certainty where doubt previously existed. For example, you are buying a house that you really love, then without warning the sale falls through. You may instinctively react with anger, frustration, and sadness. By practicing Kabbalah you must switch off these baser reactions and look for a happy, helpful reaction. Perhaps this house was not meant to be your home, and you will find something even better. You must turn all bad reactions into good ones. This may at first seem like a giant leap of faith, but if we believe that only good can come from bad, then we are allowing light into our lives. As a result of positive thinking the higher realms will intervene to ensure positive outcomes.

To me this is essentially what lies at the heart of principles such as 'cosmic ordering' and Wiccan spells. By placing good, wholesome, inspiring thoughts into your mind, you should eventually reap positive rewards. By reacting differently you shut out darkness and good comes forth.

If good does not come forth immediately then perhaps that is because you need to struggle for a little while to learn. To a Kabbalist any and all obstacles in this life are nothing more than an opportunity to grow. So no matter how hard things get, if you rein in your reactions, think positive and embrace hard times, you will be on a fast track toward the elusive enlightenment and eventually happiness.

Love

We all love a bit of love! And similarly to many of the other beliefs I have covered in this book, modern day Kabbalah is definitely on the love train. Love, it seems, is the most powerful thing we have got going for us. Love, to a Kabbalist is light. Light is love, they are one and the same. It is the highest currency we have and to act with love in our hearts for others and ourselves is a jolly good start toward defeating the darkness and the opponent.

In this world we have a distinct choice as to whether we choose to embrace love. Yet many of us do not recognize this option. We see love as a distant relationship that we can only form with a potential lover, close friend or family member. We categorize love and attach conditions to it. We use love as a bargaining chip and threaten to withdraw love should something not go our way. We jealously protect our love and only allow certain people to see it, feel it or even know we are capable of it.

If love is light, and light is what we desire, then we must remove these human made obstacles to feeling and giving love.

Love is what connects us to the very highest spiritual world of Atzilut. It is what we must try to invoke when we look at all other human beings as 'divine beings'. But it is also more than this. It is what we should allow our lives and our actions to be ruled by. For in acting in everything we do with pure love, we are acting in pure light. Hey presto, upon doing so, you are achieving a Kabbalistic dream. In acting in love then you are always thoughtful, considerate and slow to react. To love others and to love the planet and to love ourselves and to show this in our every action is by no means easy. Yet it is the quickest, most effective and certainly most pleasant way to achieve your enlightenment.

The Four Worlds and the Tree of Life

The four worlds make up everything that ever was and ever is. There are different dimensions within the four worlds. These worlds and dimensions and the links between them make up a map of spiritually, the universe and absolutely everything.

We interact with the other worlds spiritually or via our emotions and actions. We currently live in the world known as Assiyah. Assiyah is basically at the bottom of the 'Tree of Life', with all the other worlds being 'above' us. The Tree of Life is the Kabbalistic name for the map that demonstrates the four worlds and dimensions. Assiyah is pretty cool in that we are profoundly affected by what goes on in all of the other worlds.

Everything that goes on in the other zones filters downward to us, where it all mixes up and creates existence as we know it. Because part of our entity exists here as well as in the other worlds, we can access the benefits of the other worlds if we learn how to. This is fundamentally what Kabbalah helps us to do. By accessing the power of these other worlds we become better people, who act thoughtfully, properly and with spiritual purpose. So let us do a run down of the four Worlds and see what they each have to offer us.

Atzilut

Atzilut is the World where everything as we know it begins. Atzilut is the source of the light, it is God himself, it is the creator, and it is the manifestation point of everything that ever existed. Atzilut sits at the top of the Tree of Life and feeds its light downward all the way to our realm of Assiyah. However, by the time the light reaches us it is quite transformed from its original state.

Atzilut is a place where things are not separate. In Atzilut nothing exists as a single personality. Nothing dominates over anything, it is all one, it is pure and simple, but also divine and all knowing. If you were to go there as a soul you would become encompassed within the divine light. You would not exist as a single entity; you would become part of the light, part of the source. Your personal knowledge would be general knowledge and you would not think or exist as an individual. I imagine that if you were to return here you would feel nothing but peace and tremendous harmony with everything that has ever been and ever will be. Indeed you would be everything, you would be existence itself, you would be God and God would be you. Scary eh!

B'riyah

B'riyah is the world of thought. The light from Atzilut filters down the Tree of Life to B'riyah, once it is in B'riyah it transforms and becomes conscious. B'riyah is a world of the intellect, of ideas and of thinking. It is from the world of B'riyah that we get our original ideas. My idea about writing this book would have drifted down to my mind from B'riyah. When Sarah Jessica Parker was cast as Carrie in Sex and The City, this inspired move no doubt came from B'riyah. When Moet and Chandon became 'Moet et Chandon' the sparkling idea that gave birth to their world renowned champagne came from B'riyah. Any and all ideas start here, even the ones that go wrong. This is not because B'riyah gives us rubbish ideas, but that sometimes we execute them wrongly, get them confused or misunderstand what we are supposed to do. Oh, and being emotional creatures, that can cause our ideas some problems too.

The ideas that come from B'riyah are said to be very weak in the first instance. That is why according to Rabbi Esther Ben-Toviya, we so often forget our thoughts. I am sure that there has been many a time you have been dying to express a thought, or idea, but when you get the chance the thought has disappeared from your brain as though it had never been there in the first place. Rabbi Ben-Toviya says that the reason we lose some of our thoughts is because we are not connected to them emotionally.

The ones we do feel an emotion about stick with us longer and are acted upon more strongly. That is where the next world comes in.

Yetzirah

In the world of Yetzirah our ideas from B'riyah become inspired by our emotions. So ideas become stronger depending on how we feel about them. If we are terrified of spiders or wolves then our thoughts are led by fear. The more fear we feel, the stronger our thoughts are in our minds, and the more we act upon them. The same goes for positive emotions such as love or desire. It is unlikely that a thought will be acted on, or thought about for long if we do not have any emotion attached to it.

In Yetzirah emotion joins with thoughts to give them weight and superior meaning. When they filter down to us we are more likely to act on those thoughts that we feel emotionally strongly about. I, for example, have had a hundred different career paths come to me in passing as ideas, however, until I decided to write I never felt emotionally strongly enough about any idea to actually do much about it. I have filled in plenty of application forms and even got onto courses, but the pull was not there to see it through. Perhaps I was being divinely guided to write, and to eventually write this book. Because once this idea came into my head I have never looked back. I was emotionally hooked and therefore the idea became an action. I am sure you can think of an example in your own life of something similar.

Assiyah – where we are now

Assiyah is the only World that is divided into two parts. These are the spiritual and the physical parts. On this plane of existence we are both of these things. Our physical selves walk, talk, act and do, whilst our spiritual part encompasses our thoughts and our feelings. So whilst Assiyah can be differentiated into two distinct arenas, we have these arenas deeply embedded within us. Assiyah is also closely linked with the four elements water, air, earth and fire. These are elements are what make up the physical world, and are the four components of our planet earth. In Assiyah there are also other important defining factors that do not exist in the other worlds, these are, time, space and self-awareness.

Everything I have described about Assiyah is not new to you. It is the world you are familiar with and without these various things such as earth, water and time, you would be somewhat lost. Well happily, or not, these traits are all specific to Assiyah.

The other worlds are very different to what we are used to. We are not talking Star Trek different whereby you land in your shiny spacecraft and are confronted by crazy jungles, red rock and ugly aliens, I am talking mind bogglingly different, beyond normal comprehension different! Nor do you need space travel to be able to access these other worlds. They are all around you, and when you want to get to them you can. Not physically of course, physical stuff is just for us humans. But mentally, emotionally and spiritually you can connect to the other worlds.

Assiyah is a world of action and things are made here. Different aspects of the other worlds come to our world to be made.

An emotion such as love may come to us from all three worlds, yet the actions that show love are made here in Assiyah. So whilst your spiritual self loves your partner, it is only through the world of Assiyah that you can kiss your partner, buy a home with them or make a baby with them. In Assiyah emotions, thoughts, ideas and spiritual yearnings are transformed into actions that are visible, quantifiable and measurable.

In some respects Assiyah seems to be a playground, or learning zone where thoughts can be processed through actual physical deeds. Ideas, and emotions are given a creative physical incarnation where spiritual beings (us) get to experiment with love, lust, fear, sadness, ambition, family, hot, cold, broken bones and our connection to our true selves.

It seems to me that Assiyah is a training ground for testing how well a soul copes with the physical reality of its soulfulness, whilst being distracted with a million and one physical and emotional distractions. By employing Kabbalah we can make our lives in Assiyah all the more meaningful and better lived. By being in contact with our divine self, as well as our physical self we have a trump card over those who live purely for fast cars and women! By embracing spirituality on Assiyah we can take advantage of a connection to our true selves and hopefully live more valuable existences.

My Kabbalah Week

Ok, this is much the same format as what occurred when I became a Buddhist for a week. I basically spent some time trying really hard to be a good Kabbalist, not reacting, defeating the opponent and trying to change my somber mood from downbeat to upbeat, a significantly difficult task I might add when I have just got back from holiday and have to go back to work!

In the very first instance it all went horribly wrong. I reacted! On this particular day I was waiting at London St Pancras train station to catch a train home after a long, hot and sweaty day of traveling, visiting and having a headache. I arrived at the station to find there was no train for half an hour. Fair enough, I thought, and went to the toilet, bought a nice Chai Latte and before I knew it half an hour had whizzed by. On attempting to board the train I was informed I could not board that train as my ticket was only valid on trains after 7pm. This meant that I could not get on the 7pm train. In fact I had another 45 minutes to wait. I was tired, grumpy and flustered, and boy did I let the train attendant know it. Not that I reacted by screaming and shouting. Instead I got all huffy and abrasive and tried to protest that nobody had told me the limitations of my ticket (which they had not). She still would not let me on the train. I reacted further by muttering under my breath and waltzing off with my pissed off princess hat on. I then attempted to lure another attendant into my grips by whining to him about letting me onto the 7pm train. He was having none of it, so I huffed and puffed and stormed off all over again.

Need I say that I made a right twit out of myself? I reacted very badly toward two people who were simply doing their job. As soon as I sat my princess ass down to wait I realized what I had done. But I still felt irritated and began to think that all the staff were evil and on power trips. Under the strain of the circumstances I allowed myself to sit and quietly fume. Once I began to calm down I started to rationalize my behavior. I knew I had been in the wrong, but I told myself I was tired, I had jet lag, I was frustrated, and anybody would have acted the same way under the circumstances. Aha! Classic Opponent thinking.

Basically I had been a bad girl, and then allowed myself to believe that I could not have acted any other way. I think we all know that I could have, quite easily. Had I not reacted with petulance and frustration I might have seen the opportunity given to me. This was a chance to be polite in the face of opposition. It was a chance to absorb the crappiness of the situation but not allow it to faze me. I could have been polite to the train staff, who knows, they may have appreciated that and let me on the train out of sympathy! Instead I went with my immediate primadonna, drama queen reaction and no doubt exuded darkness to anyone and everyone around me.

Now I have been working on my 'issues' with patience since I did this same thing for Buddhism. This event showed to me that there is always room for improvement, but also that reacting, in this instance with impatience, breeds nothing but negativity. If only I had just sat and thought of it as an opportunity to relax, to be with myself, to absorb the events of the day. I had the opportunity to not react and I blew it.

It seems this non-reacting thing is a bit of a stick in the guts. It is actually very difficult to do and needs to be cultivated over time. In many ways it is a bit like anger management and involves changing the way you think and see things, though rather than doing this through counseling or psychiatry, you are doing it through spirituality and no doubt for a different reason.

As the week progressed I was offered more and more 'opportunities' not to react. In some instances I did very well. I found I was more patient, and kinder to those around me. By not reacting to things, I would come up with a better solution than going bonkers or getting huffy. Often the solution was to help others with a problem, rather than getting upset with them for having a problem. Sometimes, especially in personal close relationships there can be a lot of blame, and where there is blame there is usually some recrimination. By cutting out reaction, you cut these things out totally. This circumvents the need to argue and you tend to get to the heart of matters quicker, healing can begin and we can all move on.

My example of this comes in the guise of my wonderful other half James. He too was no doubt suffering the holiday blues and I came home one day to find him in a real state of confusion and upset. My gut reaction might have been to question him as to why he was upset when everything was fine, perhaps I would get a bit defensive or accusing. When I realized he had had a beer, I felt like blaming this for his mood and then blaming him for drinking the beer. Instead I did not react. As a result I was more open to what needed to be done to make him feel better. In the past, such a situation might have led to an argument, which would likely have nothing to do with anything (I am sure you have all been there with spouses, kids, siblings and housemates). But matching frustration with frustration is of course liable to be the Opponent's handiwork and can be explosive.

As I did not react with emotion or stress, things worked out rather well. As a result of non-reaction I was no doubt guided by my divine half up above to be kinder, to listen and to be patient. I felt that by denying my human need to react I let love in, and I discovered that it is a more powerful feeling than ranting, raving and slamming doors! I gave James some Reiki healing and left him sleeping on the bed. I tidied up the house and got on with my own thing, so much happier knowing that I had let Light in, where normally darkness might have prevailed. The next day he was fine, much happier and even thanked me. Ladies, I do believe I may have found the key to domestic bliss!

Non-reaction seemed to be a real stickler for me this week. I had certain terrible events occur at work, and in one instance was nearly convinced I might lose my job. I swayed precariously between reaction and non-reaction on this one. One minute I would think positively and consider that if I did lose my job it was meant to be, I could finish my book and it would all work out lovely. The next minute I would be feeling utterly defeated and panicky about the situation. Some time later I would attempt happy thoughts again and try to recognize that nothing was going to happen, nobody was going to lose their jobs and that normality would inevitably prevail!

In the end the positivism won out and it came to pass that I had overreacted with regards to my potential unemployment. In fact I had reacted so badly that I realized that it was only me who had considered the possible loss of job. Nobody had said that to me, nobody had even hinted at it, I was in many respects caught up in my reaction without even realizing it. So whilst I thought I was reacting to the possibility of losing my job, the actual thought of losing my job was the reaction to something else entirely. Tricky, tricky opponent! This non-reaction malarkey is a hard slog, but in my week's worth of practice I can certainly see that it comes endowed with many excellent benefits.

My Kabbalistic practice was fraught with danger this week as I realized how ingrained it is to us humans to react. It is what we have been doing since our conception, when our parents' sperm and egg reacted to each other to form our tiny fetus selves. Reaction is possibly even more difficult to conquer than that other thing I had problems with on my Buddhist week 'Delusion'. Inevitably Kabbalah in theory is picture perfect, and in action it is impressive, but to remember to not react is a heck of a thing. Honestly though, I think it is worth a go, permanently.

For me Kabbalistic thought is central to many other spiritual thoughts that have derived from it. It feels good to me, it feels right, I feel that the 99% is worth striving for and the Opponent is certainly worth defeating. Having been led by him for the majority of my life, I reckon it is time for a change of mental ownership. I am taking back the rights to my brain and upping my vibration to become a fully-fledged Light headed version of me!

Kabbalah – High-Heeled Conclusion

In this small chapter there is only so much I could fit in. Indeed I have likely created a hybrid of Kabbalistic thoughts, with information retrieved from a number of Kabbalistic areas. And as I may have mentioned several times, this is complicated stuff. The Worlds are infinitely deep and profound and when you are diving in deeply, then the assistance of a tutor or group might become necessary, especially if you intend this to be a lifelong affair rather than a brief and enlightening fling. Many of the books I have come across, including the simplest ones, are still complicated and heavy going. The best by far (in terms of simplicity and workability) are the ones produced by the Kabbalah Centre, these really get across the Judaic, original message as it relates to modern civilization and modern people. I can see why Madonna got hooked! If you fancy something heavier, then there are plenty out there, and I am talking big books, tiny writing, both sides filled, very few pictures. I guess when you are trying to fill in 99% missing from a previously unheard of picture many; many sheets of paper will be required!

I personally really like Kabbalah; it fits in well with my version of existence. It echoes the sentiments of my favorite parts of Spiritualism and Buddhism to some extent. When I tally it up alongside my best bits of Shamanism, Wicca and any other faiths it fits very nicely, giving shape, form and structure to them all. Plus Kabbalah seems modern and reasonable when taking into account it is no doubt one of the oldest belief systems featured here. For my personal version of the world, religion, belief and faith, Kabbalah is certainly an inspiration and a very detailed, specific approach. I love the fact that it allows you to live in the real world and that life's challenges are to be met head on. It is refreshing to see a faith that promotes living and that lets you get stuck right in. I like that we are allowed to make our own mistakes, and that these are analyzed without recrimination or everlasting damnation! We are prompted to do the right thing, with little imperative other than happiness. I adore the realistic, down to earth approach of the Kabbalah Centre and how spirituality is boiled down to good behavior, respect and love. Yeah, some of the theory gets a little bit tricky, but at the easy end we can see that life is about living, learning, loving and having a good time. That, my friend, is what I am talking about!

High-Heeled Healing

Spiritual healing is how I got myself here. My spiritual mending came in the form of Reiki, and as you will see from my Reiki section, I speak highly of it. For me it mended something that I could not put my finger on, and that I am sure medical science could not have put their white-gloved finger on either. Yes, they may have dosed me up on antidepressants, or sent me off to see a counselor. But the responsibility I took for myself by seeking spiritual attention blew any form of western therapy out of the water. Not that I am dissing the medical brigade, but sometimes, I do believe, there are certain symptoms they have no decent medication for. I believe that used sensibly, alternative healing practices and daily spiritual practices can keep a host of physical, mental and emotional problems at bay. For those of you already suffering any form of illness, disability or personal internal strife, these healing techniques can help you manage and hopefully minimize whatever it is that ails you.

Healing as a concept may possibly sound a little pretentious, hippyfied or downright bizarre to you. If that is the case then think of it like this, healing is a form of help, it is aid and it is assistance. Healing is a wonderful accessory to all round good health. I won't claim it cures cancer, because I've never had cancer and so I don't know that, but I do know that it alleviates a host of symptoms and beyond that it helps keep you on a straight and narrow path of good physical, mental and spiritual health. This chapter is a quick glance into a handful of treatments and activities available to you as you step gingerly toward your chosen spiritual path.

This chapter instead focuses on some fun and intriguing curealls that you can embark on separately from any belief system you choose to have. Meditation and yoga are superb examples of this. Both practices allow you time to be in your own mind and your own body, shutting out distractions and stresses. They may not cure cancer, but they will calm your mind, alleviate depression, help you cope with pain and acts as a positive step toward fixing yourself, though of course these both require some effort on your part.

Other unexpected delights such as Feng Shui can help realign your lifestyle from the materialistic outside in. Making your living space more pleasant and a better thought out place to exist in. Reiki and crystal healing are treats for the girl who likes to lay back and let someone else do all the hard work. The amazing after-effects of these treatments, considering all you did was relax and daydream may surprise you.

When I started writing The High Heeled Guide to Enlightenment I did so entirely for myself. This book was my little bit of therapy that started off by documenting a spiritual journey that occurred as I attempted to fix what was wrong in my life. This path to modern day enlightenment proved itself to be a wonderful antidote to the common stresses that contributed to a larger feeling of unhappiness. You are probably aware of the fact that life is very hard, good times come and go by the minute. It can be difficult to focus and be entirely rational all the time. PMT, exhaustion, traffic jams, petty arguments, boredom and repetitive routine can all significantly impact your well-being. It is easy to lurch wildly between moods and a bad day can easily slip into a bad week, a bad year and if you are really unfortunate; a bad life.

Sometimes in the midst of all life's difficulties it is nice to put your feet up and be spoiled. High Heeled Healing shows that you need not go to the beautician, spa or hairdresser for luxury pampering treatment. You can pamper your soul in equal style without lifting a finger. Healing treatments are like a detox for your spirit, it removes all of your toxic mess and all you need to do is show up for the appointment!

Chakras

I first learned about chakras through Wicca, though they are used in Spiritualism, Kabbalah, crystal healing, Reiki and no doubt many more forms of healing. The idea of chakras originates from Hinduism and the chakra points are used extensively within the traditional Indian healing medicine of Ayurveda.

It seems the whole world of spiritual pursuits has caught on to the idea of chakras and is using them to improve their own teachings. It is only a matter of time, I am sure, before the Pope includes them in one of his addresses from the Vatican (or maybe not!) Before I begin chattering away about treatments such as Reiki. It is important you understand what a chakra is and what they can do for you.

So, what are they essentially? Well a chakra is not something you can see, however, once you become more familiar with your own chakras, you might even become physically or psychically aware of them. Chakras are the energy centers of the body, and there are seven of them. Some more spiritually attuned people claim to able to see them, but for your regular gals like us it's probably best just to imagine them. I tend to imagine the chakras as beautiful flowers that can open and close at my command. So once you have conjured up a suitable image of your chakras then you must place this image on seven bodily spots. Each chakra has its own color and each one provides different benefits for you. The chakras help to regulate your body's energies and emotions so keeping them in tip top condition that is essential for your sanity and happiness. Starting from your head downwards the chakras are located in the following positions.

The Crown Chakra – Violet is located on the very top of your head, the same place where a very young baby has a 'soft spot'. This chakra is powerfully linked to the universe, to knowledge and to the wisdom of our earth and beyond.

The Brow Chakra – Indigo is located in the centre of your forehead, or where your 'third eye' is. This is linked to your intuition, spirituality and psychic ability. It helps you to 'see' the whole truth of what is around you, and helps you to access inner knowledge.

The Throat Chakra – Blue is located at your throat. It is key to your ability to communicate through the vibrations that resonate as words from your voice box. Language, creativity and expression all stem from here.

The Heart Chakra – Green is located behind your actual heart. Unsurprisingly it relates to love, compassion and balance. It also helps keep a fair balance between opposites such as, male and female, mind and body.

The Solar Plexus Chakra – Yellow is located at the soft spot where your ribs meet at the base of the sternum. This chakra is often referred to as 'the power centre'. It rules your personal identity, your energy and your will.

The Sacral Chakra – Orange is located in your lower abdomen. It is linked to your emotions and to your sexuality. It assists us in making links with new people, helps creativity and is the central place through which your sensuality and sexiness stems from.

The Root Chakra – Red – is located between your legs, around your perineum – oh err missus! This chakra is related to your very existence on this planet. As our 'root' it is what keeps us grounded and aware of the world around us

Blocked Chakras

Not quite the same as blocked pores, but not entirely dissimilar either. Imagine that nasty spot you had and how it occurred. It is likely that it came about due to a number of things; poor diet, forgetting to take your make up off, hormonal influences, or too much chocolate. As the pore became blocked, it also became unhealthy. What started as a self-regulating breathing hole in the skin, loses its ability to cope and starts to get angry, larger, redder and nastier till it eventually pops and oozes its contents out.

A chakra can get blocked in the same way, perhaps through lack of attention to your personal needs or because you are carrying a lot of stress or illness in that particular area of your body. It may be that a failing relationship is causing you heartache, or stress at work is building in your solar plexus, or maybe an argument with your mother, when you said horrible things, has caused your throat to tighten up. All these things and many more may be causing you to have a blocked chakra at the relevant position (heart, throat, solar plexus). If you do not clear the chakra, then it is likely, to become more and more of a problem, just like the spot, until it pops, oozing out a vile outpouring of anger, emotion and physical illness. At worst you might develop a constant blockage, similar to a stubborn blackhead. This will keep you blocked off; eventually making you feel stale and bitter on the inside.

The good news is that chakras can be treated through self-healing, meditation, crystals and reiki. You would not suffer a boil on your face willingly, so why suffer a boil in your emotional centre when you can easily consult an expert?

Any of your chakras can become blocked. Sometimes they sort themselves out quite naturally, without your interference. Other times they can become blocked off for years, resulting in out of character, unhealthy behavior. You will see later in this chapter that Reiki or similar treatments can sort these out for you. It is worth contemplating the various areas of your body that each chakra relates to. Do any of them feel tense, or perhaps underused? Chakras that are blocked can cause innumerable psychological and physical problems to their owner. Don't be scared, of course most people go their whole lives without even considering the meaning of the word chakra, never mind do anything about clearing them. It may be that those people suffer from this, or not at all. Inevitably, even those of us who do cleanse and pay due respect to our chakras, still end up with blocked chakras. That is the nature of this stressful, up and down life.

I recently underwent a crystal healing, which was wonderful and I left feeling pure and delightful. My chakras had all been cleared out and I felt utterly untroubled. However after a tense week at work, I was soon back to being blocked up and in need of a spiritual steam bath.

The best thing you can do is to simply be aware of your chakras and when you have the time perhaps meditate on clearing them out.

One trick my father taught me through his Wiccan pursuits is simply to imagine a pure white or golden light flowing down from the heavens. The light flows over your body, at every chakra point it stops and opens the chakra. The light is good and healing and enters each chakra and removes any negativity. When you have imagined this for each of your chakras, you then envisage a cool shower pouring healing water down onto you and the water passes over your body and closes up each chakra, leaving it cleansed and nicely cleaned out. This is great to do after a stressful day at work, or in preparation for any irksome events.

If you trained in Usui Reiki you will be taught how to clear out your chakras using Reiki energy. You may just fancy buying a selection of crystals that relate to each chakra and carrying them in your handbag or keeping them under your pillow. In her handy book *Crystal Prescriptions* Judy Hall tells us that chakras can be rebalanced and unblocked using crystals the same color as the chakra. This is an easy and fun way to clear the gluts of stress that build up in your chakras. Think of it as an MOT for your soul, without the complication of taking your car to a garage and potentially being ripped off by the dodgy garage geezer man. Oh, and you get a handful of lovely, colorful stones to play with to! All you need do is from time to time place the relevant crystals onto each chakra point and allow them to wizard away your internal badness.

Chakras are certainly a valuable piece of physical/mental/ spiritual information to be aware of on your path to enlightenment. They help you shape your life from a physical perspective; by looking inward for some much needed solutions. Numerous books can be bought on the subject and of course a plethora of websites exist. It seems the chakras are currently undergoing a resurgence of fame. I would suggest you jump on that bandwagon and use the information wisely. Looking after your chakras is akin to a beauty regime for your soul, keeping a host of dysfunctions, negative emotions and potential Vesuvius like outbursts firmly at bay!

Reiki

Reiki is a spiritual hot water bottle that I cannot speak of highly enough. My personal trip into Reiki literally transformed my life. It is also partially responsible for sparking off my adult journey into my own spirituality, which in turn led to this book. Without wanting to sound overly amateur dramatic, I am not sure where I would be had I not gone searching for an answer to life's woes and inadvertently put my faith in a Reiki practitioner.

The truth is, I was feeling seriously low, I will not go so far as to say depressed, but I had spiraled into a state of ongoing misery that was certainly taking me lower by the minute. Furthermore, my behavior was erratic; I made some wonky choices and did a few things I am not proud of. You could say I was having an early midlife crisis. Nothing made me truly happy and the things that did were valueless, like drinking, partying and spending cash on trash. I was self-obsessed and could not see beyond my immediate desires. I felt utterly hard done to, and was blaming everybody else for what essentially was my own problem. I was lost.

Even now, I am not sure how I got there, I can pinpoint one or two bad choices, but how I came into a state of utter questioning and confusion about my life I cannot be completely sure. This state of disillusionment was casting a dark cloud over everything, my relationship suffered under the weight of my gloom. I felt utterly compelled to abandon life as I knew it and go traveling to any country that would have me. Meanwhile, my poor friends, and darling James, who all have the patience of saints, stood by and listened to my droning, month after miserable month.

So what pushed me to the point of turning to Reiki for help? Again I am not certain of that either, but I knew I desperately needed something, and quickly. I was sick of being miserable and somewhere deep down I must have known it was me that needed changing, not everything around me. I did not know what I wanted and was growing bored of my own incessant whining.

My boyfriend and I had reached several crisis points, although there was something in his beautiful face that kept me where I was, and thank God, Goddess, Great Spirit, Buddha and the angels for that!

I made declarations about being happy, yet had no idea how to fulfill them or make happiness a reality. I was at a stalemate, trapped in a mental limbo that I could not shift out of. My emotions were caput, inside there was a swirling mass of turmoil, but outside I was robotic, tearless and devoid of any deep feelings. It was like my heart had shut down and my brain just could not be bothered. The only thing I enjoyed was driving, listening to loud wild music and fantasizing my life away.

What I needed was a push to remember who I was. In all the fogginess I barely remembered my own name, let alone what I wanted out of life. Where had my sweet natured self gone? And who was this gloomy, sullen, secretive person who now inhabited my body? I look back on this time with sadness and awe. I have come so far in less than a year, and it all began with that first Reiki session with the wonderful Reiki Master Lynda Small.

I had considered Reiki before, but never felt a serious compulsion to do anything about it. With the state of my life spiraling out of control I desperately reached out into the bright lights of internet world, found myself a Reiki healer and got booked in for the following day.

My arrival at Lynda's home for my first session felt so easy, despite the unsettling circumstances of turning up at a stranger's house then telling her I was super stressed and might just crack at any moment. She was, however, sympathetic, kind and thoughtful. She did not offer a solution but explained that Reiki could help realign whatever was wrong with me, be this spiritual, emotional, mental or physical.

My first session was the start of a whole new me – or indeed the revival of the old me. This was mixed in with a new spiritual yearning and the beginnings of a supreme self-awareness. I realized after day one that I had been vastly neglecting myself and reflecting in other people's glories rather than my own. I had taken past problems onto my shoulders and was still painfully carrying them. I had a habit of dragging these hurts round with me, and as a result could not always see the good that had come out of them, or the opportunities that lay ahead. I had been living for the sake of appearances, rather than for the real me, and as a result the seeds of resentment had grown twisted and deep. I realized that in many ways this was my doing, and that I had to release all of these pent up hurts and emotions to enable myself to move on. From the first session through to the fourth I continued to have similar realizations, the walls around my heart and mind dropped away and I started to see the truth of my predicament. It was not anybody else; it was not my job, my friends or my partner causing the problems. It was me. I was in a devilish rut but Reiki was a saving grace.

That is when I really came to realize my true self. I started to remember what I loved and what made me happy, I pursued these things with an open heart. This included forcing myself to commit to things that I believed in, but that I did not always act upon. I reigned in my drinking and partying lifestyle. At age 28 I had been indulging in full on partying for well over ten years and I knew it had to slow down. It was no kind of life, waiting for the weekend all the time.

I realized that I had to look beyond my ingrained habits and fears. I did other things that I had abandoned years ago, I spent time thinking, I listened to music uncritically and enjoyed genres that I would possibly be ridiculed for in my role as rock chick girlfriend. I hugged a tree when no one was looking, I spent time with family and friends, for me rather than out of duty, I started writing instead of thinking about it. I went on a crazy girls only trip to Dublin and let off some steam.

I spent time thinking about the little me inside, the little girl I once was, my heartfelt love of animals and the planet that I had left behind when I stepped out of primary school. I considered my skills and talents and education, I read books and watched films and reacquainted myself with a world I had almost forgotten. I looked after me for a change and it was just what the Reiki Doctor ordered!

Reiki helped me to realize that living more for me not only made me brighter and happier, it was better for those around me. I was afraid that pursuing my needs would push those around me away, but I realized that not pursuing them made me unhappy, and that my unhappiness would truly push them away. I came to remember what a wonderful partner I had, not only had he put up with my misery guts self, but he loved the new happy me even more. He was more than pleased for me to spend time pursuing what I loved, and in turn that gave him time to get on with his love of music. As a result when we did spend time together it was so much more interesting, checking in on what the other had been doing and enjoying a good old gossip about it all. This is a luxury that many couples forsake once they move in together, but having reclaimed it I can say that it's great for the soul and great for the soul mate!

Reiki also provoked some other unexpected results. For years, like many women, I had been reluctantly dragging myself to the gym and forcing my body into fast paced, high impact aerobics.

After my second Reiki session my body refused to have anything to do with it any more. I became embarrassingly uncoordinated, my joints ached and clicked, whilst my mind drifted and yearned desperately for an end to the class. At 28 years old I wondered what on earth was wrong with me physically. I took this query to Lynda who informed me that it was a healing crisis, and that I could expect strange things like this as a side effect from the Reiki. It was only then, and several rounds of aerobics later that I realized that I detested these classes. I despised the rigors of jumping round a room to some terrible dance track. I suddenly found the whole thing pointless, draining, vain and an utter waste of my time. So I stopped, and I took up yoga classes instead. As a result the gym became an asset rather than a pain in the ass (literally – think of all those squats and star jumps!). I can now venture back into certain classes and actually have fun and no longer do I think life is over if I cannot get Liz Hurley's stomach.

To some this might seem a small change, but for me it was an escape from the grim psychological pressure I put on myself to get fit, lose weight and tone up, all of which I mistakenly believed I was doing for myself. This change was an unexpected gift that has vastly improved the quality of my life.

Reiki, in many respects opened my heart. Life had taken its toll and over several years I had closed up, copped out and allowed doubt after doubt in. Reiki dispelled all this, and quickly. I felt close to the abyss, yet the laying on of hands and the good intentions of my practitioner pulled me straight back, setting me on the path of a happier, more fulfilling, opportunity filled life.

I felt a reawakening to spiritual energies too and was fortunate enough to see my third eye whilst meditating; I could only imagine where this renewed spiritual interest might take me.

Thus far I have completed Usui Reiki 1 and 2 and I am amazed by the power it has to make my boyfriend fall asleep, whilst preventing him snoring! Reiki saved my sanity and brought me contentment that even in any future times of stress I will reflect back on to find my centre and continue to reach for the stars!

My experience of Reiki is of course not indicative of everybody. We all have different issues to contend with. Some of these you may be aware of, others you may not. During my recent Reiki 2 training Lynda pointed out to me that I had a problem with my left shoulder. I was adamant that I did not. Later that day, when I left Lynda's home and got in my car I realized that every time I changed gear my left shoulder was actually quite painful and awkward. It also dawned on me that it had been like this for a good few weeks, but because the pain was not constant it had not really registered. That night I had trouble sleeping as the ache really kicked in; it was as if the Reiki was going all out to attune me to its mystical powers! To ensure I got some sleep that night I did a little self-healing using techniques you learn when you train in Usui Reiki Level 1 and I soon nodded off! So as you can see Reiki is handy for the little things in life alongside the more significant mental breakdowns.

What is Reiki?

Mikao Usui developed Reiki in Japan at the start of the twentieth century. Based around a set of precepts and meaningful symbols Reiki aims to treat all the human bodies' ills, though it can be used on plants, animals and the environment too. The Reiki precepts are particularly meaningful as they are the foundation of the practice and help form a purity of mind that allows a person to be a better channel of Reiki energy. The precepts reflect the religious and cultural background that Usui came from, the precepts are gentle reminders of how to live well and peacefully.

Reiki Precepts

Just for today, do not anger.
Just for today, do not worry.
Just for today, be humble.
Just for today, be honest in your dealings with people.
Just for today, be compassionate towards yourself and others.

Reiki is a holistic approach to self-improvement, resulting in a balanced mind, better health and assisting the body's ability to heal itself. The word Reiki comes from a Japanese word that literally means Universal Life Energy.

That pretty much sums it up, as a Reiki user I cannot think of a better way to describe what Reiki is. I know when I do it I am calling on unknown forces from the universe to channel their way through me for mine or other people's benefit. You could believe that this energy comes from the universe, the stars, from god, angels, fairies or Santa Claus. I am not sure that its origin is that important, the fact is I cannot say where it comes from, but the results are spectacular.

Mikao Usui certainly uncovered a mysterious yet practical source of health and wellness and for that I believe we should all be grateful. It well may be the same energy that Shamans tap into through plants and drumming, or the same source that Wiccans call on in their spells. Perhaps it is the same energy that Jesus used to cure the lame and bring folk back from the dead? Reiki no doubt originates from the great unknown, but like so many other things that cannot be seen and that science cannot ratify, it certainly exists and as far as I am concerned it definitely works.

As a form of spiritual healing Reiki is a very flexible system, it cleverly works around you and your needs. The Reiki practitioner is not 'the healer'. Instead she or he is the conduit through which Reiki energy passes. No person can direct Reiki energy to any specific place. Reiki has a mind of its own, so whilst you may go to be treated for the pain in your bunions, it might be that the Reiki has other ideas and instead goes to help your stress levels, self esteem or period pains. No Reiki practitioner can claim to control the energy, although it can be directed at a person, it cannot be given a purpose.

A Reiki practitioner is merely a vessel for Reiki, and anyone who claims otherwise is either on an ego trip, or has been badly misinformed.

Another classy little trick of Reiki is that the person receiving the Reiki need not be in the room. Reiki can be sent anywhere in the world, it is simply a case of the practitioner setting their intent that a particular person receives it.

I have of course experimented with this, using a good friend as a guinea pig. I sent her the distance Reiki with the intention that it was for her highest good. I did not tell her I was doing this. I later informed her and asked if she had noticed anything. She did say that she had been in a foul mood all morning but around eleven am, the same time I sent her Reiki she felt much better. The work related problems that had been stressing her out were no longer a problem. Who needs happy pills eh!

Reiki is a very spiritual practice, although some practitioners believe in the spiritual side more than others. My Reiki teacher was keen to talk about her connections to spirit; angels and personal guides who she believes help her. In learning Reiki myself I have had a great many experiences that I simply cannot explain. These include seeing lights and orbs flashing round the room, in broad daylight and I was of course sober! I have felt the temperature in a room drop to an unbearable degree of coldness, when there is no good reason for that to happen. Lynda informs me that this was a guide; I have no other explanation so I hasten to agree with her. I have felt this since, in one instance I was freezing cold before I went to sleep, in spite of two duvets and a cat to cuddle. I awoke in the morning inspired, motivated and brimming with happiness and ideas. I have closed my eyes and seen visions of angel's wings. I have treated people and had reported back to me magical and mystical experiences. I have tuned in to other people's pains, problems and feelings.

I am not suggesting that Reiki is all fairies and flower folk, but if you want a direct route into a deeper spirituality then I do believe that Reiki can assist you onto that path. If you just want the annoying pain in your elbow sorted then it can do that too. Depending on what you want and what you are ready for then Reiki can truly help.

What can you expect from a treatment?

If you are going to take the Reiki plunge, and I recommend that you do, then ensure you find a trusted and well-respected practitioner. The best way would be through word of mouth or through a large reliable database such as The UK Reiki Federation or the Reiki Association. Your chosen practitioner should make you feel comfortable, the fact is they will be placing their hands on you for an hour, if you do not feel right then move along and find someone who makes you comfortable. A good practitioner will have a chat with you and explain what will happen while answering any of your concerns. Reiki is not a counseling service, but this little chat will set you both at ease and give the Reiki practitioner an idea of where you may need extra treatment.

A very good practitioner will be able to follow where the Reiki wants them to go. I have been taught to do this and it is a strange and instinctive process. The Reiki directs the practitioner rather than the other way around. Recently after a Reiki session a friend reported that when I had my hands on her stomach she felt a swirling mass of energy. She felt the energy dissipate and move down toward her hips, and as it did this I moved my hands to follow it, the swirling mass then left her body. I had no idea I had followed any energy, I just moved my hands instinctively when it felt right. It seems to me that something was tapping into my Reiki instincts and ensuring that the Reiki went to the right place at the right time.

Reiki practitioners cannot and should not diagnose illness or problems; it is not within their powers ethically or legally. However they may be able to tell that something is not quite right. So their comments might be rather generic such as 'do you have problems with your knees?' Depending on your needs, the practitioner will either go through a standard set of hand positions, or possibly vary these depending on the client. There are different hand positions depending on whether you have Western style or Japanese style Reiki, however the benefits all work out the same in the end so do not be too concerned about that.

All you have to do is lie back and relax. Reiki is not intrusive, no one needs to get naked and the practitioner does not touch you anywhere they shouldn't! Be warned though, your tummy might gurgle. I have found this frequently whilst being treated myself and whilst treating others. Often this gurgling starts near your throat and moves down the stomach as the practitioner works her way down your body. Needless to say any decent practitioner will be used to this, so don't be embarrassed or feel the need to excuse yourself! The reason for the gurgling is basically that new energy is being introduced to your body, this pushes the old energy around and as a result your tummy acts like it has not been fed in a very long time!

You may find yourself a little tense on your first treatment, but once you feel more comfortable with the process and the practitioner you will experience enormous relaxation, possibly fall asleep or experience a variety of different effects.

Some people find that Reiki gives them a massive emotional release, they may cry or become upset, this usually passes quickly and relaxation resumes. Some people feel the energy passing through the practitioners hands into them, others don't. When being treated I have experienced all manner of things, often my mind would wander off to stunningly beautiful places or on crazy little dreamlike journeys. Physically I might feel very cold or very hot, one time I felt tickly pins and needles across my back for the whole session, it sounds awful but it was actually quite pleasant. Other common experiences might be seeing colors and lights, feeling a variety of emotions, falling asleep, or experiencing involuntary movements as the energy passes through. Reiki might induce a meditative state of mind, or you may see relevant and pertinent images in the mind's eye. Whatever you do experience you can discuss with your practitioner.

The wonderful thing about Reiki is it carries on working for hours, days or maybe months after the treatment depending on your individual need. Immediately after a treatment you may feel dozy or disorientated. Be sure to drink plenty of water and relax, no gym sessions or heavy lifting should be planned for that day.

A slightly annoying effect of Reiki is that you may need to make a few dashes to the toilet, or possibly wind up with what is known as a Reiki cold. If you do need to urinate more than usual, or end up with the sniffles, this is all good, it is just your body's way of pushing the energy around and removing nasty toxins. It is normal for any symptoms to subside after a couple of days.

Some people go through a 'healing crisis' after receiving Reiki; this might occur physically or emotionally and could last a little longer. This sounds scary but it is a fantastic thing as it means that deeply rooted issues and ailments are amending themselves. You might find yourself inspired, motivated or unusually creative. Alternatively you may suffer mood swings, feel sad or abnormally tired. All of these effects are temporary and are the outward symptoms of your body and mind becoming healthier and happier.

Reiki is given to you with pure love and with the intention that it is for your highest purpose. It is not harmful and cannot be given with bad or evil intent, it cannot make you ill and it cannot mess with your head. Reiki rocks, simple as, it may save your life or get rid of your headache. Do it ladies!

Learning Reiki

Reiki was originally designed as a self-treatment tool. It is well worth learning simply to administer a bit of Reiki love and light to yourself. You can also extend this service to your pets, houseplants, friend and family. If you want to go further then the second level takes you to practitioner level, whereby you can set up a practice and do Reiki for payment if you so please. Whilst the third and final level transforms you into a Master Teacher, at this level you can teach others and you are fully empowered to all that Reiki can offer. I am currently sat happily in the middle at number two and it is a comfortable place to be. I can treat my mates, my pot plants and myself. If I want to then I can get insurance and set up a practice.

You can learn western or original Japanese Usui Reiki, there are some differences in technique but the healing effects are the same. If you do want to learn then find yourself a reliable Master Teacher and get on in there.

As a tool for self-treatment Reiki is superb. In the past year that Reiki has been part of my life I can see distinctly how it has helped me. I have come on literally leaps and bound.; I have found my calling in life, that sounds so clichéd, and yet it is true! Only today I remarked to James that I could not imagine being truly unhappy ever again. Learning Reiki has ensured that I am always connected to that wonderful source of magic and healing. Once you are attuned to it, it will never leave you. You will always be able to use it on yourself whether it is a quick five minutes in the office during a stressful day, or helping you though medical or mental emergencies. That said if you break your leg, get yourself to the hospital first and think Reiki later!

Reiki is a marvelous gift; I cannot rant and rave enough about it. Do yourself a huge favor and have a treatment, see how you like it! Reiki is the new spiritual 'Rock 'n' Roll', it is the new black, it is cool for cats (literally and other animals). Reiki is.... Well, honestly, Reiki is my personal savior!

Crystals and Crystal Healing

Crystals are little powerhouses of miracle. Not only do they look pretty, but they can also do a fabulous patch up job on a huge variety of illness and ailments. They are the superheroes of the rock and fossils world. Perhaps you collected them as a child, or maybe even have a few dusty specimens lying around your home, lost at the back of the kitchen drawer or tucked inside a handbag you stopped using four years ago.

As a young girl I was pretty impressed by them, not for their healing qualities but purely because they shimmer, they shine and they are far cheaper than so many other forms of platinum set bling! Now I adore them because of the secret talents they keep well hidden beyond their glossy coats and smooth shiny surfaces.

For those of you whom until now the term crystal usually goes hand in hand with 'Swarovski', this section is sure to be an education. The non-Swarovski variety of crystals does not come embedded into jewelry, watches, handbags or clothing. Despite their lack of attached glamour, designer labeling and expensive cost, crystals of all shape, form, texture and color are powerful. Crystals are used by healers to help balance the body, fight illness and to promote good health. They are also used in practices such as Feng Shui to counteract negative energies.

In other instances you may have nothing physically, emotionally or mentally wrong with you (here's hoping!), but perhaps need a dose of bravery, communication skills or charm for an interview, first date or work meeting. If you know your crystals, or you know a book that does, you can dip into that and find precisely the 'brave-making' stone required, slip it in your handbag and hey presto you get the small confidence boost required! Other uses might be as diverse as using crystals to help you remember your dreams by slipping the appropriate gem under your pillow, contacting and communicating with your angel (for the more spiritually aware of you), facilitating out of body experiences (even I am not that advanced yet), promotion of fertility, or for other day to day needs such as concentration, improved organizational skills, calming, sex drive, appetite suppressant, self awareness, keeping you safe from mobile radiation, encouraging intuition, soothing PMT or assisting detoxing. You name it and there will be a crystal that can help fix it.

I am far from being a crystal expert, but luckily I know a few books that are. Every time I drop into a crystal selling shop and pick up a crystal I go home, leaf through the book and see what my newfound gem can do for me. What is especially interesting in doing this, is that the crystal I am attracted to, is generally always the one that I most need at that moment in time. For example, during a recent period of my life I found myself gazing into a box of mixed crystals wondering which specimen to purchase. I was going through a phase when I had a whole lot of things to say, but could not quite find the will or the words to say them. I allowed my intuition free reign, and instead of picking the nearest bright pink gem or one that matched my outfit, I went for a pretty but unassuming baby blue rock. At home I looked up the meaning and lo and behold it was of course relevant. My baby rock turned out to be a Blue Lace Agate. According to the Crystal Directory in Judy Hall's superb Crystal *Bible*, Blue Lace Agate is effective for healing the throat chakra, thus "allowing free expression of thoughts and feelings" – perfect!

Each crystal, be it polished or rough, has impressive qualities that seem to scream out to your subconscious and urge you to pick it up. Long gone are the days when I pick out the biggest or brightest. These days I may be nudged toward one that is not such a pretty color, or one that's smaller than its neighbor. On some level I am not picking it for its beauty or size, but it is picking me as it knows it can help bring about whatever change or cure I need at that precise moment.

Now how this happens is anybody's guess. Perhaps our bodies

can somehow sense the properties of the crystals and somewhere deep in our DNA we know which one would be best for us, or maybe our Angels or Spirit Guides are prompting us? Either way it makes for a very effective healing tool. It even works if you do not know what you need. Just go with the flow and pick a crystal, when you find out what that crystal represents it might teach you something about yourself you had not realized. When I picked my Blue Lace Agate I was not aware that I had been holding so much in, but upon reading the Agates description I realized I was desperate for help in those particular areas.

Crystals come in a variety of exciting forms, of course they will never beat the intricate nature of the clear crystal swans, ducks and bears that clamor for attention in the window of Mr Swarovski's shop. Yet, despite this debatable flaw, their shape and form is rather less ridiculous and somewhat more practical. Tumble stones are the basic pebbles; they are usually polished and smooth, though you can buy the rough rock too. The main difference being that a polished Rose Quartz is like a pretty marble-ized piece of pink gum that is shiny and sleek, whereas the rough version is still pink but with harder grainy edges and is like something that just washed up on a beach. Either variety is fine, and whether your stone has been given a polish and scrub up, or not, it will still hold the same powers.

Besides tumble stones, crystals come in all manner of shapes and sizes, and of course they also come attached to jewelry. So if you are not the type to have lumps of rock interfering with your minimal and modern maisonette, you may be open to wearing a polished piece of something set elegantly in a ring or around our neck. You can buy large pebbles, heart shaped crystals, skull shaped crystals, big whopping chunks of crystal, slices of crystal, animal shaped crystals, pyramid shaped crystals and for the Wiccan minded amongst us you can also get crystal wands and balls. I personally stick to tumble stones or mid-sized chunks, although if anybody wanted to buy me a large Amethyst

Geode for the corner of my living room I would happily accept (hint, hint James)

Crystals can be purchased in the most random of places, if you do not have a local hippy shop selling crystals, then try a children's toy shop, or even the local museum. Although the local museum / toyshop may not label them up with their reputed healing benefits, it is likely they will house a spectacular variety of crystal types.

The best collection I saw was in the kid's section of the London Museum of Natural History. Not only was this a great collection of all kinds of color, texture and size, it was also far cheaper than many of the holistic shops I have bought similar from. Bargain hunters out there pay attention to this. The Internet is also awash with a variety of crystals and bought in bulk they can work out extremely cheaply. If for example you need a whole wad of Amethyst to counteract negative vibes at work, in your car and at home, then it's worth looking for wholesale on eBay or similar. That's what I did and it was nice to have a few left over to pass onto friends too. I recently purchased a pack of five Amethyst tumble stones from Amazon for a silly cheap price.

Crystal Healing Experience

My experience of crystal healing was at a gorgeous treasure trove of a crystal shop near my home. The shop is truly magical. There are crystals everywhere and the atmosphere is so peaceful, so relaxed and for a shop it is quite awe inspiring. The power of the crystals asserts itself as soon as you enter, and in my opinion it stays with you once you have left. Lucky for the owner that she gets to work daily amongst these sparkling little wonders!

The treatment room upstairs was similarly decked out with hundreds of crystals, and the atmosphere of peace was inescapable. What made the room all the more special for me was the beautiful painting of a white Pegasus horse hanging on the wall. The last time I had been to the shop this painting had been hanging in the shop downstairs, but now I was face to face with it.

Bear in mind my guardian angel (Celebrielle) had come to me in my Spiritual Development classes as a winged white horse, and you will know why I was pleased by this beautiful coincidence. I asked the owner if she had two of the paintings, one upstairs and one downstairs, but she said no. She had intuitively felt that the painting had wanted to be moved upstairs and it was literally the day before that she'd hung it up in the treatment room. This for me was a coincidental affirmation that I was in the right place at the right time, and that my guardian angel would be carefully overseeing the process.

The treatment itself was extremely relaxing, as my eyes were closed it was hard to know what was going on, but I felt a variety of crystals placed upon and around me. The therapist seemed to be walking around the treatment bed, and I believe using a pendulum dowser to decide what areas needed treatment and for how long. About half way through I totally zoned out. It was like I dropped into a very deep meditative state, wherein I had some fantastic ideas relating to this book and my own future. Furthermore I had a deep consultation with myself about the term 'boundaries' and what that might mean. I chatted to myself for quite a long time, and enjoyed this internal dialogue immensely. Once the treatment was complete I remembered the entire conversation I had had with myself. What followed led me to believe that I was no doubt not the sole party in this conversation, and that the guides, spirits, angels and pixie folks were no doubt dropping their little ideas and thoughts into my head for me to mentally chew on during this relaxed state.

Afterward the therapist went through her perception of what happened. She stated that I had several chakras blocked off she used the crystals to realign them and to ensure my bodily energies were running smoothly.

I was most intrigued by her next comments. She said that I was being very specific with my energies and very focused, which is true. She also mentioned how I was keeping people at arm's length and that there were certain people I was blocking from my life. This chimed in extraordinarily well with my own deep thoughts about boundaries. In reality I have been rather exclusive of late, wishing only to spend time with certain people, and seriously avoiding others. It is nothing personal, it is just what I needed to do at that point in time. I guess I am so focused at the moment that spreading any of the Alice love around right now would be spreading me too thin. Due to this I am likely to be a little more aware of not becoming a total recluse and I may occasionally show myself to the world. Who would have thought a bunch of glorified rocks could be so very insightful!

After the session I felt quite 'out of this world' and very much like my head was in the clouds. I found myself drawn to my little garden where I gardened for two whole hours, a feat never seen before by the likes of my fairly well manicured hands! I was informed that the symptoms of a crystal healing could go on for days, much like the symptoms of Reiki. And indeed they did. I believe the crystals shifted some energy about and this worked its way through my system via a few mood swings and emotional outbursts. Indeed I believe I suffered a fairly significant healing crisis.

The crystal healing was Friday, on Saturday I was tired and generally suffering from a lack of energy, thankfully it was summer and the day was spent sunning myself in a friend's garden. I would like to say that on Saturday night the crystal healing made me more susceptible to alcohol (I would like to blame them for getting drunk), but in reality I think it is more honest to say that I simply drank too much on a near empty stomach. Sunday I suffered for Saturday, though the suffering did seem more prolonged than usual. Monday I was emotional and crazy. I became quite overcome by sad stories on the news. I also had a random fit of tears regarding my desire to live in America (bear in mind I had just come back from the good old US of A visiting relatives). Tuesday I felt foggy headed and miserable, symptoms I have not been subject to for a long while. I was also a little on the sensitive side, and rather negative too. It is now Tuesday night, and following three cups of Yorkshire Tea, one after the other, earlier this afternoon, I felt much improved. Yorkshire Tea cures all, spiritual fact.

My crystal healing experience, reminded me very much of a Reiki session but with more going on around me. The results were similar, as were the moods and emotions I experienced as a result. The therapist was good enough to warn me that I might feel the urge to cry or become upset, and that I should just go with it, which I did with gusto. The crystal healing did temporarily stall my positive thinking and replaced it with a more distressed state of mind. However I trusted that it was fleeting and that once the energies had worked their magic I would be left feeling stable, happier and more comfortably aligned to my own energies.

The only physical symptom I encountered was a very vague ache in my womb area. I have had some problems with late periods and various PMT symptoms, so I do hope that this ache may be related to fixing that! The ache did start the same day as the crystal healing and has died down significantly along with the other experiences; this makes me sure that some good has been done. A week following this strange dull ache I have actually noticed another intriguing and possibly related symptom, I have been fantastically horny. Perhaps the dull ache was actually removing some blockage I may have developed 'down under'. The therapist had mentioned that I was closed off in my lower region charkas. It seems Alice has been all work and no play! The crystals are clearly having none of that, and I had previously felt my sex drive had taken a dip over winter, and was still flagging come spring, however with the help of a few strate-gically placed rocks it seems my zsa zsa zuu has come out of hibernation and is purring along happily – Yee ha! Now that is a great tip and a wonderful side effect for bored couples or those who want a kinky boost! Sex and the City eat your heart out!

Crystal healing is particularly special, because unlike Reiki it can be used to direct energy at specific symptoms. Every single crystal has its own magical properties that treat a different symptom or problem and healings can be conjured up especially for an individual and their particular needs. You can choose to do this yourself with the help of a handy crystal directory, or you can go to an expert to do it for you. Crystal Therapy is closely regulated and accredited, any crystal healer should have been in training for quite some time and have certificates to attest to this. Crystal healing's intensive power as a holistic therapy is affirmed by this rigorous training and certification system.

Do it Yourself Crystals

Purchasing crystals for personal use is the cheap and easy way to harness the power of the rock in your daily life. Once you have purchased your perfect array of life improving crystals you must cleanse them and make sure any nasty vibes they have picked up on their way into your possession are thoroughly removed. Cleansing a crystal is a simple act, although this depends on time of the month and what accessories you have lying around your home. I am by no means suggesting that at certain times of the month you may be incapable, I will leave accusations of that sort to your gentlemen friends! However what I will say is that at certain times of the month, I am referring to the time of the full moon, your crystals can be left in moonlight over night to help empower and clear them of any dirty vibes.

Even simpler than any of the above is cleansing your crystals using dried sage. Sage is a fantastic purifying herb that can be used to clarify people, homes, emotions and all kinds of objects from jewelry through to tarot cards. Sage smudge sticks can be burned and the crystals should be wafted through their smoke. Be warned that the smell of burning smudge sticks is identical to the smell of marijuana (I am reliably informed) so perhaps best leave this till a time your parents are not due on a visit! I am sure it is hard enough explaining your general life choices to them without also trying to convince them you have not recently turned into a ganja-smoking pothead!

Using crystals is as easy as you want it to be. You can get some great books, or you can go with your intuition and grab the stone that calls to you. I have filled my house with Rose Quartz, this crystal promotes love and all things loving. I see no harm in chunks of it being anywhere and everywhere I can find a space. It is in my car, my bed, my handbags and a whole bowl full of it in my living room.

Other crystals I have collected over the years sit around and occasionally I pick one out and carry it with me that day. I am not a crystal freak who knows all the names and benefits of every last stone under the sun and beneath the earth. But I do know that having a lump of something in my pocket or handbag can be reassuring and helpful. I recommend you to go out and pick up a few and see how you go. Crystals can give you confidence, calm your nerves or lessen your headache. They are cheap, cheerful and charming. For spiritual bling, shimmer, shine and magical properties look no further!

Feng Shui

Feng Shui is healing for your home. By arranging your possessions and furniture to be aligned to the contours of the energies of your house you can access untold good fortune, happiness and wealth.

Feng Shui has been popularized, and to an extent bastardized by the popular press. You may have read an article which advises you to move things to certain positions or to ensure that your back window on the east side is left open with a yucca plant beneath it on the seventh night of the 3rd month at 2.18pm for ten minutes. Needless to say, much of what you read in the general media is so condensed and pulled out of all context that you may as well put a frozen turkey on the roof and be done with it!

Feng Shui is not a process that can be easily generalized. Good Feng Shui is mapped out according to you very specifically and uses your personal astrological details. So where you place your antique chest of drawers is very much dependent on what time, where, and when you were born!

More precious than your pin code, your astrological details are key to your soul in so many respects. Charted out correctly these details can help you in both your interior decorating and in achieving your life purpose through the correct placement of mirrors, crystals and wardrobes. Feng Shui is classic spiritual style multi-tasking; get a great looking house and a great life in one fell swoop!

I was charmed enough to induce a real life Feng Shui, Master, Mr Thomas Coxon to my home to furnish my precious abode with a Feng Shui consultation. Taking this step was somewhat daunting. I had no idea what this might involve. I had already given him my astrological particulars but would he want to snoop in my drawers? Would he find some embarrassing evidence of my slovenly ways behind the sofa, or something even more embarrassing under the bed? So to be sure to spare myself the blushes I had a good tidy up beforehand. I need not have bothered! All

Thomas did was wander round each room and check out positioning of major furniture. He then set to work.

It took hours. And in spite of this I am still none the wiser as to how to pronounce the said service – Fong Shway, Fong Shooey, Fingy Whatsit?

Thomas uses a combination of Chinese and Tibetan Feng Shui to come to his conclusions. The purpose is to harmonize the energy of rooms and the positioning of people and things within those rooms so that you can gain the very best influences possible. Although there is some commonsense value in not cluttering up your hallway with bicycles, boots and smelly socks if you want to welcome in the positive energies and create a 'harmonious' home, it is not just about getting the best from your hallway space. Feng Shui can be used to design buildings, in renovating older properties, for problem solving particular areas of your life, and improving business, profits and relationships. It is a bit of a cure all, a life enhancer, and if moving my kitchen table to a different angle means I'll get a pay rise and improve my lung function, then why the heck not? Sure, I'll have a go at that!

I was somewhat cynical as to what effect the Feng Shui would have. I am not so in awe of spiritual pursuits that I automatically believe them, and often I need to see the evidence for myself. So let us dive right in and see what Master Coxon conjured up for me.

Luckily the overall positioning of the house and the things around it were pretty good. This was a relief as had the house been facing south it could have meant the breakdown of my relationship with James. That would have been bad! This ominous potential break up was worked out in accordance with the prophecy of our individual birth charts in conjunction with the detail on the various Feng Shui charts, compass directions and energy flows. Indeed, we have a good few years in this house before any bad influences start to occur. Because there is a train line opposite the front door, this will mean that in around ten years time we might want to think about moving. The train line, because it rises upward, acts as an obstacle to the smooth continuation of our lives. Anything can be slowed down and affected by that. As I do not intend to be here in ten years time, I will not give that much consideration right away. Luck was apparently on our side and thankfully the things that needed changing were not so substantial as upping the foundations and moving.

Now here comes the most amazing bit. I am happy to declare that several years of battling my inner demons and apparent random PMT has now been resolved. I learned from Thomas that I had been sleeping in a 'conflict' zone – ouch! This meant my poor old head was stuck in a nasty place, receiving bad energy influences for eight hours a night, every night, for about three years. The first thing we did upon learning this was to move the bed to a more preferable position. Several months later I can say that I feel so much better. I had not actually realized I felt so rotten before. Since moving the bed I feel revitalized, positive and living with me is far easier on poor old James.

I do believe that moving the bed position has opened me up to an inner sunny disposition! I have more patience and am less likely to resort to any negative behavior or thought patterns. I can see now that the 'conflict' zone was making me irritable, impatient and critical. I had been moaning about bizarre mood swings for several years, though I had blamed these on my lady cycle. I now firmly believe that the blame lies squarely with the rubbish bed position.

It is actually freaky how much change has occurred. I can see so many areas of my life where I did feel conflicted, and this was often evidenced in erratic behavior. Now I am so much happier. I cannot explain it, but it has worked. What I thought was simply my negative internal mental processes have been completely transformed since I moved the bed. I certainly do not think that moving the bed has had a 'placebo' effect, especially because I was not truly aware of the extent of the conflict that was affecting me.

Nor would I ever have guessed that the cause of it was something as utterly random as the position of my bed! In retrospect, of course I can see what a grumpy arse I was then, and what a relative angel of light and happiness I am now!

What really is annoying though, is the fact I was never happy with that bed positioning. It never felt right, and yet for years I did not move it and kept sleeping in a place I was not happy with. Thomas explains that in Feng Shui we should go with our instinct. If your head and heart tell you to move a plant pot, just go ahead and do it. Do not sleep with the enemy as I had done for so many years.

My new bed positioning opens up positive energies toward family and friends. As a result of sleeping with family and friends, sorry, sleeping in the friends and family zone, I have seen my familial relationships change and transform for the better. The various changes are quite apparent to me. I am a lot more relaxed and so much happier.

I am in more contact with my various relatives and have rekindled a closer relationship with my Dad. As a teenager I was forever on the phone to him nattering away. As I got older that dwindled out to just the occasional phone call every so often. Since I have been sleeping in the new position we talk regularly, it's cool! Another wonderful plus is that I am getting a far better night's sleep. Actually that is a bit of a detriment as the sleep is so brilliant I am really struggling to wake up in the morning! James purchasing an industrial sized alarm clock has not even solved that one; although for some things there are no spiritual answers.

Thomas gave us lots of little tricks and hints as to where we should place various items to gain the greatest benefit for them. This included placing copies of my book in certain areas of the house, or James placing copies of his album in others. It does lend a kind of random higgledy piggldeyness to our decor, as I should place copies of my book on certain walls, under light switches or in windows. Now this is not always aesthetically pleasing, however I am sure I can find are ways to disguise CD's stuck to walls or pages of paper fluttering away midway between the living room and kitchen!

One thing I found particularly interesting was concerning James's music. Thomas informed me that every single thing in the house that related to music, would relate back to James's music career and have some effect on it. So in theory if we have a stack of CD's in an area that held negative energy, this would affect his music career negatively. As our house is chock a block with musical images, artwork, books on music, CDs and musical instruments, this is quite a challenging and potentially detrimental situation for James to be in. Happily however, this does not mean a massive internal redesign.

A little bit of amethyst stone goes a long way in terms of counteracting bad influences. The advice was to purchase a big bag of amethyst crystals and place the stones wherever a bad influence was occurring in a room. This helps to neutralize the energy so that it cannot have a bad influence on your life. This led to a bulk purchase of amethyst on eBay and hours of fun for my cats who both adore finding the little purple stones and knocking them across the room! I wonder if there is a Feng Shui to work on cats?

Feng Shui is a complicated and in-depth subject. Think about how much clutter you have in your home. Many of those items lying around forgotten about in drawers, or underneath the bed, are equally subject to a variety of influences. Photographs, for example, are a minefield. Even if they are tucked away in an album, underneath the spare blankets at the bottom of a barely used wardrobe, they could still be having a powerful effect on your life, possibly in a good, and possibly in a bad way. This depends on the area of the room they are stored in and how that section correlates with your personal birth chart.

Complicated stuff, and all the more reason why it is better to get a Master in. It is actually very hard to do a Feng Shui report justice without a major overhaul of cupboards, boxes, wardrobes, drawers, furniture, colors, rearrangement, and some considerable upheaval. Indeed Thomas advised me to do his suggestions one at a time spaced out over several months. Apparently making too many changes in one go can lead to chaos. Indeed the very thought of attempting to organize my wardrobe is the ultimate definition of chaos, so I totally know where he is coming from! There are still many small changes I need to make, and definitely several more amethyst stones to lie around the place well hidden from the cats! But all in all I would say Feng Shui is a little bit of a miracle.

As for the use of Feng Shui on your path to enlightenment, I say go for it. There are plenty of good books so that you can DIY yourself some solutions, or if you can afford it, and believe it is worthwhile then I would definitely recommend a visit for your local Master. For all those things that doctors, counselors, plasterers and painters cannot fix, Feng Shui has an intriguing answer. I know that moving my bed has had a profound effect on my wellbeing, and for that alone I am eternally grateful.

Feng Shui does not directly make you more spiritual, but within a holistic approach toward enlightenment it certainly helps. It creates a better environment for you to be spiritual from and irons out the unseen wrinkles in life that get you down and prevent you from achieving your full potential. Feng Shui is spring cleaning that reaches parts a duster just can't touch!

Yoga

Yoga is prevalent in Hindu and Buddhist culture, although now it is perhaps more famous for being a gym bound, DVD based, pseudo-spiritual, muscle defining activity. In popular culture, yoga is the slinky celebrities' best friend. Modern day myth states that Madonna practices yoga dawn till dusk and even the boy-toy television program Jackass featured a skit in it where Johnny Knoxville, surrounded by beautiful yoga toned women, loudly farted his way through a yoga session. Yoga is more than just a stretching class down the gym. When I talk to people about yoga they seem convinced it is little more than a great technique to get flexible and toned. Yet yoga is so much more than this.

The Ancient Yogis used yoga as a means to an end, and that end was not the acquisition of fantastic triceps, although of course that benefit is a valid side effect in these figure conscious times! Yoga evolved to enable Yogis to maintain strict control over their bodies and minds whilst bringing their earthbound physical human parts into better alignment with their spiritual beliefs and selves.

Yoga is the union of breath, body and mind. It was not devised as a 'keep fit' tool, nor was it ever supposed to be just about the body. Yoga is a physical, mental and spiritual exercise that on a basic level improves the Yogi's ability to sit and to meditate. By enabling this meditation the Yogi becomes closer to God. The fact she has a body to die for is little more than a pleasant side effect of great health and massive discipline!

We can probably all access a yoga class very easily and at a great price. If a gym did not do yoga then I would not join. Indeed I just left a gym because the yoga there was simply not good enough.

The sad fact is that enlightenment will rarely be discovered in the yoga room at your local health club. Especially not whilst the room next door pumps out loud music and the occasional whoops and hollers as the energetic body combat instructor whips her class into an adrenaline fuelled frenzy!

Knowing very little about yoga, except for the fact that I like it, I met up with the founder of Sun Power Yoga, Anne Marie Newland. Anne Marie is just too cool. Shame on anyone who says that us women cannot have it all, Ms Newland proves that we can – and some! The woman was at the very first Sex Pistols gig! She was already spectacular and we had not even started on the yoga yet! In this one lifetime she has already existed in several fascinating incarnations. Perhaps most strikingly she was a punk in the seventies, she hung around in the very middle of the punk scene, she was a fashion designer with a penchant for the psychedelic, she was a dancer, and at one point she was the drummer for Toyah Wilcox. Not bad going in one lifetime! Most of us only manage to carve out one persona, and even then sometimes that one persona is a little rocky! I am sure that Anne Marie is working on one persona per decade. In her current guise she is a Yoga Guru with her own brand of Yoga, Sun Power Yoga. Besides this she is a mother and is possibly one of the coolest, most charming and feistiest people I have had the pleasure of meeting on this journey.

Yoga means Union. I know I already alluded to that fact but this is something I have been told to stress to you by the lovely Anne Marie. If you learn nothing else about yoga whilst reading this section then do try to remember that one fact. Yoga does not mean body toning, it does not mean stress relief, and it does not mean relaxation. Many people turn up at yoga class seeking toned tummies and stretchy torsos. Some people may wish to relax, whilst a very few turn up looking for a spiritual opening into life. The fact is that yoga can give you all three if and when you are ready to accept them.

Anne Marie has created a mixture of the types of yoga that she has practiced, Astanga and Sivananda. To this potent concoction she had added her learning from being a professional ballet and jazz dancer, the result is Sun Power Yoga.

Anne Marie is a very spiritual person, and her advice and words of wisdom are impressive. She lives life laced up by yoga and spirituality, a combination that seemingly works well for her. She certainly does not preach the spiritual and life changing effects of a regular yoga practice to her students, but when one of them is ready to talk or discover more they often go to her. In this respect she practically embodies a modern day version of a waiting, patient Buddha!

I was intrigued to discover what a modern woman's take on yoga would be, and I was sufficiently impressed. I believe it is important that the world continues to update and improve upon our ancient relics. And although some believe that if it is not broke do not fix it, if we really lived by that theory then we would all be watching tiny portable black and white televisions whilst cooking our dinner over a fire in the back yard!

I was excited by the prospect of seeing this new, dynamic, female designed yoga in practice. Essentially yoga was designed for Yogis, Yogis were men, they were monks, they had very little to do with the ladies. I believe it is utterly apt and proper that somebody like Anne Marie shakes yoga into the 21st century gives it a touch of punk rock and modern dance and helps a new generation of women utilize its valuable properties of Union.

To this end I attended a Sun Power Yoga session taught by Anne Marie and I can say that two days on my body still feels the burn! Sun Power Yoga is fast, graceful, exciting and challenging. Sun Power combines traditional yogic breathing and mental focus with modern spurts of energy and dance like percussion as you move through a series of truly dynamic postures.

For me Sun Power Yoga was a fantastic way to bring spirituality out of my head and into my body. Yoga's modernization by Anne Marie has certainly done traditional versions justice. I am sure that in this respectful modernized format many more people will be drawn to yoga's benefits and potentially start their own personal journeys toward enlightenment.

Speaking of enlightenment, Anne Marie kindly gave me a cute little vest with her Sun Power logo emblazoned on it. Above the logo was the simple and glorious word 'Enlightenment'. A little mini testament me thinks to the fact that of all the yoga classes in all the world, I had to walk into Anne Marie's! Enlightenment indeed!

Yoga is a precious sport that truly helps balance out the mind, body and soul. It is so easy to neglect the body when a person starts upon a spiritual path. The body suddenly seems irrelevant as you come to discovering a greater truth about yourself, the universe and enlightenment. However as soon as you let your body go you will be yanked away from your spiritual path to deal with the more earthly phenomena of bad health, colds, flu, migraines, weight gain, athlete's foot, tummy troubles, hangovers and sprained ankles.

No matter how spiritual you are, you are just as liable to suffer illness and injury as all the other mortal creatures surrounding you. This can be a shock to the system, particularly when one's head is literally in the clouds, dancing with spirit or concentrating on angelic pursuits. Rather than being stumped and shocked by a surprise return to your physical self, you should embrace your physical self as part and parcel of your spiritual whole. Your body is a wonderful spiritual gift, and if you wish to do anything, including seeking enlightenment then you need to treat your body well for it's the vehicle through which you must work.

I know that I let my health and fitness slip to write this book. My mind kept saying that there were far more important things to worry about than whether or not I got to the gym. Which is partially true, people are living lives of misery famine and torture. However, my path is not to be miserable or tortured or live in a war zone. For what I am doing with my life I need to keep a reasonable degree of health, otherwise I am no good to anyone, spiritually or otherwise. Sadly this advice from myself has come a little too late, here, at the end of my journey I have found I have lost my fitness, put on a couple of pounds round the old waist and generally have less energy. As a result I now have that to worry about that whilst I get my body into better physical health. You, however, have been warned – lucky you!

A Yogi would not allow this level of detriment to occur to their physical selves because they know that to be in peak spiritual condition they need to feed themselves well and ensure the body is active and capable.

On a spiritual path to enlightenment it is important not to get too lost within your own mind. It is lovely to know that there is more to life than your existence as a human, but whilst you still are a human there are certain things you should be doing to make your stay in your body a better, happier and more productive one. Keeping your body in check is one of these, that includes the very obvious eating healthy and getting enough exercise.

By bringing yoga into this you are creating a better bridge between the spiritual self you are discovering and the physical body you have always known. I tend to start each yoga class off by mentally dedicating the session to my spiritual journey, and using the session as a thank you to my guides and angels. In doing this I work a bit harder and am constantly reminded that I am not just there seeking great abs, but that there is a greater purpose to my attendance. As a result I often leave a very active session feeling as though I have had a wonderful sleep and awoken feeling energized, peaceful and ready to take on the world.

Yoga is an all-round work out that touches upon every part of your multi-faceted being. It can teach you a great deal about yourself, and the focus on breath and meditation helps to induce an immense state of fabulousness.

Yoga is the ultimate personal training buddy for the glamorous and high-heeled enlightenment seeker.

Shamanic Reiki

As I feel I owe my now well-balanced mind to Reiki, how could I turn down the opportunity to undergo some distance Shamanic Reiki? As a Reiki practitioner I know it is quite feasible to send Reiki over great distances to reach whomever you desire. Having written a chapter about Shamanism, I am also well aware of Shamanic healing traditions and Shamanism in general. Both subjects fascinate me equally and so seeing how the two work together is doubly intriguing. When Llyn Roberts, co-author of *Shamanic Reiki* contacted me to offer a long distance healing session how could I possibly turn such a fantastic opportunity down!

Llyn is based in the northwest USA, whereas I am in the UK. Although this makes things a little slower and slightly more complicated on the practical end of things (overseas phone calls) I found that with the help of a handy phone card, there was no hardship whatsoever. In the first instance I was required to send Llyn some items so that she could connect with my energy. This made her job easier as she would be able to read me from the items, as well as send healing forces using them as a conduit. These included a photograph of me, some hair strands, an item of clothing and a sample of my handwriting. Had Llyn been a man I had met on the internet this request would have been quite frightening. But as I was to learn Llyn was far from frightening, indeed she is probably the nicest person I have ever had the pleasure of speaking with over the phone!

The first phone call...

I did not really expect to have a phone call with someone and build much of a rapport in a ten-minute slot. However Llyn has such a soothing way about her, and such a kindly voice that I did feel we established a rapport, possibly even a bond after our first short call. The call was for the purpose of setting up a spiritual link and a communication channel between us going beyond the words that were spoken. The first few minutes were spent in silence; this was followed by a chat about me and what I was hoping for and needing within my life. Llyn made a very strange situation easy for me, she was sweet, caring and encouraging. She also made me feel like she really understood where I was coming from and what I desired from life. I finished the phone call happy that I had spoken with her.

Now from the phone call till the time of the Shamanic Reiki conclusion lies a period of two weeks. In this time Llyn works her magic. This magic, involved Reiki energy being beamed toward me through the objects I had sent. Unlike normal Reiki, Llyn engaged her spirit guides as she focused on the objects; she then waited to see what emerged into her mind, feelings or through other bodily sensations. Such things could be very relevant, for example, had I been suffering premenstrual tension or cramps, she may have picked up on this. If I was depressed, paranoid or feeling particularly happy she may have sensed or seen these mental states within her own mind. She would possibly have known their root cause and what would be helpful spiritually and practically to assist. Llyn uses other Shamanic based tools such as animal cards to help discover an animal ally which represents the qualities and energies I may be in need of.

Another quite unusual bit of magic Llyn would perform is an absentee Shamanic Reiki journey. This involves Llyn journeying into imaginary realms in her mind to envisage me, and the things surrounding me. Anything that occurs in such a journey is often deeply symbolic and sent from the spirit realm to help bring about healing, balance and insight in the client's life. Because this is Shamanism it is likely that there would have been drumming, rattles, chanting, candles, sacred plants and other shamanic or symbolic items laying around to help Llyn to focus her healing intentions.

Shamanic Reiki, unlike normal Reiki expects an active participant. I too was expected to do several things to help the magic to help me Some of my tasks were fairly straightforward and involved thinking about my life and how I would ideally like it to be; easy as I do that all the time anyway! Although the harder part was that I was to imagine as if that life were already true for me now. Alongside this I must also pay attention to my dreams, notice unusual or special occurrences and coincidences, spend time contemplating and inviting the power and support of the four elements, earth, air, fire and water.

As a Reiki practitioner myself, this whole process was intriguing. I always did believe that Reiki, as a source of energy, is the same source that mystics, Shamans and healers around the world tap into. So it was fascinating to see the shamanic embellishments that render Shamanic Reiki so different from plain old vanilla style Reiki!

The two-week wait...

So what did I hope to gain from Shamanic Reiki? I felt I was reaching a culmination in that part of my spiritual journey, and whilst I was happy about that, I was also going through a phase that can be described as, 'so now I am spiritual, what happens next?' Into this equation comes the fact that I have changed significantly over the past year, as have my relationships, and how I like to pass my time. Due to my newfound self I was struggling to include parts of my old ways into my new life.

I hoped that the Shamanic Reiki would help me judge these situations wisely, manage them well, whilst also attracting new friends and opportunities. So in one very large mouthful that is what I thought about for the two-week period. In essence I hoped to polish off my rough edges and embrace my newfound spiritual persona more deeply and with as little fuss and bother as possible.

Right from the very start of the Shamanic Reiki process I started to have intense and vivid dreams. In these dreams I was talking with elders and guides to discuss my future and what steps I should be taking next. I do not remember the detail, but I know they were significant meetings, and I am sure the knowledge was being retained in my subconscious ready to float to the surface as and when required. I believe that the Shamanic Reiki came along at precisely the right time in my spiritual path. I felt it was here to sign, seal and deliver my spiritual life in a neat little package. I believed that Shamanic Reiki was perhaps my final step to the newly Enlightened Alice!

As the two weeks went on I began to be assaulted by crappy situations, other people's moods and a general influx of bad times. Things from years prior were bubbling up at work, my physical body felt utterly drained and my mind was going into meltdown. It felt as though I had reached a peak with this book, and with my own spirituality, and now I was rapidly descending downward back to harsh, cruel reality. Toward the end of the two-week period I felt a desperate need for renewal. I really truly wanted to be a better person, and to treat myself better. This showed itself in a huge obsession with going swimming and the purchasing of the GI Diet handbook. I wanted to clear all the crap from my body and start afresh, new spirit, new body, and new healthy insides! I felt a bit like a bear with a sore head emerging from hibernation. I had spent months at home in my jogging bottoms and with hair roots that would make a drunken Courtney Love look well groomed! I had been living and sleeping the search for enlightenment, and now I felt I needed to get back to humanism, to me and to bring my spiritual side fully into my day-to-day life.

This coincided with the writing of this book coming to an end, and it felt like I had precious little to do to achieve that goal, and yet I was prevaricating. I kept telling friends that I only had a few hours work to do, but then I would spend those few hours plucking my eyebrows or reading something trashy! In my need to feel human again my mind was in teenage rebellion mode, instead of just getting the work done and enjoying myself later, I became moody, withdrawn and happy to sit in my room watching MTV.

Things were become highly sensitive. My body reacted badly whenever I ate one of the numerous takeaways I was gorging on. Not only would my stomach try to reject pizza, my moods vividly reflected whatever I had eaten. If I had been good and snacked on apples and had a healthy salad for lunch, I was relaxed and pleasant. If chocolate slipped its way into my daily menu, as it so often does, I would grow irritable, stressed and frustrated. Not because I was worried about the calories, or my lack of exercise, but because my body was craving substantial, healthy foods, and I was giving it naught but white flour and sugar. Alcohol too became an instant no no. Even a few sips of a glass of wine seemed to bring out my alter ego 'grumpy Al'. The troubles I endured at work were dragging me down far more than ever before, to the point that I was seriously questioning my ability to perform my job, and my ability to cope with everyday work related stress.

The final phone call...

Something had to give, and eventually it did. Ten minutes after my final hour long phone call to Llyn I grabbed my bikini and headed off to the local pool for the longed for aquatic exercise. The final phone call confirmed to me much of what had been going on in my life during the two weeks. It is apparent that my life and I are totally changing. Llyn reliably informed me that when things change, other things begin to 'rub' or intensify in order to help you more clearly see and move toward your higher goals in life. Bad food rubs against the stomach and makes us angry, unhealthy or grumpy after a sugar high. Lack of exercise does an injustice to the body that carries you and to which you call home, whilst unhealthy mental and emotional habits based in outworn ideas of who you think you are cause stress for friends, family and yourself alike. Well the rubbing was well into the blistering stage for me, and in fact I reckon some of those blisters had begun to burst.

One of the first things Llyn told me was that she had seen me in her mind, clear as a picture, saying 'I need change'. I can now see that the change I needed was being catalyzed by this series of stressful events. My need to change jobs and my way of working was forcing crappy situations and challenges into my everyday working life, forcing me to try to think of a way out, or at least to consider a way to make the working day more pleasant. I had to admit that my need to enjoy a different type of social life left me feeling guilty that I was letting friends down, or not meeting their expectations of who they think I am. I was unsure of who I was myself! My growing desire to eat healthily and be healthy was making me miserable whenever I was unhealthy, and I was being unhealthy often. What I needed was change, and what I did not need was the reluctance to make that change, or the natural fear that goes with it. The only thing preventing the change I desperately desired from occurring was little old me. It was like I had an angel on one shoulder and Satan on the other, all it took was for me shrug Satan off and allow change to occur, yet I had kept him tucked close to me like a comfort blanket.

Llyn shared with me the Shamanic Reiki journey she had taken on my behalf. It was a lovely tale that involved me soaring high on an eagle's back and immersing myself in creative, cleansing light energy. She saw me eventually leave the eagle thoroughly cleansed and come down to earth where I met a bear. The strange coincidence here is that only that day I had been looking for my favorite childhood bear, Teddy Eddy. The bear in the Shamanic Reiki journey represented earthly energies and Llyn saw me and the bear enjoying human, earthbound pursuits. I understood that my mission is to bring the creative forces of the eagle down to earth to share with my human pals via the qualities of a bear – eating, sleeping, having fun and being firmly rooted in life. The bear and the eagle have become my personal 'medicines', and it is their qualities that I need to embrace to help me in my life right now.

Since learning this information I see bears everywhere I go. Bears on lorries, bears in the clouds, bears on television. I reckon I am most certainly in the bear stage right now, hence my preoccupation with human concerns, work, clothes, food, body etc. I am sure that the eagle is still around. For the two-week period of the Shamanic Reiki healing I had been enthralled to be noticing birds all over the place. I was constantly seeing them and watching them go about their birdie business. I forget, also, that I have the tattoo of a Native American symbolic bird just above my right buttock!

Whilst telling me about the journey, Llyn told me that an eagle had just soared past her window. Lucky her, I thought. I would be lucky to see a sparrow flitting over the train tracks from my window! But that aside, it was for us both, a fitting coincidence.

Frankly, it just all makes sense to me. I can see how I have been lifted by that lovely eagle and fed all this information that I have carried back to earth and placed within this book. The fact that Llyn saw me being showered in creative light is no surprise whatsoever. I do feel that this book has been gifted to me so that I may gift it to you. I cannot take full credit for the contents because I am sure the angels, spirits and now apparently the eagle have helped form every single sentence. I am along for the journey, just as much as anybody else who picks this up, reads it or passes it onto a friend. The eagle helped me get there and the bear will help me adapt to the changes that this brings to my everyday life.

The journey Llyn recounted to me had many other elements, they all matched up perfectly with where I see myself today. Even down to the desire to be healthy and treat myself better. I feel now that thanks to Shamanic Reiki the biggest blister has now burst and is well on its way to full healing. I am ready to bring myself back to the world and come out of my self-imposed, jogging bottom wearing isolation. I am feeling that I can be released from that phase of my life whilst comfortably keeping a firm grip and strong connection to my spiritual side. My spiritual journey has led me back to the original me, and this end bit simply involves sloughing off the last of the outdated bad habits.

There is one more thing that occurred which I feel I need to share with you. I had two quite stunning natural events occur, one at the very start of the Shamanic Reiki and one at the very end. On the very first day of the healing I was feeling quite grumpy and tired, I was foggy headed and feeling sorry for myself. I went out to put clothes on the washing line and as I looked up I saw that the sky all around and above me was filled with white fluffy bits. I am not sure what they were exactly, but they were certainly from some kind of a plant. It looked truly amazing, there were literally thousands of them and they shone like fluffy stars against the bright blue sky. This cheered me up immensely and I ran inside to bring James out to see for himself. By the time he came out, less than a minute later, there was not a single one left in the sky. It was not a windy day, and they had merely been floating gently, and yet in less than a minute, a sky full of fluff had vanished. I think that that was a little pick me up present for me from Mother Nature herself!

The second event occurred at the very completion of the Shamanic Reiki. Llyn sent me some on the things back that I had sent to her. My task was to organize a little ritual and to burn them whilst ushering in protection, guidance and giving thanks to the elements and spirits. After I did this I decided to take the washing in. I took the clean washing up to my room and started to sort through it. It was then that I saw the light coming through the window and moving and shimmering against my bedroom wall. I looked out the window, over the noise of the road and above the adjacent train track and there I saw the most beautiful sunset. The clouds had arranged themselves so that it looked like there was a bright sunny beach in the sky. The sun turned some of the clouds yellow like sand whilst others rippled and waved like the waves of the sea. I have lived here for four years and I have not seen a thing like that from my window before. Both events were spectacular and helped begin and end what was an equally spectacular Shamanic Reiki healing. How interesting that the Shamanic Reiki started with the washing being hung out to dry, and the events were closed by me bringing it back in!

Shamanic Reiki has given me a deeper insight into the workings of the daily grind. It has allowed me to see that bad days and worries are actually opportunities as they can push us to see what we are not addressing in ourselves. I now understand more fully how personal change can throw up all kinds of good and bad things for us to deal with so that we can move on and grow. My problem was that I needed to do a little bit of tweaking on myself in order to integrate all that I had learned and experienced into my daily life, but I was unsure how to do that in case I went a bit too far and messed everything up. I was afraid to alienate friends, to step out of my comfort zone, to jeopardize my job and to put this book out into the real world for criticism, review and comment. But now I figure what the heck, I have an Eagle and a Bear backing me up; I can do whatever the hell I like!

Today I went and got my hair done to erase those unsightly mousey brown roots and to help embrace my earthly bear like qualities – Roar. While I was having my haircut I conjured up new plans for the next intriguing phase of my life. If I am going to be a conduit for spiritual creativity and healing then I want to get started on that right now. Bring it on! For once the ideas were not conjured up whilst meditating or thinking seriously about spirit. It was aided and abetted by Gaynor my lovely hairdressing friend as she applied the bleach and as her two-year-old girl sat on my lap eating cookies.

Shamanic Reiki has shone a very bright beam of light into what was becoming a slightly tumultuous and stressful existence. It has revealed that spiritual meaning can turn up in a swimming pool, at the hairdressers or whilst filing your nails. It has helped me get ready for a plunge back into living life rather than writing about it! It has geared me up, wound my key and shown me the way forward. It has told me to 'just get on with it' and shown me how. It has given me the final spiritual tools I need to take into the human world of bread, butter and fancy oversize handbags.

Ladies, the Eagle has landed and the Bear is ready to rock!

Healing Conclusion

Personal healing may come simply from having some faith. Faith in itself is sometimes sufficient to lift us up to a better, healthier life. Faith can cure many of our hearts ills and can guide us back to the path of life that we need to be on. If you feel you need to reach beyond faith and have some more specific healing then the examples I have given are ones I have found to be useful. As you have seen each of these healing techniques has played a vital role in my high-heeled path to enlightenment. We all have past hurts, scars and issues that could do with disappearing, either for the sake of spirituality or for simple self-improvement and self-esteem. Once we have dealt with what harms us we are free to move on with life and go in whatever direction takes our fancy.

What I aimed to do within this healing section is not to tell you which healing to go for, or which ones work best, but hopefully to demonstrate to you how alternative healing therapies can help turn your life around, physically, mentally, emotionally and most important spiritually. To heal is to embrace happiness and if nothing else comes of it for you then you could not really ask for anything more.

If your life is not in need of being turned around, then I hope you will see how things such as crystals can be used as accessories to help with the day-to-day strife that we all encounter. There are many more alternative healing techniques available, perhaps you will find something entirely different that is perfect for you. There is a massive world of healing to choose from including all manner of exciting techniques, be these ingesting herbs, getting your feet manipulated or having needles stuck in your back. I am certain that if a particular technique calls to you then you should follow your intuition and it will have the desired benefit.

On your path to enlightenment, healing is a spiritual perk that may just get you to your destination that little bit quicker, and with a jaunty spring in your high-heeled step.

High Heeled Divination

If you are not sure what Divination is then I guess it can be described as a form of good old-fashioned fortune telling. Fortunately the stereotypes of 'fortune tellers' and old Romany Gypsies gazing into balls, reading tealeaves or predicting your imminent demise via the tarot are not what I refer to. Modern day, realistic divination techniques are not so intriguing or so blasé as that. Divination, to my mind, is a way of using a variety of different tools to reflect back to you your current situation and what may be likely to occur in the near future.

For the modern day female, divination techniques can be viewed as a complementary therapy. Like an aromatherapy massage is seen as a holistic (hippyfied) version of physiotherapy massage, tarot might be seen as a hippyfied version of counseling or life coaching.

Divination techniques are ones you can harness at home to help get a better perspective on your life. They are perfect for self-guidance, to help assist difficult decision making or to bond over with your girlfriends. In these following sections I want to introduce you to some extremely old techniques that are trans-ferable to your life. Not only can all of these be tremendously useful, but by practice and active engagement you can make progress with your own high-heeled path to enlightenment.

As you become more familiar with each tool, your eyes will be opened to how amazing the planet can be. Divination can help you to contact that great mystical divine and in the process learn a little something about yourself.

Tarot will have you wondering how a pack of cards with pretty pictures can be so insightful into your work dramas, whilst astrology may take your breath away as it seems to recognize the complex mix of strife and happy times you have been through recently. Palm reading has its quirks and curiosities that will astound and intrigue.

All these tools when used for a glimpse into the future, or for guidance, might very well have a significant effect on you. This may be enough to push you further forward on your spiritual journey, or at the very least to keep you entertained for an evening of informative frolics.

I know that in my life such tools have done just that. I can vouch for the fact that they have certainly enhanced my own development and understanding of enlightenment. Whether you pick up the cards for a bit of fun, or choose to wave a pendulum over your friend's pregnant belly, be aware that these are powerful spiritual tools, and be prepared for amazing, fascinating and insight filled good times.

High Heeled Tarot

I have been practicing reading tarot cards since I was fourteen and was taught the art by my dad and stepmother. Tarot is an ancient art of divination or fortune telling that can be used to help guide you through any situation in your life. To me tarot is less fortune telling and more about opening your eyes and allowing you to see a current situation from a fresh perspective. It can be a great counseling tool for use with friends and loved ones, helping them to make the right decisions for them, or showing them a better direction by which to achieve goals and improve relationships.

Some people see tarot as being associated with the dark pagan arts, or even as a means of invoking black magic. This is entirely the fault of its negative portrayal in film and media, and in reality is an utter nonsense. For me the tarot has always been a steadfast and reliable friend. In my experience tarot does not foretell death or other ominous omens; rather, the cards work in a constructive way to help you better your own life.

Some people believe that tarot is a means of communing with the dead. Some clairvoyants may very well employ tarot cards to assist their readings, however that is more of an embellishment and it is likely that any medium would have the ability to contact deceased loved ones with or without the aid of tarot cards.

Tarot may very well help sharpen psychic abilities; i.e. if you are quite intuitive, then tarot can heighten that experience. Some people pick up mental images or thoughts whilst using tarot that relate to the person they are reading for. It is my belief that tarot helps to open channels that are otherwise closed. It may also be that tarot cards act to attune you to other people's worries and anxieties.

Clearly there are many theories that could explain how tarot cards actually work. Kabbalists might believe your divine self is guiding you; Spiritualists may see it as your personal guide or angel, whereas Shamans would believe that the Great Spirit played some part. Whatever the cause, the effect is the same, and it's often remarkable! All it takes is an open mind and a willingness to employ some intuition, gut feeling and common sense.

Tarot cards for me are like an infinitely sensible best friend. Imagine you are stuck, you do not know whether to go left, right, or straight ahead. The tarot can help you make that (metaphorical) decision. They will take into account what is best for all involved and tell you how to make the best of the upcoming future. They are always objective and they always tells it like it is. Tarot cards are a caring and honest agony aunt who just happens to be able to second-guess your next move and lets you know whether or not she approves!

Tarot cards never lie and they never exaggerate. If you are doing silly things the tarot is not afraid to tell you, as well as giving you an oversight of the possible consequences. Tarot can look at your relationships and let you know what can be improved and how, they can tell you what kind of day you have had, and how this may affect you tomorrow. What they cannot do is inform you that on the 14th March 2012 you will be visited by three dark suited men, one of whom will be your future husband and that after a brief liaison you will be happily married with three children, two dogs and a holiday home in Marbella. A psychic may possibly be able to tell you that, and may use the card as a basis for their visions, but in my experience the tarot cards are never that specific when used alone.

Getting Started

My first pack of tarot cards is what I fondly see now as my 'baby pack'. Despite this I still use them and treat them with as much respect as any of my other more sophisticated and bling! tarot cards. These cards were the Astrotarot cards by Russell Grant. They are bright and colorful with fantastic little cartoon style pictures. I would recommend them to any beginner. They contain the major arcana (the main tarot cards Wheel of Fortune,

Empress, Magician, Death etc), alongside western (Libra, Aries etc) and Chinese astrological signs (Dragon, Rat, Dog etc). As you are likely to be familiar with the meanings of the astrological signs then a pack like this is a fabulous place to start. Alternatively you may fancy something that is a bit more 'you', and there are thousands of packs available to choose from. These range from more traditional cards to crazy modern variations. Images can be powerful, colorful or plain old fun.

To choose a pack you must make the decision in accordance with your gut instinct. My second pack was bought for me, and although some people recommend being bought cards, I would not. Although it was a lovely gesture, it is important to be able to relate to the cards and feel an affinity with the images. The pack that was bought for me was never easy for me to use. The damn things were too big for my hands, so when using them I would get paper cuts, and the images were far less complex than I required. The imagery of the cards is very important for getting a sense of their message. There are so many options and just like a good lipstick you must find one that's perfectly suited to you. Amazon, eBay and specialist spiritual shops are your best bets to find your special pack. Always try to get a brand new pack so nobody else's vibes have affected them.

Once you have a tarot pack you must treat them like a beloved possession. I am not the best at this, but I like to think my cards know me well enough to forgive me. Some people are quite religious in how they treat their cards, keeping them wrapped in silk and carefully stored away. Silk is supposed to keep negative energies away from them, although I think that is just scaremongering. I have never wrapped mine in silk and I certainly do not think this has affected their usability. One rule of tarot that I do try to follow is not to let other people play with your pack. Unless you are reading for someone, then I would not let people touch them or even have a quick flick through at the images. Also keep them away from children, who in my experience are quick to scatter, tear and drool on them at will. I believe the cards need to attune to their owner, so keep them close to you and do not let people fiddle with them!

Whenever I get a new pack I carry them round with me for a week or so, taking them everywhere I go in a bag. Once my tarot babies and I have bonded I tend to keep them in a part of the house that is definitively my space, so a personal desk, handbag or your underwear drawer would all fit the bill. And if you want to wrap them in silk then go for it. If Paris Hilton can accessorize her pooches I cannot see the harm in prettying up your pack!

It is important to remember that the cards all have a general meaning, but as you get more experienced this will twist and turn and change with each reading. I do not know how this happens but it just does. Do not worry, you will find it comes quite naturally and it is often more reliable to go with your instinct about these things. It is possible to have the exact same layout of cards for two different people, and for it to be interpreted very differently for each. This is less than obvious and is definitely an acquired skill, with plenty of practice you are sure to develop this over time.

I find the best way to practice at the very start is by giving yourself readings, using the book or pamphlet that comes with the cards. Getting yourself a decent tarot reference book also helps. *The Tarot Bible* by Sarah Bartlett is useful reading for any beginner and a great reference for any experienced tarot reader. Within this book you will find a fuller guide and dozens of excellent spreads and layouts to get you started. You could start by pulling out one card a day, look up the meaning and then allow yourself to ponder that all day. By doing this you soon get a good grasp of the basic meaning for all 78 cards, how they relate to situations and most importantly what the card means to you.

You could memorize the meaning of every single card if you were that way inclined, but that does not necessarily mean you will be any good at tarot reading. What you need to do next is just let loose on a few willing volunteers and see what happens. I often feel when I first lay cards down that I do not know what they mean or how they relate to each other. I have a momentary panic where I worry that the cards make no sense. This soon passes and once I get going the reading seems to flow naturally from my lips, without any significant effort.

In many respects I think the key is to lay your cards on the table, open your mouth and seeing where your intuition takes you. This can be daunting, but you may be surprised. It is like opening a channel to some crazy cool powers and letting a higher intelligence speak through you. Whether this is your own subconscious intelligence, or something a bit more mysterious is up for debate, perhaps it is collusion between the two? Either way your new diplomatic, eloquent and insightful self will impress you.

I often find that once a reading is completed I totally forget what I have said to that person. I go on autopilot; say what needs saying and then it drops out of my head. This is actually rather convenient as I have enough mental clutter of my own without adding that of all my friends!

Don't pressure yourself to be amazing straight away. If you can't get to grips with the tarot then get an expert in who can. Tarot readers are well worth employing for your girly parties and often leave you with plenty of conversational material for the evening after the reader leaves! Of course make sure that you find a trusted reader, word of mouth is usually best for this. Above all remember that tarot is a lot of fun and is a great enhancer to a girly evening, or a fabulous guide for a friend in need.

Reading for friends

Yes, you know that Kelly got dumped last week and Dawn is suffering a bout of terrible wind and bloating, yet in spite of your insider knowledge it is still possible to give a valid reading that may surprise you with its perspective on the situation. When reading for friends I would be as open, honest and direct as possible. Feel free to relate things to what you already know about them, but make sure you say you are doing that. Let them know you think a particular card represents their new job, pay rise or the fact they are trying to get pregnant.

Tarot is a two way process and it is great if the person who is being read for gets involved occasionally, not to prompt you, but to offer their own insight.

I have found that, particularly with friends, tarot cards can act as a real counseling aid when a friend is in troubled times. If you know and trust one another, the tarot can be like an objective third party chipping in with an opinion, perhaps one that's different from your own and to hers. Always be ready to be astonished, and never expect that the tarot will say what you want or expect it to.

For example, you are reading Becky's cards and you don't like Becky's new boyfriend. They are already on the verge of splitting up and Becky is miserable. You may hope or expect the cards to advise that they break up and move on. It makes sense to you and Becky is definitely edging that way. So you dip into the cards for affirmation of what you think you already know! It is in instances like this that you might be very surprised. The cards may read differently, to the point where you question them and believe they may be wrong. But that is the charm of tarot; it never follows what you expect, much like life! The cards might say that Becky is suffering some stress at the moment but that it will make her stronger and in turn make her relationship stronger. It may be that this horrible stale patch in her relationship is a make or break, and just when all looks lost something will happen that pushes Becky and her boyfriend back together.

Don't be afraid to act on news that you could never have foreseen. It may be that Becky's beggar of a boyfriend turns a new leaf and the pair of them live happily ever after. You may even grow to like him. Even if that is not what you want or what Becky expects to hear!

When reading cards for friends you must also be careful not to manipulate or change the information you are getting. You may think you know what is best for someone, but you could be very wrong. Just go with what it says and use it as a bonding tool to get to know each other better. The cards are a magnificent addition to your friendships, and taken in a positive light-hearted manner they can render up some amazing results without anybody getting hurt, scared or manipulated.

Warning: Treated with too much reverence or taken too literally the cards can be dangerous. Once upon a time a good friend of mine had the Death card arise in her reading. My protestations that this did not mean actual death fell on deaf ears. She happened to be in a bad place and was probably borderline depressed. Years later she told me that she spent a good few months after that reading absolutely terrified she was going to die. Needless to say it is now ten years later, she is alive and kicking and just gave birth to a beautiful baby girl. She is utterly loved up, happy and living the good life in Australia. This showed me that you must be careful who you read for and how you read for them. Inevitably it is not the tarot that is dangerous but the way it is read and how it is understood. Ensure that you are fully acquainted with the cards and confident in your interpretations before reading for others. Cards such as death or the devil, have many connotations that are actually very positive. If you believe a friend is vulnerable, or likely to take the tarot negatively then do not read for her, wait till she is in a better place and less likely to take anything too literally.

Reading for yourself

This is something I find almost impossible to do. I hate to read for myself because I simply change the meaning of the cards to suit whatever I want to know at the time. If I asked 'Does he fancy me' and then I get a card that says 'hell no' I would find some way in my crazy little head to say, 'oh Lordy yes he is quite enamored, he thinks of you constantly and will no doubt woo you very shortly'. As a result of my wayward imagination I now only read my own cards when I have my reliable *Tarot Bible* to hand. By doing this I can look up the specific meaning of every card.

When reading for others the meaning of cards can be fluid and influenced by the cards around them, but when it is just for me I have to be strict to ensure I do not fantasize up a large lottery win or long vacation to the moon!

As I have got more experienced I have got slightly better at implementing a little objectivity. But if the cards do not read as I want them to I tend to get frustrated and that is when Little Miss Imagination enters. This is particularly true if I am asking about a subject I am emotionally attached to, involved with or stressed about.

To avoid your own overactive mind ruining a reading I would always recommend keeping a good guide to hand. This is also an excellent way to learn the meaning of the cards for beginners. Do yourself a weekly spread and with the help of a good book you will quickly begin to learn the meaning of the cards and how to interpret patterns.

Who Not to read for

I am not being self righteous and snooty by telling you who not to read for. I have committed most of the following tarot sins myself many a time since I laid hands on my first pack a very long time ago. I know how easy it is to get carried away with the power and intrigue a tarot pack can wield. However, if I advise not to do it, it is for a very good reason and because of hard earned experience!

I find it difficult to read for my other half, it is too close to home and he does not like it either so it all gets a bit awkward and weird. If you do wish to read for a partner, then I suggest you do a generic reading that incorporates both of you. Alternatively, keep it very specific regarding work, career, holidays, and potential new car. You may even wish to do a relationship spread, which can be very revealing and get you both talking about areas that may otherwise have been neglected. It is often surprising how tarot can bring unspoken problems to the surface and help you to resolve a variety of niggling issues.

If a partner does not want to be roped into a reading then let them be. Many folk (particularly men folk) are not always as amenable to tarot as us enlightened gals, and nobody should ever be forced into a reading no matter how much they love you!!

I would also advise you not to read for any potential sweetheart, crush or new lover. Things can get messy and your heart may very well overrule your head. It might be that you use the cards to get what you want rather than to offer up an objective genuine reading. I am not accusing you of being an arch manipulator, but it is dangerous ground. If the object of your fantasies likes you enough, things are bound to progress without an innuendo laden Celtic Cross spread. Repeat after me 'tarot cards are not sex aids'.

People who are going through a major life upheaval, or who are not mentally well, are not people you should be reading for. By mentally well, I mean those who are depressed or dependent on drugs/alcohol, suffering an eating disorder or any other disorder that means that they might be a bit manic, vulnerable, negative or prone to gloominess. Only read for people who you know to be stable and mentally resilient. I would not advise that you read for friends who are grieving a death, they may expect more than you can give them, and it may not be the ideal time for them to be consulting the cards. Remember the cards are not a party trick so do not read whilst you or others are under the influence. I speak from personal experience; you need your head firmly screwed on to do a decent job!

One or two glasses of wine to be sociable are quite acceptable. And you can have as many as you like after you have finished a reading, but try interpreting anything after a bottle of white and a couple of shots and you are a better woman than me if you make any sense! With the cards comes responsibility, if drinking and driving is a criminal offence, I reckon drinking and fortune telling should be outlawed too. Don't get me wrong, I am no angel and I have 'drink read' many a time before. We all know that alcohol makes you believe you are funnier, cleverer, and classier when downing that fourth double vodka. The truth is you may be slurring, glassy eyed and giving someone terrible advice. When drunk put the cards down and back away slowly.

The cards tend to have a life of their own regarding when they want to make sense, and they can have a tendency to 'act up'. They can be tricky beggars and if you use them unwisely, misuse them, or you ask them a silly question, they will happily give you a stupid answer back. For colorful pieces of cardboard they are quite adept at making their displeasure well known!

So ladies, if you are out on the tiles, on the pull, or simply feel like showing off then leave the tarot at home. There is a time and a place - you know what I am saying!

Oracle Cards

Oracle cards are similar to tarot but a little softer round the edges. They do not contain the same stark imagery; instead they are generally prettier and girly. They are also a lot easier to read, as they tend to have words written on them to describe the meaning of the card i.e. Support, Travel or Love.

The most popular type of Oracle cards are Angel cards, but there are many other variations available too. If you feel you will not get on with tarot then angel cards may be perfect. The tarot can be complex, whereas angel cards are a lot more user friendly. They are also preferable to be used for a friend who is a bit down in the dumps. With the angel cards there is no danger of sticking her with the death card then trying in vain to explain to her that everything is going to be OK.

There are loads of oracle cards to choose from, the images are wonderful, supremely positive and slightly less pagan and arcane than the tarot. They also tend to be themed quite nicely, if angels are not your thing then you can get fairy packs, unicorn packs, dolphin packs, 'have a nice day' positive affirmation packs and all manner of other variations.

Having come from a background of tarot, I must admit that at first I thought angel cards were a bit wishy-washy and, dare I say it, childish. I believed that because I use a heap of interpretation in tarot, angel cards, which can be more self explanatory, were therefore inferior. However, I now concede that I was wrong. Angel cards are equally open to interpretation, although because they are straightforward this extra interpretation may not always be necessary. They are also absolutely brilliant for on the spot answers and daily reading. Tarot can be a little bit complex when answering questions, but angel cards tend to pop you with a very relevant answer there and then.

If you require a beautiful pack, with honest, inspiring and straightforward meanings then these are for you. Use them as I have recommended you use tarot, with great care and respect. Use them daily, monthly or randomly and/or out of the blue. However you choose to use them, I am sure you will be gifted with delightful answers to your little woes and sensible guidance for your bigger life altering choices.

High Heeled Astrology

Hands up who else reads their horoscopes daily only to forget the content within five minutes of reading! I am undeniably guilty of that. Sometimes I will read several different horoscopes in a variety of newspapers, websites and magazines, and I swear that none of it sticks in my head for longer than 30 seconds. Unless something particularly rings true then my astrological day is generally outright forgettable. This scatterbrained reading of the daily horoscopes does not however, make astrology valueless or a waste of time.

Astrology has been used since time immemorial to help plan, structure or predict the future. It is an incredibly useful tool to inform you about your character, temperament and when to expect significant happenings and/or changes.

The reading of the alignment of universal bodies, sun and moon do not show us our exact futures, but they can predict noteworthy periods of time, upheaval and personal transformations. 'How in the heavens does it do that?' I hear you cry. 'I thought it was naught but a load of twaddle, bunkum and baloney,' I hear you exclaim.

Well as we know from reading this book that what some people consider to be bunkum and baloney are at the heart of enlightenment (sort of). The only reason they are considered that way by the establishment is merely because they are not understood. Sure enough there are a whole gaggle of cheesy 'astrologers' out there who wear bad wigs, dress like children's TV characters and speak using as many describing words as the thesaurus holds, but that does not mean that what they say is untrue. It just makes those particular astrologers a little bit peculiar with a bizarre sense of fashion. Yes, astrologers seem to be characterized as crazies, but that is the media for you! And although editors love to push astrology to the back pages next to the made up problems and crosswords, it can actually be quite a serious and life influencing subject.

I believe the problem with newspaper and magazine horoscopes is that they are very generalized. They aim at all Librans, or all Scorpios or all…insert your star sign here. There is no accounting for exact day, time or the area of birth in these mass-produced documents. Yet all these details make a tremendous difference to a realistic and convincing astrological reading. I well know this from forcing my poor mother to scrabble around her house searching for well-hidden evidence of my specific birth time.

Astrologers say that from the day we pop out into the world, indeed from the very second we burst onto the planet, our futures are somewhat plotted. This does not mean that had you known astrology at age 13 you could have avoided the death of 'Poodle' your much loved Rottweiler, or that at 28 you could have known better… But had you been aware of astrological influences then you may have been able to understand the rough patches, for example, and instead of downing one too many drinks at vulnerable times, you could have planned your fortunes better, thus avoiding abstract social humiliation! With astrology as your guide you can choose the perfect time to apply for a new job, or seize the day when an astrologer gives you the nod and wink that it's an ideal time for star crossed lovers to attempt seduction and try this out on the object of your affections.

I will explore this more throughout the chapter, and hopefully provide some basic understanding of how astrology works.

Prior to this I must say I am not entirely unimpressed by mass-produced astrology. It can, on occasion, be very accurate. Lyn Birkbeck in his weighty book The *Instant Astrologer* describes mass produced sun sign readings as being like a map that shows a town address, whereas a full on astrological birth chart describes the nooks and crannies of your home. I personally find the daily horoscopes to be most precise when I am going through a happy or successful period of time in my life. Perhaps in those instances you are living to the very highest expectations of your particular star sign, therefore you are more likely to see the generic truth in the otherwise sweeping statements.

Strangely enough (chalk this up to another handy coincidence) my stars were absolutely spot on today. They warned me against discussing homecoming plans with a relative as they may get excited, and my plans might change. Unfortunately I read my horoscope not long after that exact incident had happened. I rang up my mother informing her of plans to visit our family in America with her, only to give it some thought later, leading, of course, to a change of plan. Had I read the horoscope first I may have done the thinking first. Then again I may very well have read them, taken notice, enjoyed a nice cup of tea, promptly forgotten the warning and gone on to ring my mum and do exactly as I did!

I guess astrology, like anything else can only help you so far, the leg work is down to you, much like a personal trainer, life coach or therapist. So let us explore the serious side to those pretty twinkling night-lights.

The science bit

OK I lied, officially there is no science bit, well, no officially government endorsed science bit, in the western world at least. Astrologers know only too well that their art is very much validated by experience, faith and ongoing visible examples of astrology working. In that respect if you are half hearted about your belief in astrology, the best way to make your mind up would be to get a decent chart made up and see for yourself. If you do not fancy that then remember this, astrology has been used for thousands of years and it has not gone out of fashion yet!

Studies have recently proven that electromagnetic waves and the position of the moon all affect human moods, so why not the sparkling dots in the sky too? If nothing else we can see the twinkly dots. I would not know an electromagnetic wave if it smiled, waved and honked its electrified horn at me! I appreciate that the stars are so far removed from our daily existence it is a wonder we even notice them anymore, especially those of us who are city girls. And yet the thought that their positioning could affect our chance of promotion, or may explain why we feel tearful or exuberant on a particular day is an intriguing prospect.

For a really great and easy read about how astrological bodies affect our daily lives pick up *Destiny vs. Free Will* by David Hamilton PhD. David Hamilton really gets to grips with explaining how we are influenced both astrologically and by other galactic phenomena such as magnetic storms, eclipses and asteroids. Dr Hamilton refers to many scientific studies and demonstrates that it would be arrogant of us to presume that the widespread galaxy and universe has no correlation to our everyday lives.

We are simply tiny beings that are pulled and poked by events beyond our control on a daily basis. Most times these are events that we can see such as a traffic jam, a decision made by someone else about us, or your partner arriving home drunk and disorderly. All these things are easily understood by our brains. We can make sense of them, we see, hear or feel them distinctly. Astrology is not so obvious or clear-cut. Astrology allows us to predict when these unseen prods might come our way, although sadly it does not inform us what guise these will arrive in.

These various prods and pokes are generally referred to as 'transits'. A transit is seen as an astrological effect that lasts for a set period of time and helps bring about change. Some transits are good, and others are more difficult to deal with. If you are aware of them you can plan around them, ride out any storms and choose appropriate times for work, play, sex and shopping!

Astrology cannot give you a definitive guide to your life, but it can help you track your progress and wisely contemplate future decisions. Lyn Birkbeck describes it nicely by referring to the individual as being like a little boat out on the sea. The boat has free will to try to get to her destination. But depending on the conditions, weather and crew of the boat, her journey may be influenced significantly. Astrology can therefore be harnessed to help your little boat along and to move it successfully past fog, wind, rain and drunken, lecherous sailors.

Lyn Birkbeck's book provides a CD-ROM that will work out your own personal birth chart, alongside romantic and transit timeline profiles. For those who want to splash the cash you could perhaps find yourself a real life astrologer to draw up a chart for you and give you the professional low-down. I would only advise you to avoid expensive premium rate phone lines, or any internet astrologer who contacts you with a 'free reading'. I have haphazardly had contact with several of these, they seem quite genuine but type their name in Google and you will realize what a dastardly near miss you have had. If one contacts you offering important messages just for you, or messages about imminent events that you could miss out on if you don't pay for a reading immediately, then please, please, please turn off your computer and find something else to do.

Having just completed my experimentation with the Lyn Birkbeck astrological profile I can say that it made both interesting and slightly harrowing reading. It was a real mixed up bag that I am sure does actually represent me awfully well. The results made me think deeply about my behavior and the way I present myself, and I can honestly say that there was a great deal of truth represented on those pages. At times it felt that Birkbeck had somehow gotten into my brain and was revealing to me my own inner truths. This was unsettling but incredibly enlightening. I can see myself more clearly as a result, both in terms of strengths and flaws. This, as a form of proof is powerful.

Examples of areas that really shone out were both specific to my character, whilst he also made some comments about my parents and childhood that were highly accurate. The reading pinpointed my current career as a writer, and also stressed that religion would be what takes me to a successful career goal, which, using this book as the obvious example, it is.

If you have paid attention to my ramblings you may be aware that I have been on somewhat of a spiritual journey of late. This was also totally reflected in my chart, including the fascinating point that I seemingly have exceptional psychic skills. Apparently these are psychic skills that I have previously manipulated in social settings. However, as I was not really aware until recently that I had any sensitive or psychic side, I will stress that any manipulation was unintentional. That said, it might explain my occasional intense reactions toward people, or the frequent feeling that I already know a person's personality when I meet them, these feelings generally proving to be correct. Plus now that I know I may have unconsciously been manipulating people, I will of course persevere to use my super powers only for good. These are only a few examples of my soul laid bare, and quite frankly I learned a hell of a lot in the half hour or so it took me to read through.

Although the science behind astrology cannot as yet be dissected or laid out on a laboratory chart, I am without a doubt convinced. Perhaps most convincing were the parts that were not so flattering. If Lyn Birkbeck's chart had simply told me what an all round great gal I was, I would certainly be inclined to agree. But the darker, hidden aspects of my character that the chart revealed, truly exhibited to me the validity of astrology. These charts are something that I will return to often to help in times of personality crisis or strife. If the truth be told I am actually officially stunned by what the Birkbeck profile has revealed. It has truly been an eye opener and a valuable tool to making the most of my attributes, keeping a check on my weaknesses and hopefully living happily ever after.

In the name of good research and just to be doubly sure I purchased myself another chart from the well-known London Astrology Shop. The shop is a popular Covent Garden haunt and despite being tiny is usually packed to the rafters with the occult curious and fortune seekers. Without going into detail and boring you, I can say I was equally impressed. The Astrology Shop runs a different program individually designed by their head honcho. The main difference between Birkbeck and The Astrology Shop's charts lies within the interpretations and articulation of the documents produced. This was so slight and in the end becomes only a matter of preference over whose written voice you prefer, the facts were pretty much identical. Again I felt an overwhelming feeling that the writer had somehow infiltrated my character. The accuracy level from the general characteristics to the nitty-gritty details was jaw-droppingly precise.

I was most astounded when I looked to the past. The London Astrology Chart included transits that occurred all of last year through to a year ahead from now. If you read my Reiki section, you will see that last year I was a bit of a miserable wreck, my life has progressed onward and upward to where I am today, and hopefully will continue to be even more positive into the future. Last year I felt weighted down with life changing decisions, and I was scuffling through my days stressed and unsure of what I wanted to do, or who I wanted to be. This was accurately reflected in my chart, which said that currently I am going through changes that will influence my life well into the future and that my spirituality is being reignited. Which of course I hope is accurate, indeed much of my hopes for the future lie within writing this book, a book that a year ago I had not even conceived of.

To show you exactly what I am talking about here are a few extracts from the transits I had for last year. Around the 22nd of February 2007 I was at a time of 'self-doubt, super sensitivity and confusion in my dealings with people', err, yeah spot on! Around the 30th of May 2007 I was apparently lost in 'idealistic dream plans that sound like a good idea at the time'. That could not be closer to the truth, in fact I spent a good deal of May 2007 in wonderland, wishing up a billion scenarios and fantasizing my life away. Between January and October last year my misery guts self is well documented by The Astrology Shop, it makes painful reading. However, the transit between 31st of October and 7th of November 2007 marks the time of my, 'Saturn Returning; the coming of Age and Maturity'. This also happens to be the time I screwed my head back on, conceived this book and started the journey I am now on.

Looking through into 2008, the transits are much more positive and reflect my more sane and happy existence, including such helpful transits as, 'Establishing the structure of my life for years to come', and, 'better organization leads to growth at work and opportunities at home'.

The picture painted is freakily accurate, at the time of writing this I am currently in a transit called 'Personal Freedom Brings New Friendships and Partnerships'. As you may well imagine my adventures writing this book have brought about many new working partnerships, and I appear to have snagged myself a few new friends through my various new associations!

Following this I am now an astrology convert and will be running off star charts from now until infinity. Though astrology cannot tell you day by day or deed by deed, it can give you a hugely reliable heads up to coming moods, trends and thought processes. The sheer size and scale of the universe has always been mind boggling to me, however, as we girls are often informed, size does not matter. And in no instance has this ever seemed more relevant. It is not about the information you receive; it is what you do with it that matters. The information in itself does not predict the future, but by acting wisely on the information, you can ensure things go your way more often.

What makes my mind boggle now is not the universe's vastness but the sheer genius and wisdom that apparently emanates from the universe and that has such a far-reaching affect on little me! I feel really quite touched that in the great, huge, gigantic scale of things, I do matter, and that my otherwise insignificant thoughts and actions are reflected and charted by the sparkling stars.

High Heeled Palmistry

Of all the divination techniques I have covered, palmistry conjures images to me of Romany Gypsies traveling around Europe whilst touting their palm reading skills. In my mind's eye I can picture their elaborate caravans, floating skirts and golden-hooped earrings. From this I imagine the outstretched open palm of the hand as a basis of hidden knowledge, just waiting to be interpreted and my destiny revealed. I can almost hear the beautiful Gypsy lady with her long dark curly hair whispering of family tragedies, marriage and children to me in exchange for a palm crossed with silver.

In reality this was not to be. My face-to-face palm reading came in the form of an altogether different type of brunette. This one goes by the name of Frank, and as far as I can tell he has no Romany connections whatsoever!

Frank Clifford is an expert of the palm and of astrology, so much so that he has his very own school of palmistry. Although he may travel the world it is not via horse and caravan, and he does so for the purposes of charities, conventions and publicity no doubt. When not teaching at The London School of Astrology, Frank delivers personal readings to a wide variety of clients, many of whom are not there to discover their future spouse, or whether they will have three or four children. Oh no, palmistry in the hands of Frank is a serious business. He has clients fly in from abroad to see him, and their concerns will vary from meat and bones business queries, to more spiritually based curiosity readings such as my own.

Part of me was intrigued to find out about my potential future marriages, number of children, and holiday homes in the United States. But alas it was not meant to be and none of that information was received.

Frank explained that such information is almost impossible to gain from the palm of a hand. Although important relationships are to be found there, it follows that these may not necessarily be marriages, or indeed children. He told me about a client of his who has two 'marriage' lines on his hand, and yet had never been married. Instead this particular person was devoted – or in some respects married - to his parents.

The variety and volatility of relationships in this day and age is very different from a hundred years ago, when divorce, cohabiting and same sex relations were nearly unheard of. Most intriguingly it may be that somebody you have never been in a relationship with will still show up on your hand as a significant 'relationship'. Although that person may never even know you exist, their existence has in some way been important or transformative to you. So whilst you may now be totally over your obsessive teenage crush on Michael Jackson, Michael J Fox or Marilyn Manson, your hand may very well show you up by still carrying a record of that crush embedded deep into your flesh. It seems that these people have inescapably scarred you for life! The same can be said for any kind of deep friendship or close family relationship.

Frank ushered me into his thoroughly modern home and although I was impressed by the clear love of music that was well documented on the walls, there was nothing in way of palmistry paraphernalia at all. I had at least expected some ancient weighty book dedicated to the palm, or possibly one of those awful alabaster hands with the lines drawn on and labeled. But again, I was wrong in my assumptions entirely. We settled into the conservatory, furnished with a sofa, table and exercise machine and got down to business. Frank takes palm prints using a mini roller and water-based paint, which thankfully washes off very nicely. The readings he does are based on a mixture of astrological charts and the actual palm print itself. It is not entirely necessary to use a print, but apparently for what it shows, and does not show, it can be easier to use than an actual fleshy, sweaty palm!

Despite the lack of future predictions I was not at all disappointed. Some predictions were made, although these were read alongside the various astrological transits that had also been worked out. Palmistry is not the same as a psychic reading, it is not the fate and fortune style readings of your typical Gypsy Rose. It is useful day-to-day guidance that maps and charts your life and where it is likely to go. Whilst astrology uses transits, palmistry, compliments this with such transits being differently marked on the hand. Career wise my hand was particularly telling. And indeed Frank did make some loose predictions, although he appeared embarrassed about the fact he thought he sounded like a psychic by making them. He said that in around six to eight months from the reading I would go on a life-changing journey overseas. He saw a lot of activity around me at about that same point in time, and possible family trouble the following January. Though some of this I certainly cannot see clearly, I can also see how such things might be due to come about. I do hope that my James will take me away in four months time for my 30th birthday, but family trouble come January is anybody's guess!

(Note: I have to interrupt proceedings here to say that I am currently editing the book and it is several months after I wrote that last paragraph. I now know what this tremendous overseas voyage is to be! Yes James took me away for my 30th, but that was not it. Indeed James and I have planned to go overseas at Christmas, to the USA, to Las Vegas…and yes dear reader, we are to get hitched! I think that pretty much sums up that particular life-changing event and bang on the correct timescale too. I am currently one month away from that particular holiday and I am more excited than you could ever know, Viva Las Vegas!)

Other interesting points of the palm reading surrounded the career of this book, Frank thought that I may not go on to write many more, and that another path may open. So if you are really not keen on my writing style, or do not understand how this got published in the first place, then lucky you, you may not have to put up with me again (at least not for a while)!

That said there are already small opportunities opening for me in my life, which in the future, if they blossom, could make intriguing career developments. Without boring you rigid any further with my potential future life, I can say that the palm reading was an interesting experience. It certainly rang very true, and done in tandem with the astrology makes for a superb overview of life direction.

Frank has written a good handful of palm-reading books and guides and he certainly knows his stuff. Palmistry was more matter of fact than I had expected, which in turn helps make it far more accessible and believable. For fun times go see a palm reader at the seaside, for facts go see someone like Frank!

High Heeled Mediums and Psychics

I have found that whilst being on a spiritual path to enlight-enment, the assistance and insight of psychics has been extremely valuable. Whether this has been in the form of spiritual life coaching and / or a predictive service, the use of psychics has strengthened my own belief that there is so much more to life than meets the eye.

It is my personal thought that seeing a psychic is similar to a young warrior visiting a Shaman, or a religious devotee going to a guru or sage for worldly advice. The correct psychic can shed light on your own path, and future possible events.

I believe that when you leave a psychic, you should leave feeling refreshed and confident that you have been given a wonderful glimpse of another world, a world that we cannot yet fully grasp, but that clearly resides all around us.

I have enjoyed a few readings myself for the benefit of reporting back and I have mainly been very pleased by the results. The small skeptic in me always doubts the ability of a stranger to glimpse inside my life, and yet, they have managed to do so with both ease and finesse. If you do not wish to learn the tarot for yourself, and do not have the time or requirement to develop any psychic ability, then finding a very good psychic is money well spent.

I recommend that you go to see a psychic for a form of spiritual counseling. Ask questions of the world in your head before you arrive and hopefully some answers may come to you during your session. Of course it is tempting to have a full on Spanish inquisition of your career progress or love life. But I whole-heartedly recommend you go for more than just a run down of your future prospects. Go with an open heart, knowing that the information being given to you is being given for a reason. Know that some friendly guide, passed loved one or loving angel is allowing you a glimpse of information for a specific reason. Treat this gift with reverence and say thank you in your own way. If the information comes from nowhere obvious, then just be glad and grateful.

I must, however, stress that some psychics are not all good, considerate caring people. I am lucky enough to have my teacher and friend Deborah Chamberlain as a psychic. Because of Deb, I know exactly what a first class psychic is. However, there are those out there who are not so warm, friendly, caring and considerate as my Debs! Sadly I know this from first hand experience. I also know how damaging it is to run into one of these. I can assure you that a bad psychic will leave a disgusting taste in your mouth. As I have recently learned…

In the process of writing this book I have been told by a psychic that James is not the one for me and that I will split up with him in the autumn. This stands at odds to what Deb told me and what I learned for myself in my Life Between Life regression. However, in spite of this prior knowledge that James and I are sound and stable, I was quaking in my three inch heeled snake print boots. I was incredibly upset about this, to the point that I actually became ill. What made it worse was that I did not tell anybody about what the psychic had said because I felt so silly. I believed that it was my fault for asking a psychic about the relationship in the first place, I really did blame myself. I felt like my world was crumbling round me and everything I had built over the past seven years was in danger of dissolving in the autumn. It is a wonder I did not split up with him there and then just to get it over with!

Two days after the reading I could not take it anymore and rang James in floods of tears and confessed all. He however did not think it was my fault; he believed the fault lay with the psychic. Such a sensible young man!

The more I thought about it, the more I realized I had little to worry about and that James and I were as strong, if not stronger than we had ever been.

I wrote to the psychic to inform her of this and to let her know that I was reluctant to believe the part about James and me. Her response was simply that my response matched up with her prediction. Her full prediction had been that James and I were currently very happy and that I believed he was the perfect man for me. She then comes out with the radical premonition that in the autumn I would leave him... No explanation, no counseling, no softly softly, just bold as brass, and downright factual. This in itself was particularly rude. I expressed I was happy, and that I did not want to think or believe we would split, and yet, she came straight out with the prediction again. The least she could have done was accepted how I felt and not mentioned it again. I could not believe the gall of the woman!

Now my hard learned lesson is this. That psychic was basically talking a load of cabbage and bananas. If James and I do not make it through the autumn, then she is incredibly cruel and irresponsible to tell me that in June! I did not need to know that now. Should we break up then she still will not have redeemed herself. Yes, she may have proven her psychic skills, but her human and people skills will still need some serious improvement. In many respects her actions could plant a seed of doubt that grew and established itself until, like a self-fulfilling prophecy, it comes true.

A good and kind psychic would not do this to anyone. We live in a world full of vulnerable people, and to treat people and their relationships in such a thoughtless and disposable manner is really not good business. This reading devastated me, and I am a strong person. Lord only knows what it would do to someone who is not emotionally tough or someone who was going through a vulnerable time in their life or a moment of self-doubt.

I was lucky to have the back up of a strong man and a strong, kind-hearted psychic, my friend Debs. Not everyone has that. When going to see a psychic, go with your instinct. I wish I had listened to mine. Before I had this reading all the signs were screaming at me not to have it. I was initially supposed to meet with the psychic in person, but on the day I turned up in Oxford, whilst she was in London somewhere (about 2 hours driving distance away). My 'misreading' of a website meant I went to a an event two months early and turned up in the middle of a Scout camp, full of tents and tiny young boys wearing toggles. No wonder the guy at the scout camp gate looked confused when I told him I had press passes and asked him where I should park!

I decided to request the reading by email. Although my guts were churning as I did it. And yet, like a fool I continued on this treacherous path, determined to get my reading for my research. I felt ill when the reading arrived via email and my best friend had a horrific nightmare about it. She dreamt that it told her all kinds of terrible things about her life, saying that she would never find love and she would be alone forever. Eventually it was sat in my inbox and my stomach curdled as I went to open it. Yet again I ignored my gut instinct and ping, with a press of a button it was in front of me and before you could say 'psychic attack' I had read it! I then spent days agonizing in emotional turmoil. Silly me. I should never have read it.

Part of me is angry because I was told something I did not want to hear. Some things are best left unsaid, these include the topics of death and disaster. I would prefer these things to be a surprise to me, and I would rather have my free will left intact so that I can choose to act how I need to at any given moment, rather than being orchestrated by somebody claiming to see my future. No person, psychic or not, has the right to take that away. I have the simple human right to live unfettered and unflustered by oppressive psychic predictions, and dammit, I intend to invoke that right!

There is little good to come out of this situation, except that I have learned a great deal and I can pass this onto to you. I will consider that I have 'taken one for the team', and I hope you all appreciate it, learn from me and don't make that same stupid mistake yourselves!

From now on I will only be taking my psychic needs to the one person that I know and trust (Deb of course). I advise you to do the same. Don't ring expensive telephone numbers and do not get readings by email. Your future and any contact you might hope to make with your deceased loved ones are both incredibly precious, important things, and you should give them the same respect that you'd give to anything else that is dear to you.

Yes, psychics can help renew your faith in the other side, and they can guide you on your life path, but fall into the hands of a wrong one and you could live to seriously regret it. Use your intuition and do not feel obliged to go through with a reading if you do not feel safe, contented and relaxed.

If in doubt, don't bother, it is not worth the heartache if you end up in a similar situation to me. If you know a great psychic, go for it! If not grab yourself a pack of angel cards off Amazon and let your loving winged helpers do the talking!

(Note: Just to clarify it is now mid-November, the leaves are well and truly off the trees and it's bloody cold. I believe this classifies as winter. My relationship made it through autumn unscathed and as you will know from the palm reading section James and I are planning a tryst to Las Vegas at Christmas to get wed. Proof if anything that psychics can be so very, very wrong)

Divination Conclusion

Why these varied techniques work is very hard to say. If you want answers as to why your life is mapped out on your hand, I am afraid I cannot give that. Similarly I cannot explain why the stars in a certain position can be mapped to make meaningful predictions of your foul moods and character traits.

With tarot my guess is that there is a little helping hand from the guardian angels / spirits / guides, but can I prove that? Of course I can't.

My theory is that we have been gifted these things to use as we will, to interpret and to plan for the future. There is more to this planet than you, I, or even Barack Obama knows. I am not talking about secret governmental plans, but on a basic energy, spirit, soul level, it occurs to me that not enough research has been done (that we know of).

I fear that just because something seems to be nonsense, or does not fit into a scientifically prescribed view of the planet it is thought not to exist. Those people who do believe it exists are often ridiculed or marginalized. And yet, they continue to think it, they also continue to work it and prove the validity of it through their work.

Although divination techniques may not be a mainstream, easily accessed service, I cannot see why in the future they could not be. Many of the professionals I met tended to make their skills available as life coaching services that are open to anybody who can stump up the reasonable fees. The psychic world is certainly a growth industry. Holistic and psychic services offered commercially are being transformed slowly to become as commonplace as the perfume section in your local department store, with holistic psychic centers such as Psychic Sisters opening in places as unexpected as Selfridges and Harrods in London.

If the trend continues, and if such things are carefully regulated, we may all benefit from a local palm reader, astrologer or tarot reader, to help guide us through the ups and downs of life. Who knows, before we know it the doctor could be recommending such facilities to the general public. In fact I actually know a doctor who does!

In my experience these things, alongside healing techniques such as Reiki can be restorative and transformative. They can help structure and order your life in a manner no anti-depressant or money splurge can touch.

All of these things mysterious, mystical or magical as they seem are likely to be rooted in some kind of as yet unknown science. Or at least in the future science may be able to offer an explanation for them, taking away their 'mystical' qualities, but verifying that they do exist. Divination, to me is only as bizarre as radio waves or television. Certain technologies confuse the hell out of me and I sincerely believe that in many respects they should be impossible. Although a scientist can explain to me how a photograph works, can they really, really explain why it works? Can they really, really explain, to my satisfaction how a video camera can be pointed at George Clooney and that via waves, or encryptions on a CD his image can pop up on my big screen, his perfect, like for like image, so that he is there in all his wondrousness on my laptop. Can anybody please explain that? The thing is, that even if you do, I still won't believe you, because though you might be able to explain the process, I do not think you will be able to tell me why.

And it is the Why that really bothers me. Why is my life apparently mapped out on my palm, or why is Brad Pitt apparently smoldering away on the box in the corner? I do not know the why to any of these questions, but if they exist and I can see they exist, I must believe them. I do believe them, they mess with my head and cause me great confusion, but they exist, they happen, they are real, I believe them. This proves that I don't have to understand to believe; the next step from this is that I don't have to see to believe. Maybe in some instances belief should come first? If we can't understand and we can't see something, yet we feel it, know it, experience it, then who can say that it is not true. Some food for thought there ladies! Now moving swiftly on from this philosophical muddle...

Divination is an exciting benefit of a spiritual path. By using this gift we can make better-informed choices. In my life divination has provided bagfuls of clarity and confirmation. Sometimes that is all that is needed. If confirmation is not forthcoming then direction and suggestion are equally as helpful.

Ensure you use respected resources and well-known practitioners. Be eternally grateful for any wisdom you do receive and remember that it is given to you to use wisely and for the highest purpose of everyone involved.

As pleased as you may be for the 'heads up' you are about to receive, the fact you have received anything at all is a little miracle.

The High Heeled Conclusion

So do you need to get your life re-heeled? Sometimes it can be tempting to carry on clomping around in the same old comfy, yet sexy, knee high boots for a few more weeks, prolonging the original heel, saving money, but inevitably making horrible dents in your wooden flooring!

If it is time for a change it need not be that you have to pack in your beloved kitten heels for a new pair, you may simply need to visit a cobbler, get some polish and add a bit of lustre. You may find that although the heel is worn down, the essence of the shoe remains the same, given a bit of thought and TLC you can bring about a revival, before you know it people will be asking where you got your new shoes!

OK that was a slightly drawn out and over-egged pudding of a metaphor but I do hope you see what I am getting at. You are the shoe, you may be a bit knackered round the edges, a good dose of inner searching and refinement of your soul could bring about some wondrous changes inside and out! Before you know it, you will be good as new, better than new, enhanced by your new set of beliefs, hopes and spiritual yearnings. You will have a whole new 'sole' or soul so to speak! Sorry!

I am so pleased that you have read this far. Enlightenment is a bit of a farfetched goal in a century when obsessions can go no further than the nose on your face, literally. Let's face it, some people in our society live and die never thinking beyond their looks, their clothes, their hair or their handbag. The media tends to encourage this; occasionally throwing out some images of those less fortunate for us to fawn over. Whilst on one hand we may be moved to see Scarlett Johansson photographed with the poor and needy in far flung Africa, we may very well shed a tear and psychically pat Johansson on the back. On the other hand we are only too pleased to turn the page and check out Gap's new summer collection, or learn what exactly Britney's mental state is that morning.

We can all be very selfish, we may care dearly for our immediate friends and family, but we cocoon ourselves off from reality, safe in our healthy eating plans, mortgages and Tuesday night gym sessions.

We do not have to go out and save the world, nor will the world stop turning if we do not save ourselves from our habits, vices and misbehaving ways. Yet we are so distracted the majority of the time we do not stop to think about what we might be missing. There is more to life. All it takes is a few moments for you to let all the mundane clutter of life slip away and allow something miraculous to catch your attention.

I can advise you, from my personal experience, that seeking some form of spiritual truth is well worth the effort. My journey toward enlightenment has officially been going less than a year at the time of writing this, however if I look deeper I can see it has always been just below the surface waiting to bubble up and enthrall me.

Since starting this book my life has changed immeasurably. I am more content and happy than I ever expected to be. There are still things that worry me, or cause me pain, yet my spiritual path has alleviated the majority of my previous rather petty concerns.

My spiritual path to enlightenment is of course an extreme version. I have literally immersed myself head to foot in spiritual pursuits and taken on board a great number of theories and faiths that I previously knew little about.

You might wish to do nothing more than read this book, then put it down and forget it for a few years. Others of you may be inspired to research further and try out some faiths for size. Go for whatever feels right, grab at it hard and trust that enlightenment can be an answer to whatever hardships are bugging you today.

The benefits I have reaped have gone far beyond a belief in the afterlife. I am overjoyed in my relationship with James, I have been lucky enough to receive so many insights and to realize that he truly is a soul mate and that we are in the right place at the right time. That beats anything else hands down. Spirituality has brought me new ambitions, goals and fantastic new ways to help achieve them. A year ago I was miserable with no clue where life would take me next. I now have definite aspirations and an ability to avoid that pit of misery that I had previously fallen victim to. I am positive and I expect doors to open and for me to step through them willingly, confidently and with huge pride.

Enlightenment will not bring you fancy cars, high fashion, diamond rings or tropical holidays, but if those things are meant to be in your life, then enlightenment can push you in the right direction to receive whatever amazing gifts await you.

Most importantly enlightenment can help you remember who you are. My spiritual journey has been a real trip. I have become a full and whole person, entirely conscious of my own mind, my wants and my desires.

In many respects I feel that I am in the driving seat and I am directing my future with the help of friends, guides, angels, family and a great dose of renewed self-esteem. I am not sure that a top psychiatrist could achieve the same fantastic results in such a short time and for so little cash!

Ladies, if you are having a crisis of self, forget rehab, forget detoxing, forget makeovers, instead step into this book and find yourself the peace and comfort you already possess in your heart and in your soul.

I hope I have demonstrated to you how alternative spiritual pursuits can help ease the strains of fast paced modern living. What you find or choose to believe in is entirely down to you. There is no prescriptive 'truth', none of it is verifiable, and essentially you can take bits of any belief and craft them into your own shape. To me spiritual belief is utterly creative and entirely moldable by the individual who believes it. It is yours to do with, as you will.

Never before have women had so many opportunities

available to them. This is true in all areas of our lives, family, career, relationships, holidays, lipsticks and diets. There is constantly a choice to be made or a path to be followed. We aim for perfection or at the least a portrayal of perfection.

Gaining space for your soul is a welcome relief from the high-octane pursuits of day-to-day life. You are entirely free to start small, making tiny choices that will snowball into a sounder mind and better quality of life. Such changes may not be outwardly obvious, but inside you will know you are addressing a need and nurturing the soul of you that has been neglected by a desire to grow your hair, or the pursuit of Mr Right.

I am nearly one year down the road since I first started to write this book. As the year came round and the writing of this book nears its end I began to feel that my path was complete. I considered that I was now officially 'spiritual' and my question in response to that was 'OK so I am spiritual…what now?'

The answer I was given was mundane, yet enlightening. What now, came in the form of life, boring, day-to-day, uninspired life. In short I had a week from hell, people were being grumpy with me, overly critical, and letting me down. Even good people were plying me with unhelpful, harmful information. I felt stuck, slumped and incredibly human.

It was in this messy week that I realized that this is what life is. Life is charging between moments of insane, beautiful clarity and days when your hair will not straighten, the bank will not pay out any more cash, and the boss is hell bent on making you cry.

No matter how spiritual you declare yourself to be you are still subject to the human kingdom around us. This means you are not omnipotent, immortal and nor do you possess any superpowers. You are still subject to the laws of gravity, you are still clumsy and your boyfriend is just as likely to start a row about the housework as he was when you thought Buddha was a bar in Barcelona. Spiritual or not you still have to deal with the here and now. I am sure the Dalai Lama has stubbed his toe and knocked his funny bone as many times as the rest of us. Yeah, you are spiritual, but some things never change!

Living as a more enlightened human being involves knowing and maintaining some degree of spirituality through all the crap. It is taking that enlightenment and making it work for you. You cannot put a request to the universe and then sit back and do nothing, nor can you ask your angels for help and expect to wake up and everything be better, bolder, brighter. Living spiritually is getting on with the day-to-day, using your intuition and sniffing out the right track, the right choices and the right people.

Prior to my week from hell I had been fantasizing about my future career, life possibilities and how to escape from the here and now as quickly as possible. I was being impatient again, a trait I should have sorted out way back in the Buddhism chapter! My spiritual journey had got me so amped up I yearned for the next phase. I totally forgot the basic spiritual premise that I must embrace life moment by moment, be grateful for what I have and remember that there are always more lessons to be learned. One thing I struggle to learn, but that is so important is that I must be happy right now, if you cannot be happy right now, then you may never be happy. All we have is now, this moment – so smile!

It is not all bad news of course. One year down the road and I am far happier than I was. My spiritual path has given me deeper insight into who I am and what I need. I hope my version of enlightenment will assist me to carve out an interesting career, create a happy family and give joy to my sweet-hearted friends.

The last thing I want to think is that my purpose is complete, or that my life should be better. Could it be better, of course it could, I could be on holiday in the Maldives or St Lucia... But should it be better? No it should not, not right now.

Yet with the guidance of spirituality and enlightenment I must trust that everything in my life is precisely how it should be. I know that the universe has got my number, and when it seems that it does not have my number then I must figure out why. So, last week I had a terrible week. But the effect of that was to bring me back down to earth, turn off the fantasies and get on with the job in hand. The universe had my back, it just sometimes has a very funny way of showing it!

So, the answer to the question: 'so I am spiritual, what next?' goes as follows. Nothing happens next, there is no poetic or wondrous answer. We live in a fast past goal-oriented society where achievement and the possession of success is paramount. There is no trophy for achieving a spiritual life, you do not win anything, or at least nothing visible. You get on with your life and you become a little more or a little less spiritual by the day. Some days you feel like the universe is at your feet, while other days the world will be on your shoulders. There simply is no spiritually endorsed what next? All that does happen is continuation, constant growth and plenty more lessons to learn. By embracing your own spirituality you will be better equipped to handle whatever life has in store for you. You will be in touch with the inner you, and more able to create an ideal life and achieve your personal life purpose. But I'm afraid honey that the bumps in the road will still be there. It is your job to realize the innate and precious value of what you have, hold it close to your heart, contemplate it every day and keep on dodging life's bullets! Life will rock, then it will suck and on and on and on

A final brief note on coincidence

Having read through every page and word very carefully I am sure that you will have now formed some further opinions on coincidence. Hopefully you will have grasped why I felt it important to raise it as an important subject right back at the beginning.

My personal belief regarding coincidence is a little complex and probably draws on several of the various beliefs I have touched upon in this book.

Do I believe in fate? Yes I do. Do I believe in free will? Yes, I believe in that too. I reckon that we have a basic plan before we come to earth in this incarnation. We may plan to open a clothing shop, become a fashion editor, be a mother or teach the world to sing. Either way, we have a personal mission. I believe that we prearrange significant meetings, or catalysts that will help push us onto the right path should we get distracted. We might choose our parents or friends or that one day we'll walk into a club and meet a soul mate that will push us beyond ourselves until we achieve something wondrous.

Once we are on the right path I believe that more and more coincidences will open up to us, gifting us with amazing experiences and the right people at the right time. I know that once you try to be more aware of these coincidences then the better they will work for you, and the faster you will progress toward whatever success or spirituality you desire.

It is important to remember that we learn significantly from every person we ever meet, they are all given to us in the hope we will benefit from their actions, be they good or bad. Perhaps we can follow their example, or their challenges to us will prompt us to follow through on delayed plans.

Their presence, no matter how brief, intense or horrid is there to make you become more yourself. Sometimes their advice may be terrible, but it is your challenge not to listen to it. Occasionally they will hurt you, talk about you behind your back, or damage your self-esteem. It is your job to rise above it. People are all part of the spiritual puzzle and your path to enlightenment.

If you pay attention and use what you learn then you can achieve precisely what you came to earth to do. This will often involve knock backs and rejections, but one day it will all become clear.

In my early adult life I was convinced I should be a model, people told me I should and it seemed to be a way to achieve a visible form of success. The coincidences I encountered were not willing to let this happen. As well as the fact that I felt utterly sick to my stomach anytime a casting director wanted to see me for an audition. In spite of this I tried and I tried. All that was available to me was 'glamour modeling' which went against every grain of my being.

I tried to force myself into a mould that simply was not for me, it was difficult and often treacherous what with dodgy photographers and perverted 'agents' to contend with. Nothing I tried was working and the day I decided to stop I felt so completely relieved.

The day I picked up a pen and paper and started to write it all just happened. It came easily. Magazines snapped me up as if I was Shakespeare himself, websites clamored to have me interview the stars, I may be vaguely exaggerating here, but it was a great start all the same! All along I had been told that writing was a difficult industry to break into. Here was I, no journalism qualification, writing as a Live Music Editor for a respected UK magazine, as well as an international travel site and some crazy rock music fanzine! I guess that this particular path was 'meant to be', 'happened for a reason', and was 'oohh what a coincidence!'

The coincidences piled up and here I am now with a book, a publisher and a very excited self! Not that the modeling episode was a waste of time, I have some lovely photos and I learned a great deal about myself. Inevitably though, the fates were not for it. Strangely enough during my time posing for glamour mags, I came across a whole slew of writers. It felt I was constantly tripping over them and I was secretly envious of their abilities and position. Then I picked up a pen and paper and the rest is history...

You must remember that other people learn and experience from you too. None of us are really hugely conscious of it, and I do not think anybody, except crazed megalomaniacs, wander round believing they are working under the direct orders of the Gods. However, once you recognize coincidence in your life, you may be able to recognize when you have had some effect on others too. Coincidence is not all about what happens to me, me, me, it might be that you are a significant contributing factor in other people's life decisions, and that, my friend, is quite a responsibility! More often than not though, you will barely be able to perceive how you may affect another person, but just to know that you do, or that you can, is enough to help you become a better person, thus speeding your own journey toward enlightenment!

I do also believe that we can totally ignore coincidence and fate if we choose to do so. We may very well have a plan to live a full and fruitful life, but throw it all away due to our own reckless behavior and because we ignore the signs and opportunities thrown our way. In such instances all I can say is better luck next time. It may be that through thoroughly messing up one life, you will be more likely to do a better job on your next incarnation. However, all we can really concentrate on in this life is this body, this mind and our plans for the next fifty years or so.

Once you open yourself to some form of spiritual growth amazing and miraculous things will occur. Part of the trick is recognizing them and not missing a trick. Some of the miracles may be very tiny, even very annoying, like missing a bus. However, had these baby miracles not occurred, your life would not be as you now know it to be. You might be a very different person, living elsewhere, with a different partner or career. If you have not seen the film *Sliding Doors*, I recommend you go hire a copy and watch it.

My personal journey has seen me grow and realize my potential. From a purely earthly perspective I have learned to deal with people and the world around me better, I am happier in my own skin. Opening to such a path will bring the right people to you at the perfect times.

It was coincidence that meant I turned up to a Reiki practitioner who also happened to be involved with a blossoming spiritual development business. It was coincidence that saw me at her door at the exact right time for me to get the help I needed and progress to where I am today.

I have just arrived home from a holiday that was choc-a-block with coincidence, although these were coincidences of a very different sort. I was taking a little time out of writing to refresh myself and think about… well to avoid thinking at all. Prior to the holiday I had met my personal angel and my spirit guide through my spiritual development classes.

I went on holiday expecting these entities to be silent partners. However at every twist and turn I was given little reminders of their existence. My angel, who came to me as a horse with wings (a Pegasus called Celebrielle) was everywhere. I walked into a craft shop to be met with a giant painting of a winged horse lunging toward me. In the shop I picked up a greeting card, unaware of its content, only for it to tell me my Guardian Angel was with me and always would be. I turned to my left and saw a painting of what could only be Archangel Michael; the artist confirmed this for me. Only a week prior to that I had learned all about the Archangel Michael and his powers of protection. So fresh in my mind was he that I had invoked him several times on the plane journey to protect me from horrible turbulence.

Whilst trundling around doing my sightseeing, images of winged horses popped up everywhere, with the final one being the most breathtaking. On leaving the airport after a 24-hour delay I looked up to see a tremendous wire built Pegasus hanging above my head. I had been at the same spot the day before, though I had not noticed this amazing life size sculpture. On the day that the plane did actually arrive on time and was not hit by lightning, I was privy to the giant 3D image of my lovely Celebrielle.

It is fair to say that 'they' do not do things by halves, and when you open to a path of enlightenment and ask the universe to bring you all good things, the volume of tiny miracles that happen every day, in every way, may surprise you.

Whilst on this holiday images of Native American Indians also began to inundate me. I had a sneaking suspicion that my spirit guide was a Native American, and this suspicion was confirmed over and over again throughout the week. At first I took the imagery I stumbled across to be very basic, unmeaning coincidence. After all I was in America, home of the Native American, it is not so peculiar that imagery exists.

Clearly unimpressed by my lack of faith I was gifted a marvelous coincidence in the form of the wonderful American Indian fellow that I mentioned way back in the Shamanism chapter. On visiting Beale Street, home of the blues in Memphis, the first bar we walked into also housed this chap, not only was he very talented, he was charming, funny and classy. He made a beeline for James and me, and when James went outside for a smoke he came and serenaded me with the blues. On his break, he joined us at the bar and we chatted for a long while. In that brief meeting I felt confirmed in my belief that my spirit guide was a Native American, as did James, who realized that point without me even prompting him, that boy knows me so well!

These holiday 'coincidences' were not necessarily life changing, nor did they take me away onto a different path. What they did do was act as timely reminders and confirmations of the path I was already on. Overall it was a marvelous holiday, everything went perfectly, even when it went wrong.

I opened myself to anything happening, and anything did, all positive, all delightful and all seemingly wrapped up in one happy coincidence after another.

Indeed one very happy coincidence happened to James. Following our holiday taking an abrupt extension due to an unforeseen 'act of God', James found himself to be very frustrated and understandably angry. He was due back at work on the Monday and because of the delay he would have no time to rest at home and get over any jet lag. I did try to placate him by saying I was sure it had happened for a reason and that maybe we would end up having fun? Sometimes though in the thick of it, such well meant words sound a little stupid even to the most spiritually hardy of us all.

However, and here comes the coincidence and magnificence, it did all work out OK. James had been hankering after some technological hardware all holiday, and yet it had fiendishly eluded him. My darling family rescued us from the airport and my uncle asked if there was anything we needed in the USA seeing as our stay had been elongated. James made a little joke about the techno gadget he lusted after. Only for my lovely uncle to say 'OK, lets go get it now!' It turns out the only shop that sold this gadget in the entire of the state of Kentucky, also happened to be in my relative's local mall, a ten-minute drive from their home.

Had the darned plane not got hit by lightning James would still be without his beloved piece of computer wizardry… and no doubt he would still be sulking. Not only did we get the bit of tech hardware, but we also spent some time with the family, we watched some great cheesy comedy films on a big screen, drank home brew and the next day after a breakfast of gargantuan proportions (waffles, bacon, strawberries and cream – only in America) we got to shoot guns in the back garden – yee ha!

Methinks that these bits of coincidence were especially for James, what more could a boy ask for! Sometimes it takes a pain in the ass to happen for something really cool to spring from it. I am also pretty happy that next time I start spouting my hippy mantra, 'everything happens for a reason', I bet you ten bucks James will not need convincing!

Coincidence should never be overlooked, as it is the calling card of the spirits, angels, pixies and Gods. It connects us to the divine, and to the divine within ourselves.

In Michael Newton's books on past life regression he says that when we come to earth, we leave some of our energies behind, and we can communicate with these energies through our thoughts and our meditations. We can also communicate with the energies of other people, we are all interlinked and woven together intrinsically in ways we do not know and cannot perceive.

Perhaps this is how our subconscious manages to usher the right people to us at the right time? Perhaps the bit of us left behind sees what we need and has a quiet word with somebody else's left behind bit. Between them they conjure up an ingenious plan that sees you entering into somebody else's life just when you, or they need it.

Perhaps by this route we also manage to conjure up wonderful things via the law of attraction and positive thinking. I believe that we can make happy coincidences come to us through thinking positively and putting mental requests into the ether.

I recently placed an old Elvis Presley album on a shelf because it looked pretty. Within two weeks it came about that we booked that trip to the USA to visit my family, and whilst there we drove to Graceland and saw Elvis for ourselves. Having now returned from that holiday, I can say that Graceland was one of the most amazing experiences of my life. I arrived there fairly nonchalant about the whole thing. I was not an Elvis fan and had no urgent desire to visit his family home. I went because we were in the area and it seemed a fun thing to do. However, having traipsed through his home, viewed his things and felt the bizarre divine vibe that permeates Graceland I can say that I am an Elvis convert.

Being given the opportunity to feel an almost religious love and sadness within the King's former home, has opened my eyes to the power of emotion, and the intensity of the people's love. Standing over Elvis Presley's grave I felt my guts churn and my lower lip wobble. I walked away and cried my little eyes out. I cannot for sure say what that was all about!

Maybe I connected with the tragedy and the grief of millions, maybe I needed to feel the spiritual vibe that comes from a place on the planet becoming a shrine to one person's effect on that planet. Until I arrived at Graceland I had not known a religious experience quite like it. It felt like I'd been on a pilgrimage, it was crazy, emotional, overwhelming and wonderful all at the same time. Now the question remains did I place the album of Elvis on my shelf because my inner self knew I would be visiting Mr Presley, or did my placing of the album cause the universe to take me at my word and conspire to whisk me off to Memphis, Tennessee. I don't know, but the nature of coincidence is mysterious, things happen, events bump into one another and somewhere in the midst of randomness a pattern emerges and things work out in the most intriguing of fashions.

This voyage of discovery taught me the value of people, of life and of the sheer spiritual weight of raw emotion. I had heard of such things through my development classes and Deborah had told me of the extreme atmosphere she had encountered in New York at Ground Zero. I had not encountered this for myself, but thanks to the pelvis shaking King of Rock 'n' Roll, I now have. Long Live the King!

I believe that by positive thinking you can attract wonderful things to you. In doing so you tap into some huge universal consciousness, and make coincidence work for you rather than being an unruly force which works around you. Recently I saw the upgraded version of my car and quietly yearned that I could have one, but with my sensible head on I knew I could no way afford it. Strangely enough that week my local car dealer called me up saying he needed my specific car for a customer and if I was willing to do that he would give me an amazing deal on the newest upgrade of my car. When I first experimented with 'cosmic ordering', I wrote a note to the great whoever spirits, guides, angels, and asked that within three months I would like to be a paid Travel Writer. Within two months I had a small gig writing travel reviews for a website at £1.50 a pop! Not exactly what I had in mind, but I did get exactly what I asked for. Other times things I have asked for have not been forthcoming, though in hindsight I can see that they were not meant for me, or that the request has perhaps been shelved for a later date...

Coincidence allows us small windows of opportunity to make a new friend, learn something new or to experience a meaningful occurrence. Coincidence is not just coincidence, it is it a bubbling cauldron of possibility, magic, knowledge and experience. Every single time it is the right person, the right time, the right place. Coincidence is a delicious and fruitful gift. If you accept and believe in it, you can turn it to your advantage. If it is meant to be for you, then by some strange and magnificent coincidence you will surely have it. Think positive and the world can be yours!

Have I shaped my own path, or did I get lucky and stumble across the precise thing I needed? Or was it a bit of both? You may be so busy looking for a reason why, that you overlook the amazing promise available.

I am sure that we all have a vague path in life, whether we achieve it or not is entirely down to us. Having a spiritual belief system makes us more astute to the signs and opportunities available. Confidence, charm and savvy will push us the rest of the way.

My background and lifestyle prepared me to write this book, though a year ago I did not know this was what I would do. I was a little lost soul, desperately miserable and suffering a late-20s crisis.

My search for enlightenment has been an education, it has opened my eyes to an array of amazing beliefs and brought me through to a place where I feel contented and focused. I believe that this all occurred in conjunction with a plan I set out before I even came to earth and that spirit guides, angels and my intuition have prodded and poked me in the right direction, until finally I am on the correct lines. I am sure this could have happened now, or two years ago, or had I ignored it, it may have happened in ten years time when I would be suffering a proper midlife crisis! One way or another I would have been prompted to go this way until I did, or until I died.

My life thus far is one glorious mess of incident and coincidence, phenomenally working with ideal timing and apparently for my best benefit. You cannot moan at that now, can you!

How to...

How to begin your path to enlightenment, you ask? Well here are my ideas of how you can start. First put down your gossip rag / glossy magazine, pick up a paper and watch the news. Magazines are great fun, do not get me wrong, but they cannot be your bible, if they are you will be damaged and straining for an ideal you are unlikely to achieve. It is not my aim to put 'glossips' out of business; my aim is to focus your mind away from celebrity baby bulges, cellulite and the bingo wings of the stars. Who cares, seriously babe, it is bullshit. Complete and utter, depressing, manufactured, steaming cow dung.

Take a few moments to re-associate yourself with what is really going on in the world, maybe you have a good idea, or maybe you forgot just how good and how downright despicable the planet we live on can be. Let yourself feel the fear for a few seconds, challenge yourself to step out of your sweet scented, body lotioned life and really consider the war and pestilence that surrounds our precious little existence. Let yourself be sad, angry, frightened. Allow your mind to appreciate what you have in comparison, and try feeling, really truly deeply feeling for those who are worse off.

Pop the little bubble of consumerism and marketing that has you in its stranglehold and defy the conventions that clutter your mind with everything but the bad. Think about the bad, feel it till you want to cry, and then consider what changes you would like to make in your life.

I believe that with spirituality comes responsibility. Yes you can still save up for some Jimmy Choos and you are more than welcome to take your best friend to a spa for her birthday. But at the same time consider life beyond your next paycheck, peek beyond this and see how the world is panning out.

Try to make a small difference in you and the places and people around you. Look for happiness but give it out too, anyone can make a dent on the grand scheme of things. Live spiritually and reflect your belief through your actions. Be a great person; be kind and caring and aware.

Buy organic and free range when you can . Do not be afraid to label yourself, and I am not talking Armani or Dior here! Be true to yourself, stick your head above the parapet and embrace your quirks. Be whatever you feel. Be a vegetarian, vegan, feminist, humanist, Spiritualist, hippy, believer, Shaman, Witch, shoe lover, hormone ridden, lip gloss loving Buddhist. Alternatively reject all labels and live unburdened by other people's expectations. You are who you are and no friend, lover, parent or media outlet should prescribe your womanhood to you.

Know that pain and heartache are always going to hurt. Unemployment, disease and disability will not go away just because you adopt an attitude of enlightenment. Try to learn from these dreadful things, make it your goal to turn suffering into solace. Know that grief will come to us all, as will various degrees of terrible luck, but also know that you will find a way through, and in doing so you will improve your functioning as a human being and as a result your immortal soul will progress.

Know that you will be aided to reach your potential, whatever that may be, signs will be given and fulfillment and happiness will eventually follow. This world is a difficult place to exist, and no, it is not fair, but it will be OK, one day.

Follow your intuition, take your chances, learn to live a little bit more for yourself and worship at whatever altar takes your fancy on whichever day of the week is suitable. You will be just fine.

Shop at the local grocer and make the supermarkets sweat. Count food miles instead of calories! Consider the future of the planet and how you can help. Switch the TV and lights off when you leave the room. Try to avoid coating your body in chemicals and opt for green organic products, or even mush up an avocado and stick it on your face if need be!

Few of us are 'born with it', but if you want to pay your hard earned money to try to 'get it', then let's not make the environment or cute little bunnies suffer as a result of 'it'. Remember that 'it' is not so important.

Meditate when you can, close your eyes and give yourself some space, even if it's just for five snatched minutes. If you fall asleep, then maybe you needed to rest, if you have an amazing vision or inspiring thought then good for you! Always listen to your gut instinct; it can save an awful lot of trouble In the long run. It can also keep you safe, it may be the voice of your angels guiding you from danger; ignore your intuition at your peril.

Wish upon a star, pray, request or cosmic order what you desire. If it is meant to be it will come to you, but be patient, it may take time or you may not yet be ready. Good things come to those who wait!

Allow yourself to fall in love, not just with a partner but also with your friends, your family, your goldfish and your potted Yucca plant. Be good to all these people and things; let them know how much you appreciate them. Show the love, open your heart, be vulnerable, do not hold back, give a lot of hugs and be grateful for what you get back. If somebody has hurt you find a way to forgive and forget, be a bigger person. Don't shout and scream and curse, just chill, listen, consider and be brave. Wish everyone you have ever known well and resolve to stop bitching, just stop, it causes nothing but harm.

Talk to your angels or your pets or your flowers. Explore your every option and do not be afraid to say yes to new opportunities. Challenge yourself every day, move beyond any self-imposed boundaries, test your limits. Keep fit, eat well, and avoid processed food (the occasional pizza is the exception to this rule as it is of course, an essential of life). Live life second, by second, by second and cherish each tick of the clock.

Put your hard earned cash toward spiritual growth once in a while, be it an interesting book or a short course on crystals. Drop negativity and know that whatever becomes of you, and whatever hardships arise, you will see them through. Let yourself grow from every experience good or bad, become wiser and do not let life bring you down. Be happy babe!

The Very End?

So what is it we are searching for in our very intimate and personal quest for enlightenment? I believe that at the very heart of our search lies the dreadful paradox of love and loss.

As human beings we live semi conscious of the fact that everything we love, we will lose. Our handbags and glad rags become faded, old and broken. Our youth decays as our waistlines expand; our hair thins, turns silver or drops out, our skin sags and our vim and vivacity slowly becomes crushed under ailing hormones, responsibility and aching joints. Many of our friends, family and partners are likely to depart this place before we do. Nothing remains unchanged or untouched by the force that is loss. Everything we have ever placed value on will cease to be. Inescapably we may lose ourselves, our senses, our physical abilities, eventually even our memories of all the things we have loved will grow gloomy. And finally we too have left; our very life essence is snuffed.

The search for enlightenment removes all of the aberrations and devastation that stems so violently and cripplingly from having loved and lost. The trauma of life may disorientate you, throw you adrift and cause you to call on God to show his face and explain. Perplexed and alone you may seemingly stumble from one inane disaster to another waiting to simply vanish from the face of the planet. Whilst some turn to drink, partying, drugs, sex and other vacuous and temporary thrills, a turn to some form of spirituality will better heal any rips in your heart.

Whether you choose to believe in a Buddha, a goddess, or a pack of tarot, any belief in the divine and mysterious will aid you in times of despair; when times are good you will be confident and exhilarated. Holding any faith, be it structured, or one that you invented from a mish-mash of theories, is enough to keep the stranglehold of doubt and bewilderment far from your mind. When the cosmetics, fancy dresses, bling and booze are no longer enough to keep your head held high, then you must turn inward and look to your essence, to your neglected soul.

Whilst physical things disappear, dull, and disappoint, a belief in a soul, means that you are never truly lost. Spiritual belief enables your concept of death and finality to be tipped up, turned over and tossed aside. Nothing dies, everything moves on. We all go beyond this earth and meet up elsewhere to a rapturous applause and a massive Welcome Home.

To believe in spirituality or to seek enlightenment is simply an affirmation of never-ending, heart soaking, bone breaking love. All those losses become irrelevant because at the core of it all lies nothing but love. A belief in an unending soul is a belief that you will be reunited with each and every single thing you believed to be vanished, your love can continue unceasingly for all time.

Embracing your heart's belief in a soul means you will allow your life to be governed by the gentle, warm, hum of love. For love is what spirituality is. And love is what enlightenment will stem from.

Enlightenment is found in love, it is deeply set within every love you have ever felt for a child, a pet, a spectacular view, a book, a lover, a parent or a friend. These things will not die, not really. In spirituality there is no abandonment, no forever suffering and no true helplessness. If love never ends then our essence continues, our ashes are long blown away but our heart, our soul and our love will be infinite.

Ladies, this has been the High Heeled Guide to Enlightenment and this can be your

BEGINNING

Recommended

All of the below are the kind and wonderful people who offered their services and time to help the stories within this book come to fruition.

I wish to extend a massive thank you to them all, they have added, color, depth and knowledge to the various subjects and I will be forever grateful for their involvement and guidance. It has been an honor.

I would highly recommend any and all on your personal High-Heeled journey to Enlightenment.

Deborah Chamberlain – Psychic Medium, Reiki Master, Spiritual Life Coach and proprietor of Inspiration School of Psychic and Spiritual Development School, Leicestershire, UK deborah.jc@ntlworld.com

Frank C. Clifford – Astrologer and Palm Reader www.londonschoolofastrology.co.uk

Llyn Roberts – Shamanic Reiki www.dreamchange.org

Lynda Small – Reiki Master, Leicestershire, UK Inspiration Spiritual Development School

Anne Marie Newland - Founder of Sun Power Yoga www.sun-power-yoga.co.uk

Matt France - Continuum Personal Development www.thecontinuum.org.uk

Thomas Coxon - Feng Shui Master

www.fengshui-consultants.co.uk

Prem Gajree – Star Crystals Shop and Healing
www.starcrystalsandhealing.co.uk

Theresa Hincks – Clinical Hypnotherapist and Life Between Lives
Therapist www.newtoninstitute.org

Lucy Gibbs BA, Clinical Hypnotherapist and Life Between Lives
Therapist www.newtoninstitute.org

Sarah Craven – Artist Extraordinaire
Email: sarah_jc@hotmail.com

References

Bartlett, Sarah, *The Tarot Bible* (Godsfield Press 2006)

Ben Toviya, Rabbi Esther *Created in the Image of God* (O Books 2007)

Berg, Yehuda *The Power of Kabbalah* (Kabbalah Publishing 2004)

Birkbeck, Lyn The Instant Astrologer Book and Software Package (O Books 2003)

Chopra, Deepak *Synchrodestiny Harnessing the Infinite Cower of Coincidence to Create Miracles* (Rider & Co 2005)

Clifford, Frank *Palmistry 4 Today* (Rider 2002)

Grist, Tony and Aileen, *The Illustrated Guide to Witchcraft; The Secrets of Wicca and Paganism Revealed* (Godsfield Press 2000)

Grant, Russell, *Astrotarot* (Virgin Publishing 1998)

Hall, Judy *The Crystal Bible* (Godsfield Press 2003)

Hall, Judy *Crystal Prescriptions* (O Books 2005)

Hamilton, David PhD *Destiny vs. Free Will; Why Things Happen the Way they Do* (Hay House 2007)

Kelsang Gyatso, Geshe *Introduction to Buddhism* Tharpa Publications 2001

Newton, Michael *Journey of Souls: Case Studies of Life Between Lives* (Llewellyn Publications 1994)

Newton, Michael *Destiny of Souls: New Case Studies of Life Between Lives* (Llewellyn Publications 2000)

Perkins, John *The World Is As You Dream It* (Destiny Books, 1994)

Roberts, Lynn & Levy, Robert *Shamanic Reiki* (O Books 2008)

Roberts, Marsha *Medicine Dance* (O Books 2007)

Weiss, Dr Brian *Many Lives, Many Masters* (Piatkus 1988)

BOOKS

O is a symbol of the world, of oneness and unity. In different cultures it also means the "eye," symbolizing knowledge and insight. We aim to publish books that are accessible, constructive and that challenge accepted opinion, both that of academia and the "moral majority."

Our books are available in all good English language bookstores worldwide. If you don't see the book on the shelves ask the bookstore to order it for you, quoting the ISBN number and title. Alternatively you can order online (all major online retail sites carry our titles) or contact the distributor in the relevant country, listed on the copyright page.

See our website **www.o-books.net** for a full list of over 500 titles, growing by 100 a year.

And tune in to myspiritradio.com for our book review radio show, hosted by June-Elleni Laine, where you can listen to the authors discussing their books.

MySpiritRadio